For Derek Ma...
With Best Wis...
from Alan Sked,
7/6/97

AN INTELLIGENT PERSON'S GUIDE TO
POST-WAR BRITAIN

AN
INTELLIGENT PERSON'S
GUIDE TO
POST-WAR BRITAIN

Alan Sked

Duckworth

To Alex and Eleanor
with all my love

First published in 1997 by
Gerald Duckworth & Co. Ltd.
The Old Piano Factory
48 Hoxton Square, London N1 6PB
Tel: 0171 729 5986
Fax: 0171 729 0015

A catalogue record for this book is available
from the British Library

ISBN 0 7156 2749 X

Typeset by Ray Davies
Printed and bound in Great Britain by
Biddles Ltd, Guildford and King's Lynn

Contents

Preface & Acknowledgments

This book is divided into two parts. The first deals with the issue of Britain's relative decline and suggests how that decline might finally be overcome.

The second part tackles specific political and social issues. The overall conclusion is that Britain is a viable political and economic unit that can look forward to stable government and economic prosperity in the twenty-first century, so long as it has the self-confidence to run its own affairs.

This interpretation of post-war Britain is entirely my own, but I would like to acknowledge some intellectual debts: to my LSE colleague, Robert Reiner, on crime; to my UKIP colleague, Gerald Roberts, on education; and to E.N. Williams for his elucidation of British constitutional history.

Introduction

The United Kingdom is one of the eight great island states of the world. Only 17 states have a larger population. It has the fifth largest economy in the world when measured in terms of gross domestic product and has £1.7 trillion invested throughout the globe. It is a nuclear power whose armed forces are the most professional in Europe. It has a seat on the Security Council of the UN, is a member of the G7 Group, has peacefully established a Commonwealth out of its Empire, and has a unique record of success in world history, both in terms of continuous parliamentary government and victory in wars. It has not been invaded since 1066, has suffered no Communist or Fascist takeovers and has seen no 'falls of regime' since the seventeenth century. Not surprisingly perhaps, many of its foreign admirers tend to see it as a success story without parallel, still a model to be emulated in all sorts of ways.

Yet at home there is a continuous attempt by commentators on the Left to write Britain off, an attempt which has found considerable resonance among a public educated by a 'progressive' teaching profession which now sees British history as a kind of thousand-year prelude to decline. Obsessed by social movements, classes, race and the subjugation of women, these commentators and teachers object violently to any kind of 'national histories' – save of course those of Ireland, Scotland or Wales, which can be exploited to diminish any remaining sense of being British or (worst of all) English. They are self-styled citizens of the world, supporters of that creature once satirised by George Canning as Universal Man. Indeed, Canning's famous couplet can still be used to describe the kind of critic I have in mind:

> A steady patriot of the world alone,
> The friend of every country – but his own.

Their *reductio ad absurdum* in the world of politics is perhaps the leader of the Liberal Democrats, Paddy Ashdown MP, who calls anyone who criticises the European Union a 'xenophobe' or 'false patriot'. He believes that British soldiers should risk their lives for the independence of Bosnia, but dismisses any idea that Britain herself could be independent with the

Introduction

argument that it is impossible to be independent in an interdependent world.

Other 'small-l' liberals believe much the same thing. They have nothing against the independence of Japan, Israel, New Zealand, Singapore, Taiwan or even Scotland, but object violently to the idea that the UK should be independent. And they find all sorts of excuses. Professor Stephen Haseler wrote to *The Times* on 28 May 1996: 'The UK is too small to be independent – in the modern global economy a nation of 55 million is simply no longer able to determine its own economic policy or deal as an equal with international capital – and it is too big to enable the citizen to participate.' In June 1996, the 'political editor' of an Oxford student newspaper wrote: 'We have an outdated dogma that we are as important as Germany and the other major players .... We are still under the impression that we are in Victorian Britain and we own half of the globe.'

On the contrary, most of us are increasingly under the impression that we are the European equivalent of Tierra del Fuego. Thus, for example, when the beef crisis broke out, the farm workers' leader, Barry Leathwood of the TGWU, was quoted in the *Evening Standard* of 22 May 1996 as saying: 'We can't take on Europe. We're small fry. We have to negotiate what the Europeans will accept.' The same attitude was displayed by William Horsley, the BBC correspondent in Bonn writing in the *Observer* on 27 August 1996. Having quoted Germany's Europe Minister, Werner Hoyer, as saying that British objections 'leave me cold', he concluded: 'Britain should think before picking quarrels it is liable to lose.'

The Britishness of most of these people is limited to their desire to be good losers. They are obsessed by the thought of our historical decline and cannot conceive that it might be reversed. Even worse, they cannot understand why we simply do not accept our fate as a province of a German-dominated Europe. Since mentally they are already inhabitants of Vichy Britain they have nothing but contempt for British resistance to this idea. The fact that ordinary British people have somehow escaped any sense of permanent doom is a puzzle to them. In the words of Professor Bernard Porter, writing in the September 1996 issue of *History Today*: 'The process (of losing an empire) had little effect on British politics .... Life in the metropolis went on much as before .... The rest of us lived through it all hardly noticing it; entirely unsinged – it seems – by the *Götterdämmerung* that was going on all around. There must, however, have been more to it than that. Nations do not suddenly lose empires without their leaving a mark.' In the *Sunday Times* of 4 August 1996, Robert Harris (coincidentally the author of a novel that depicts the Nazi occupation of Britain) insisted that the British should remember the 'D-word', i.e. their decline. Even after forty years, the memory of Suez and the catharsis that that episode was meant to represent, should, he insisted, be engraved upon our minds.

The solution all these people have to what they obviously perceive as the British Problem is self-obliteration in Europe, where, at least since 1945, they believe, the grass has always been greener. Writing in the August/September issue of *Prospect*, Simon Head expressed their common belief that whereas British diplomacy since 1945 had been an abject failure, French diplomacy during the same period had served its country well. A little thought might well have produced a radically different judgment, but since France has apparently tied her future to 'Europe', the false conclusion followed.

A true account of the relative diplomatic records of the two countries since 1945 is altogether more favourable to Britain. Immediately after the war, France was defeated over her German policy, was then defeated in Vietnam and defeated in Algeria, the latter debacle leading to the fall of the Fourth Republic. She was also defeated over the Saarland, over the European Defence Community (EDC), and over Suez (a French, not a British idea), while the founder of the Fifth Republic, General de Gaulle, was defeated on almost everything including the reorganisation of NATO (he withdrew France militarily from the whole organisation), the Fouchet Plan, US nuclear aid, and his attempt to protect Eastern Europe from the USSR. Indeed, he even managed to get thrown out of Canada. Internationally, he was totally isolated, something which hardly served French interests very well. Americans regarded him as public enemy number one; the British thought he was barmy; while France's European partners opposed almost his every move. (The West German Bundestag emasculated the Franco-German Friendship Treaty of 1963 by attaching a pro-British and pro-NATO preamble to it. In 1966 the other members of the EEC refused to accept his views on the Common Market, leading to the Luxembourg Compromise which they refused to dignify with legal status.) The Soviets and Chinese had little time for him either, despite his opposition to the war in Vietnam.

De Gaulle's successor, Pompidou, achieved little other than allowing the UK to enter the EEC in a vain attempt to control the Germans; otherwise his stated plans for the EEC got nowhere and his challenge to Henry Kissinger in 1973 over the 'year of Europe' and OPEC brought no gains for France. Giscard travelled a lot but achieved little of substance; eventually the strange homage paid him by a cannibal African 'emperor' (coronation arranged by Paris) made France look ridiculous, while his own regal pretensions ('le roi Giscard') only added to this impression. As for Mitterrand, once the episode of 'socialism in one country' had died a death, the main policy of this corrupt ex-fascist was subservience to Germany, whose reunification, however, he did momentarily resist. He has saddled present-day France with the policy of 'le franc fort', otherwise known as rule from Frankfurt. He also signed the Maastricht Treaty which 49% of French voters opposed in a rigged plebiscite. Chirac none the less continues this policy, risking a repeat of 1968. He has outraged the civilised world by holding nuclear tests in the South Pacific despite violent protests from all countries there. How all this adds up to a brilliant diplomatic record, one cannot tell. As an example of how not to make friends and influence people it would be hard to beat.

The UK meanwhile decolonised successfully, with no major hitches. She even won a war in Malaysia and took part in the defence of South Korea. In 1954 she stopped the US from using atom bombs in Vietnam in order to save those military and political geniuses, the French. In Europe she saved Greece from Communism, helped establish the Council of Europe in 1949, and in the same year assisted in the creation of both NATO and the Federal Republic of Germany. She presided over the Geneva Conference of 1954 which allowed the French to withdraw peacefully from Vietnam, and in 1955 she saved the day with respect to West German rearmament by agreeing to set up the British Army of the Rhine (BAOR) once France had scuttled the EDC. Despite the Suez fiasco, into which she had been led by the French, she quickly repaired her special relationship with the USA and cooperated with the Americans in 1958 in peacekeeping in the Middle East. In 1962 she used her influence to become the only country in the world to buy the latest nuclear weapons (Polaris missiles) very cheaply from the USA and secured the right to use them independently. Later on she was to repeat this deal with Trident. She remained a stabilising force east of Suez till 1973 and did not get involved in the Vietnam War despite US pressure and US missile supplies. In 1983 she won the Falklands War and by so doing did more for Latin American democracy in recent times than the USA, Fidel Castro and Che Guevara combined. She also negotiated a peaceful exit from Hong Kong, which apparently secured its independent economic future, negotiated an end to the Rhodesian War and negotiated an agreement with Eire over Northern Ireland. When Saddam Hussein invaded Kuwait and war broke out in the Gulf in 1991, she was America's principal ally; the French Defence Minister meanwhile resigned, and Germany refused to fight. True, Great Britain, did allow Edward Heath and subsequent Tory premiers (Thatcher and Major) to take us into the EEC/EC/EU. Yet her diplomatic record since the war has been much more successful than that of the French, or of any other Europeans for that matter, however reluctant fashionable commentators may be to admit it.

One result of their pessimism is that the UK is now in danger, for quite mythical reasons, of losing its self-respect. No flag-waving is called for, of course, but a nation without self-respect can hardly have a true sense of its own interests or priorities. For example, in the 1990s the Americans have also had doubts about their place in the world, but they have never lost their faith in America. In the mid-1990s, as Seymour Martin Lipset records, 75% of American adults and 98% of American youth said that they were proud to be Americans. The corresponding figures for Britain were 54% and 58%. The British pessimists are having their effect. But is it justified?

Part I

1

The Peculiarities of British History

British history differs from that of other countries in important ways. The British, after all, are not simply Europeans who speak English; nor are they merely a number of people who happen to inhabit the British Isles. They are the product of a peculiar national culture, which, in turn, is the creation of particular intellectual, environmental, social, geographic, political, economic and institutional influences, all of which have been historically determined. Perhaps the most important elements that have shaped the British national consciousness have been, first, government based on the rule of law through Parliament as the protector of individual liberty; secondly, political and social cohesion; and thirdly, world power. It is the combination of these three factors since the beginning of the eighteenth century which has made British history unique. So let us examine them in turn.

It was in the seventeenth century that the British pattern of government first diverged markedly from that of the rest of Europe. This happened because the crown of England – I shall deal with Scotland and Ireland later – combined both strengths and weaknesses. Regarding the latter, its power over the citizen was limited by the common law. Agents of the executive could be tried in ordinary courts for deeds carried out in the course of their duties. Indeed, the chief agents of the crown could be arraigned before the highest court of the land, Parliament, as Charles I's chief minister, Strafford, was in 1641. The writ of *habeas corpus*, which ordered prison governors to produce a prisoner for regular trial, protected ordinary citizens from arbitrary arrest. Monarchs naturally attempted to frustrate such proceedings, but ultimately failed to do so. Thus Charles II, for example, was foiled in his legal attack on his almost revolutionary opponent, Lord Shaftesbury, by the action of the Grand Jury of Middlesex which decided that there was no case for him to answer, thus saving Shaftesbury's life. The rule of law, as a result, was upheld. Three factors, in retrospect, ensured this: first, the reverence which surrounded the supposedly immemorial traditions on which the rule of law was based; second, the tenacity with which it was defended by the common lawyers and the courts; but most important of all was the protection afforded to the rule of law by Parliament.

The High Court of Parliament was the second of the chief sources of weakness of the English monarchy. It consisted of the king, the House of Lords and the House of Commons, membership of which latter body was based on some form of election. By the seventeenth century Parliament was the highest court of justice and in addition was *alone* capable of changing the law or authorising taxation. More than that, it was claiming to tell the king which ministers he should appoint and which policies he should pursue. It went so far as to wage war on Charles I, defeat him and execute him. By 1650, therefore, this embodiment of the judiciary and legislature had become more than a check on the executive, it had become the executive itself.

The scale of Parliament's success seems very remarkable indeed in comparison with the fate of the Estates in most other European countries. There, continental monarchs were either eliminating their powers or putting an end to their existence altogether. At most they were stagnating in passive reaction. There is not room here to explain in any detail why the story had a different outcome in England; yet two factors were of the greatest importance. First, the Tudors used Parliament to make, unmake and then remake the English Reformation, while, secondly, the economic and social changes of the sixteenth century enormously increased the wealth and pretensions of the classes who sat in Parliament.

There was another factor, however, that was also important in the rise of Parliament: the comparative smallness of the royal establishment. Few monarchies disposed of a smaller revenue than England in the sixteenth and seventeenth centuries, and the same was true of the bureaucracy since the administration of local government and courts of justice was carried out by unpaid local officials. Indeed, even in the nineteenth century, with the development of the Factory Acts and Poor Law Acts, British admini- stration remained extraordinarily small by continental standards. As late as 1855 there were only 18,000 civil servants, including postmen. In 1910 a French author estimated that for every 10,000 inhabitants, Belgium had 200 officials, France 176, Germany 126, and Great Britain 73. Parliament, as a result, could never be intimidated or even bypassed by a royal bureaucracy. Most important of all in this respect was the fact that the king did not dispose of a large standing army. Englishmen rightly regarded a standing army as the greatest threat to their liberties. The example of Louis XIV and of the Prussian kings, not to mention the military dictator- ship of Oliver Cromwell himself, proved that armed forces had to be controlled. After the expulsion of James II in 1688 Parliament decreed that revenue for military purposes would have to be raised annually through the Army Act. The result was that in 1745 Bonnie Prince Charlie could reach Derby unopposed at the head of Highland clansmen and that in 1744 only 9,000 troops could be found to defend the country. True, huge armies could be raised in order to defeat Napoleon, but these were soon reduced in size once the war had been won and militarism was never to be a problem for Great Britain. By 1846, Wellington was once again reporting that only about 10,000 troops were available to defend the country, and between 1873 and 1897 the army was unable to hold manoeuvres because Parliament refused to grant it money. Significantly, Great Britain did not create a general staff until the begining of the twentieth century.

Britain was even wary about creating an unbeatable navy. In the seventeenth century the Dutch navy was bigger than its British counterpart, while in the eighteenth century a combination of French and Spanish fleets could be critical for Britain's imperial defence, as the American War of Independence showed. In the nineteenth century the British fleet was cut down drastically from 214 commissioned ships of the line in 1815 to 68 in 1822 and 58 in 1835. It was the German decision to launch a naval race at the very end of the nineteenth century that finally made the British Parliament more keen to spend money on its fleet in peacetime. Thus from the seventeenth to the twentieth centuries, Parliament's refusal to spend money on a standing army or sea-ready navy seriously undermined the power of the British executive.

Yet how was such a tradition of a small bureaucracy and few armed forces able to take root so firmly in British soil? To some extent the answer is geographical. The surrounding seas had long provided England with excellent internal communications, with the result that unification was achieved very early. The same waters also protected England from foreign invasion. Unlike many a Continental state, therefore, England was not in danger of falling apart into sub-regions or provinces or of being cut in pieces by a powerful neighbour. Almost as a piece of luck, she could afford the luxury of being lightly administered, so that while 'Continental states could not survive outside the iron lung of absolutist rule, Englishmen could stretch themselves under a bureaucratic framework as light as gossamer.'

The final victory of Parliament was established by a series of enactments at the turn of the seventeenth and eighteenth centuries, the expulsion of James II and William III's wars against Louis XIV having enormously strengthened Parliament's authority. By the end of the reign of Queen Anne, therefore, it had been established that the crown should remain in protestant hands so that absolutism and divine right should no longer trouble Britain; that judges should be placed entirely outside the reach of the executive and accused persons granted more safeguards; that the king could not raise an army without annual parliamentary consent; that censorship of the press should end; that Parliament should meet regularly and often (defined to be at least every three years, leading to twelve elections between 1689 and 1715); that religious toleration should be extended; and that only a very small part of the crown's total needs should be granted for life. The rest was to be voted and audited by Act of Parliament, it being taken as a general maxim, in the words of Bishop Burnet, that a revenue for a certain and a short time was the best security that the nation could have for frequent parliaments.

While other European countries, therefore, were experiencing the age of absolutism or enlightened despotism, Great Britain was establishing parliamentary government. Paradoxically, moreover, this proved a stronger system than absolutism, despite the fact that Britain had no standing army or (before the eighteenth century) great navy. A number of explanations suggest themselves. First, national unity had been established early; England, moreover, was a judicial area with a uniform system of law. To an increasing extent she was also an economic unit; what obstacles there were to the growth of the national market were physical ones erected by nature, not customs posts set up by privileged sub-units. Economic growth had been fostered by a strong Tudor state which had supressed banditry, defied foreign power and turned the Church into a national one, the Church of England. All this meant that the nation was united to a degree unknown among the Continental states and that nationalism appeared in England (and soon in Britain) before it developed elsewhere. This sense of unity, in turn, became extremely powerful when articulated by a Parliament that represented the nation. And this is what was happening by the end of the seventeenth century. Parliament, populated by the same elites who, as Lords lieutenants and justices of the peace, ran local government and who provided a sufficient electorate to make elections meaningful, was able to mobilise the country. All that remained was for the House of Commons to become increasingly representative. And that is what came about through the Reform Acts of 1832, 1867, 1884 and the grant of the vote to women. Thus the first distinguishing feature of modern British history can be said to be the experience of continuous parliamentary government based on the rule of law – as opposed to absolutist, bureaucratic or militaristic government – over the course of three centuries.

The second distinguishing feature of British history is undoubtedly the political and social cohesion enjoyed by Britons during the same period. There have, of course, been moments of social and political tension during these centuries – one thinks of 1745, the 1790s, 1839, 1848 – but these do not appear too serious in comparison with events experienced elsewhere. In modern times Britain has witnessed no political revolutions, no foreign invasions, no occupations, no dictatorships of right or left, nor even any significant support for communist or fascist or any other extremist doctrines. No minorities have been deliberately persecuted and the rule of law has never been put aside for political reasons. This is a singular record for a European country.

In many ways this is the direct result of the early establishment of parliamentary government as well as of the success of parliamentary reform. For Parliament, once reformed, proved susceptible to the demands of nineteenth- and twentieth-century social reformers. There was little need for social critics to indulge in revolutionary action. It was also a consequence of religious radicalism. For the same religious non-conformism that challenged the absolutist pretensions of the Stuart dynasty in the seventeenth century, revived itself towards the end of the eighteenth century, led the movement to abolish slavery in the British Empire, and went on to champion social and political reform at home. This meant that socialism in Great Britain, for example, developed along different lines from Continental socialism, being always rooted in a religious and parliamentary soil. The Labour Party owed more to Methodism than to Marx, and there was something terribly British about Robert Owen's hopes for establishing 'harmony communities' and 'cooperatives'. He was, in fact, attempting to make social reform non-partisan. However, if such reform could not help but be a political issue, the fact that the British Parliament was *not* a bourgeois sham and that all political parties – another result of the early establishment of parliamentarianism in Great Britain – were willing to tackle social reform, meant that it was not until the beginning of the twentieth century that the Labour Party was formed as a separate vehicle for social advance. And even then, right up until the First World War, the Labour Party could still be regarded as a pressure group within the Liberal Party. This fact – the lack of a separate socialist party operating within the framework of the world's oldest parliamentary system before the First World War – is in itself a striking testimony to the political and social cohesion enjoyed by the British people.

It was proof, one might say, of the essentially pragmatic, unideological and moderate consensus which underlay British politics. Attlee himself guaranteed that the Labour Party would abide by this consensus when he wrote, in the introduction to a three-volume official history of the Labour Party in 1948, that it was a 'characteristically British production differing widely from Continental Socialist Parties' and 'a product of its environment and of the national habit of mind'.

If British socialism, therefore, was shaped in a moderate mould, so too was British right-wing politics. The reason for this was that national unity was never really questioned. The country had no significant linguistic minorities. True, some Welsh was spoken in the North of Wales, and in the Scottish Highlands some Gaelic survived, but Welsh nationalism was never a problem after the Tudors, and Scotland was spectacularly absorbed into the Union after a rough start. Even the Irish Question was handled with much moderation.

As far as Scotland was concerned, the Scots were allowed to keep their own system of law, their own system of education and their own Church. They were also represented in both houses of Parliament and provided prime and cabinet ministers. They more or less ran the British Empire – or so it often seemed – with the result that they had very few genuine causes for complaint. What grievances they had were mollified when a Secretary of State for Scotland was created in 1885 and a Home Rule Bill was given a second reading in 1913. Had the First World War not broken out in 1914, it is probable that Scotland would have received self-government that year.

Ireland, of course, was a completely different problem. It had a predominantly Catholic population, was ruled by foreign landlords and a foreign Church and lacked self-government during the nineteenth century. On the other hand, it was strategically vital to Britain's defences. Yet it is a travesty of history to see the British record in Ireland as one of systematic repression. For governments throughout the nineteenth century devoted themselves to reform there, disestablishing the Church of Ireland, pushing through land reforms, protecting tenants and attempting to secure Home Rule. Gladstone, it will be remembered, attempted no less than four times to place a Home Rule Bill on the statute book. Nor should it be forgotten that Irish MPs played a notable part in the history of the House of Commons during the battles to pass these bills. Still, it was left to Lloyd George in 1921 to settle the main problem, although even then he had to leave the Ulster problem unresolved. On the other hand, it simply cannot be denied that the majority of the population of Ulster felt and still feel passionately British and have no desire to become part of a united Ireland.

So much then for political cohesion. Social cohesion has also been a feature of British life and once more to a remarkable degree. For if Britain experienced no violent political changes after 1688, she experienced no violent social ones either. Thus William III's much maligned 'Dutch money men' – camp followers who had come over from Holland after the Glorious Revolution – were easily absorbed at the beginning of the eighteenth century and the British aristocracy and gentry were able to maintain their social ascendancy right up almost until the twentieth century. That they were able to do so was the consequence of a number of important factors, all of them having to do with the different ways in which their lordships channelled their social influence. They did this, for example, through their prestige in political affairs; through the extent of their landholdings; through their control of local administration; not to mention through the survival of popular deference. Two other factors, however, were of key importance: the willingness of the aristocracy to accept key political and social reforms; and the fact that they in no way constituted a rigid political caste. The House of Lords, it should be remembered, had no fixed membership and could, as a result, absorb potential rivals from the professional and business worlds within its ranks.

By the twentieth century the aristocracy no longer dominated social or political life. The middle and upper classes did that. On the other hand, the working class was now also much better organised and in 1923 the Labour Party came to power. Yet even in the twentieth century Great Britain has seen a huge degree of political and social cohesion, because of the strength of the parliamentary tradition and of the steady rise in living standards. For example, even in the 1930s people were for the most part becoming better off. More houses were being built then than are being built today. The rub, of course, was that between the two world wars two to three million Britons were unemployed. Yet that is now seen as only part of the picture and the dismal decade is no longer seen as dismal any more. In the words of one historian, 'most English people were enjoying a richer life than any previously known in the history of the world: longer holidays, shorter hours, higher real wages. They had motor cars, cinemas, radio sets, electrical appliances.' In the words of another: 'we may need to look beyond the critics and recognise the significance of a decade which saw for many the beginnings of affluence, the evolution of the welfare state and a confirmation of the stability of British politics.' In the light of such statements, it is easy to see why fascism was a non-starter in Britain in the 1930s. The success of the Nazis and Fascists in Europe lay in the insecurities of the German and Italian middle and lower classes. But the British middle classes were anything but insecure after 1931 with the return of the National Government with a 500-seat majority, the rout of the Labour Party, which in any case clearly had no idea what to do about the depression, and the maintenance of a reasonably stable if not improving standard of living. Nor did the workers present a threat. In 1935 only 18,000 people voted Communist. In George Orwell's words: 'Between 1931 and 1940, the National Government represented the will of the mass of the people.' This kind of situation was to repeat itself in the 1980s and 1990s, when, despite recessions and massive increases in unemployment to the same levels as in the 1930s, Labour again proved incapable of winning elections since those in work experienced tangible improvements in their standards of living.

It was World War II, however, that saw British political and social cohesion reach its peak and, given the post-war implementation of the Beveridge Report and the foundation of the welfare state through the establishment of the National Health Service and other institutions, this cohesion survived the war. The welfare state was accepted by all the political parties and full employment was taken as the common aim. The nation, in fact, had become a Keynesian democracy with an accepted list of social priorities. The new consensus was christened 'Butskellism' by the *Economist*, from the names of the Labour and Conservative Chancellors, Hugh Gaitskell and R.A. Butler. Everybody knew instinctively what this epithet signified, namely that there was no discernible difference in outlook between the two major political parties. This had also been the moral of a novel published in 1953 by Edward Hyams in which the hero managed to get elected to Parliament as both a Socialist and a Tory without anybody noticing what had happened.

The post-war consensus also extended to foreign policy, for in the era of the Cold War, the British had no doubts about which side they were on. The resulting inter-party agreement could therefore be satirised in the following verse:

The Bevin or the Churchill touch
Seem both alike to Danes and Dutch,
If Socialist or Tory speaks,
It's all the same to French and Greeks.

Without doubt the vast majority of Britons believed that with the creation
of the welfare state, the achievement of full employment, and the experience of rising living standards, their system of parliamentary democracy
constituted a socio-political system which communism, like fascism, could
only threaten, but never rival.

With the Bevin and the Churchill touch we come to the last of the three
broad distinguishing traits of modern British history, namely Britain's role
as a world power. This was based, first, on the creation of the Empire,
secondly on Britain's leadership in the first Industrial Revolution, thirdly
on Britain's dominance of world financial markets, and finally on Britain's
success in innumerable wars. There is no need to discuss the origins of the
Industrial Revolution, but one of its results was that the wealth of the
country plus the wealth of the City money markets enabled Great Britain
to wage war when necessary, with the consequence that she could finance
the wars against Napoleon, take on the supposed military might of Russia
in 1854 and survive two world wars victoriously. Yet Britain's position as
the world's financial centre really predated the Industrial Revolution and
went back to the foundation of the Bank of England in 1694, the creation
of the National Debt in 1693 and the re-coinage of 1696. These measures,
together with the evolution of an effective system of tax-collection during
the eighteenth century, meant that British governments were in an extremely strong position regarding international credit. Once again, the
parliamentary system played a role. The fact that the commercial and
trading elites as well as the landed ones were represented in Parliament
meant that governments could borrow money in anticipation of revenue,
since these elites had confidence that the monies borrowed would be
properly collected, controlled and repaid. Hence at many stages of the
eighteenth and nineteenth centuries, Britain was the only great power
which really could afford a war, something which, however, she tried to
avoid.

In the nineteenth century, Britain found excuses for remaining free of
European entanglements – imperial problems, no clear government majority, refusal to commit future parliaments, etc. Her wise policy was to
pursue only her own best interests by means of free hands (no alliances or
other commitments if they could be avoided) and free trade. Among many
others, Bismarck ridiculed her refusal to come to terms ('I wasted five
years of my life in the belief that England was a great power'), yet Britain's
only alliance was to be with Japan in 1902 (with the *casus foederis*
dependent on attack by *two* other powers). She meanwhile patiently
negotiated ententes, increased her defence expenditure and cut her com-

mitments. In this way she avoided European wars right up to 1914, when Europe's supra-national Habsburg Monarchy (a kind of Central European forerunner of the European Union) deliberately started a war which it knew might well engulf the whole of Europe, a probability which was made a certainty when the small nation of Belgium was invaded by the troops of the supra-national German Empire on their way to conquer France.

Only in 1955, given the threat posed by a new supra-nationalist ideology, Communism (Nazism and Fascism having been defeated in World War II), did Britain agree to station an army abroad in peacetime by creating the British Army of the Rhine. This helped bring about the consolidation of NATO, whose ever-formidable existence played a major part in ending Communist rule in the Soviet Union in 1991.

Let us now examine the significance for British history of the British Empire. It came about in piece-meal fashion and from a variety of motives. The eighteenth-century empire was the result primarily of economic rapacity, although religion and geographical curiosity were also involved. Large parts of India and North America were seized from other European powers and from native rulers. The abomination of the slave trade was a major economic factor. However, this amazing piece of institutionalised international plunder collapsed in the West in 1776 with the American Declaration of Independence and the ensuing war.

The nineteenth-century empire was different. Plunder still went on, but on a much reduced scale. Slavery was abolished and the evangelical revival brought about a revolution in public ethics. Moreover, the American War had taught rationally-minded men that all colonies would one day have to be granted their independence. Thus Macaulay, for example, could tell the House of Commons in 1833 during a debate on the India Bill of that year: 'The public mind of India, having become instructed in European knowledge ... may in some future age demand European institutions. Whether such a day will ever come I know not. But never will I attempt to retard it. Whenever it comes, it will be the proudest day in English history.' Between the 1830s and 1850s an attempt was made to start the process of educating Indians towards eventual self-rule. The Indian Mutiny of 1857, it is true, completely altered the position and thereafter India was run by the British, paying for its own defence and partly subsidising British defences. The British, however, paid for major works of infrastructure. Whether Britain made a profit out of India is difficult to say, but if she did, this was the exception in colonial history, not the rule.

The truth was that for most of the nineteenth century, the British did not want an empire, certainly not in the formal sense. Colonies cost money and even Disraeli referred to them as 'millstones around our necks'. Colonies had to be defended, administered and controlled. Nine times out of ten they provided little in the way of markets and often involved unnecessary wars. British governments, therefore, avoided picking them up when possible (the exceptions being ocean coaling-stations). Where possible, white colonies were granted self-government.* None the less, the expansion of empire had not yet reached an end. For towards the end of the nineteenth century, European nationalism, now transformed into imperialism, together with the rising spectre of commercial protectionism, forced Britain once again to expand her formal empire. The process had nothing to do with the export of capital, as critics on the Left maintained, and Lenin obviously did not understand what had happened when he wrote his famous little book on imperialism. The facts were that only 2-5% of Europe's capital exports went into the new colonies. Most British overseas investment went into independent states in America, particularly the USA, but also to places like Argentina and Peru. There was also much European investment in China, which, unlike Africa, was simply never partitioned. Moreover, many of the states with empires – Italy, Russia, Spain, Portugal and the USA – were importers rather than exporters of capital. Nor did European powers feel compelled to go to war over colonies because of investments. The Germans and French put more money into British colonies than their own; indeed, it was almost impossible for German governments to get German businessmen to invest in newly acquired deserts and swamps – far less to persuade German colonists to go there in significant numbers. Decolonisation, not illogically therefore, brought increased economic growth. Nor was it necessary to pacify the new working classes with the fruits of empire to stop them from revolting, as Marxist writers have also implied. The European workers who had the highest standards of living were the Scandinavians and the Swiss – all citizens of states which lacked empires altogether.

Other points of misunderstanding can be cleared up as well. Britain, for example, never attempted – as did the French – to assimilate her colonial subjects. She never intended to make them British, but worked through local rulers – tribal chiefs and maharajahs – to maintain public order and control. This explains why so very few troops or administrators were necessary to keep the empire going: it had the collaboration of the local elites. Eventually, these began to demand self-government, which the British by the second half of the twentieth century were quite willing to grant. Until then, to quote Professor M.S. Anderson:

> Nothing is more striking than the ease with which small, sometimes very small numbers of Europeans were able to transform the whole existence of large parts of the world. Apart from the Maratha and Sikh states few Indian principalities offered sustained resistance to the spread of British rule. When the nineteenth century ended the whole of the subcontinent, with a population already approaching 300 million, was controlled by an army which included only 70,000 white soldiers and of which a large part was

---

* The French had no concept of this, eventually using the English word, 'le self-government'. Cf. 'Le leadership'.

stationed permanently on the Afghan frontier .... Even in Egypt, where nationalism was rapidly gaining strength, a population which by 1900 approached 10 million was effectively controlled by a British army of occupation which sometimes numbered less than 5,000. Numerically most striking of all, in 1896 about 3 million people in southern Uganda were ruled by perhaps 25 British officials.

Professor Bernard Porter quotes one colonial governor in Kenya reporting before 1914 in the language of the time: 'Here we are three white men in the heart of Africa, with 20 Nigger soldiers and 50 Nigger police, 68 miles from doctors or reinforcements, administering and policing a district inhabited by half a million well armed savages ... the position is most humorous.' Clearly, therefore, the British Empire was not ruled by force.

Perhaps precisely because so few British were employed in running the empire (most emigrants went to the USA or to the white colonies or to South Africa, which was granted independence in 1910), it never really won much public support. The working classes were simply uninterested in it. In fact it only meant something when large numbers were called upon to fight for it, as in the Boer War. Most of them thought that the money could be better spent on social reform at home. Chamberlain's programme of imperial preferences and Empire Development was perhaps not surprisingly defeated at the polls in 1906 by a huge majority. Even during World War I, H.G. Wells could write: 'nineteen people out of twenty, the lower class and most of the middle class knew no more of the Empire than of the Argentine republic or the Italian Renaissance. It did not concern them.'

After the war, many attempts were made to alter this situation through all sorts of organisations and press crusades. This made no difference, for the Chairman of the Empire Day Movement had to admit that 'in spite of unremitting efforts' there were 'still many dark corners in Great Britain, especially in the industrial areas, where the rays of our Empire's sun (had) not yet been able to penetrate'. The Empire had simply failed to catch on. In 1948 a public opinion poll showed that three-quarters of the population did not know the difference between a dominion and a colony and half could not name a single British colony. This was striking proof that the propaganda of the imperialists had secured an almost pathetic return.

By 1948, however, the post-war Labour government had already made a start on decolonisation. Churchill, who had declared during the war that he would never preside over the dissolution of the British empire, lost the 1945 general election. The process of decolonisation then continued apace, in some places perhaps at too fast a pace. Certainly, independent Africa has witnessed much greater bloodshed, dictatorship and oppression since independence than before. Even in India, recent press coverage of almost 50 years of independence has been monotonously pessimistic in tone. Yet, however one judges the British record in the former colonies, the point to note is that it has not coloured British attitudes very much. Nobody wants the empire back; it was never a popular cause while it existed; it was ruled with the collaboration of the native elites and when this collaboration stopped the colonies were quickly and usually very smoothly granted independence. Britain, unlike France, Portugal, or even Holland, suffered no trauma over decolonisation. If the Commonwealth were to disappear today, very few people in Britain would even notice.

Foreigners never really understood that it was simply geography and not Empire which made Great Britain appear to be in many ways unEuropean. The very fact that Britain was an island with trading links all over the world gave Britain a different outlook from the Continental, land-based powers. Yet most of Britain's trade was with the USA and the Dominions, Germany and Latin America, not with her newly acquired colonies. The result was that the latter could very easily be given up. The final proof, therefore, that Empire was the least significant element in Britain's unique historical tradition, can be found in the extraordinarily smooth transition between Empire and Commonwealth. Britain after 1945 felt no obligation whatsoever to fight colonial wars to hang on to recalcitrant territories. She did not experience the agony of an Algeria or of a slower war of attrition such as took place in Angola. Instead, supported by a populace which fundamentally adhered to the views that Macaulay had put forward, she applied them to colonies all over the world as yet another part of the post-war consensus. The remarkable and not unflattering aspect of this process was that nearly every former colony involved demanded a British-type constitution and entered the Commonwealth. Indeed, even countries which had never been part of the empire applied to join (e.g. Mozambique) and others that had left temporarily were glad to return (e.g. South Africa). This constituted an enormous political success and said much for British rule. So, too, does the fact that, outside Europe, the world's most stable democracies – Canada, Australia, New Zealand, the United States, India – were former British colonies.

Great Britain's history, therefore, has been unique. Britain experienced three centuries of continuous parliamentary government as well as social and political cohesion at a time when she was the world's leading power. All these factors were, not unnaturally, inter-related, although I do not have space enough here to point out some of the more curious aspects of that inter-relationship. It might be argued that what I am trying to say – if Americans will forgive me – is that modern British history has been a success story without equal. Yet although foreigners often agree with this, British citizens get a very different impression from their schoolteachers and journalists. Today, we are force-fed the history of our decline, which is held to have begun in the 1870s and to have increased apace ever since. It is now time to put this concept into perspective.

Britain's Relative Decline:
The General Issues

The British still believed in their success right up until the 1960s. True, some voices were issuing warnings that, compared to West Germany, we were falling behind, but there was much to justify the popular mood. West German income levels, as we shall see, did not pass average British ones until the early 1960s. Nor did West Germany have nuclear weapons or a world role; in fact, the Bundeswehr only came into existence as a functioning army in the 1960s. France meanwhile had reached the verge of civil war over Algeria, had witnessed the fall of the Fourth Republic and, after the return of de Gaulle to power, had received a new constitution whose ultimate acceptance was still in doubt. Indeed, in 1968 de Gaulle had to flee his country again amidst student revolts and widespread strikes; meanwhile, the military had taken over Greece to give Western Europe yet another dictatorship to add to those of Spain and Portugal. The British, therefore, had reason enough to trust in their traditional attitudes and institutions, whatever the critics had to say.

None the less, there were portents of a justifiable loss of self-confidence. The political scandals of the early 1960s (although quite trivial in retrospect), de Gaulle's veto of our first Common Market entry bid in 1963 (today his press conference statement appears totally rational), and, most of all perhaps, the devaluation of 1967 (then seen as a devaluation of our national status) led many British commentators to talk of our 'decline'. Our imperial retreat after 1968, the failures of the Wilson, Heath and Callaghan governments, the apparent dominance of the trades unions by communists, radicals, or merely blinkered old war-horses, served quickly to reinforce this impression. There was soon a flood of books and articles on 'the British disease'; for many people Great Britain appeared to have taken on the mantle of nineteenth-century Turkey and to have become the 'sick man of Europe'. By 1979 there was almost no debate about this. The country was held to be practically in its death throes. The economic historian Sidney Pollard wrote in 1982: 'Britain is no longer counted among the economically advanced nations of the world. A wide gap separates her from the rest of industrialised Europe. The difference as measured in national product per head between Britain and say, Germany, is now as wide as the difference between Britain and the continent of Africa.' The journalist Peter Jenkins, writing in the *Guardian* in September 1978, had been even more alarmist: 'No country has yet made the journey from developed to underdeveloped. Britain could be the first to embark upon that route. That is what it would mean to move away from a century of relative economic decline into a state of absolute decline. Here is how it could happen.' He then outlined a scenario in which wages rose faster than productivity, unit labour costs grew, exports fell and imports increased to such an extent that it was no longer possible to finance growth in real incomes. Relative decline would thus have brought about absolute decline. But what was meant by the phrase 'relative decline'?

This referred to the fact that although Great Britain's economy had continued to grow throughout the twentieth century, the economies of other countries had grown even faster. Indeed, this was the case despite the fact that British growth rates in the twentieth century were often double those of the previous one. Thus, although British people became increasingly better off, enjoying higher standards of living and better welfare services than ever before, some other countries improved their position at greater speeds. By the mid-1980s, therefore, economists measuring economic progress in terms of GNP per head were placing most of Western Europe, indeed the Western world, before Great Britain. Given that the Empire by now had also mostly disappeared, these figures were seen by critics such as Jenkins as portents of irreversible and ultimately absolute decline. The fact that other countries – France and Germany prominent among them – had suffered much more violent swings of fortune and had managed to recover was hardly noticed. The view began to harden that the 'British disease' was incurable and that it was time for Britannia to be placed in a hospice and allowed to expire in the arms of virile young Continental nursing staff. Some commentators seemed to become possessed by a sort of national death wish. Yet patients do recover – and for that matter, even nursing staff fall ill – and today the position is much more hopeful. So let us examine the history of Britain's relative decline in more detail, examining the questions why and when did it take place. The starting point is often taken to be about 1870, so that although this book is about post-war Britain, some historical by-ways will have to be explored. History is like that, you end up having to go further and further back for clues and this simply cannot be avoided. The evidence also comes in several forms. This particular case is usually debated in terms of economics, but there have been arguments that the British disease has been fundamentally psychological, stemming in particular from a dislike of industry. This is something which we shall also have to consider.

Critics of modern Britain have often pointed to the low prestige of engineers, the bias in favour of the arts, banking, the civil service and law, as having something to do with our relative decline. Usually, Britain's educational and class systems are mixed up in this type of argument – the classical education of the public schools, training for empire rather than industry, the lack of technical education, etc. – all leading to the conclusion that Britain has traditionally lacked entrepreneurial spirit and indeed has been culturally conditioned to despise industry. On most of the questions raised by this sort of argument, however, very little comparative research has been undertaken. For example, it is not immediately obvious that a so-called 'class-system' was less in evidence in pre-1914 Germany or post-war France than in Great Britain during these periods. Nor is it immediately apparent that nepotism, the old-boy network, attachment to particular educational institutions or other features of social life have been particularly British phenomena. Nor can it be taken to be an economically irrational act to accept a job in the City or in the professions if alternative careers in industry pay less well or have to be pursued in less attractive surroundings. The choice may well be symptomatic of industry's decline, not contributory to it. Finally, it is difficult to accept, as a Canadian academic once argued, that Britain's decline was caused by her conversion to 'imperialist values' in the late nineteenth century, something which constituted a 'fundamental change'.

This particular view can be rebutted on a number of grounds: first, if such a basic alteration in our outlook did happen at the end of the nineteenth century, it is difficult to explain why it should have led only to Britain's decline. Both Germany and the USA were also converted to imperialism about this time and at precisely that stage in their economic development when they were overtaking Britain. Japan, too, became a major imperialist power in the late nineteenth century. Moreover, if imperialist values do somehow impede economic growth, it is unclear why France, which was fighting two bitter colonial wars between 1945 and 1962, should have managed to stage an 'economic miracle', while declining Britain was happily transforming Empire into Commonwealth. Finally, if Britain really did undergo such a transformation, how are her Liberal governments between 1906 and 1904 to be explained or, for that matter, the defeat of Tariff Reform? The new imperialism, in sum, cannot hold the key to relative economic decline; indeed, it cannot even explain a decline in Britain's own growth rate, since none took place. Growth in the British economy increased throughout the late nineteenth century, dipped slightly between 1900 and 1907, and then recovered by 1914.

Let us now examine another argument, that of Martin Wiener, whose *English Culture and the Decline of the Industrial Spirit, 1850-1980* was published in 1981 to much praise from reviewers. Wiener argues that the British have been conditioned culturally to despise industry, both by their men of letters and by their political and social elites. The real trouble with this sort of history is that it is unscientific; in other words, even if it can be shown that many people disliked industry and the industrial process, it cannot be shown how exactly this contributed to Britain's relative decline. Certainly, it is not good enough to argue, as Wiener does, that since most economic historians have failed to explain it in purely economic terms, we are forced to accept the cultural explanation. This is all the more evident since Wiener's attempts to prove that these cultural factors were specific to Britain fail completely to carry conviction.

His thesis is that most British writers since 1850 have been opposed to 'the industrial spirit'. Politicians, too, have displayed a preference for the vocabulary and myths of a green and pleasant land. All this stems, Wiener argues, from the fact that the bourgeois class of entrepreneurs which made the Industrial Revolution in England was soon gentrified and absorbed into the upper class with its values based on land. There was a different pattern in Germany and the USA: in Germany the bourgeoisie was not similarly absorbed, while in America the industrial spirit was not opposed. The case for this, however, is presented for the American and German models merely by assertion, and for Britain merely by random quotation.

There are further substantial criticisms to be made of the book. To start with, it is difficult to accept the argument that only British intellectuals opposed industrialism. For example, one study of American literature discovered that in 'the entire body of American fiction ... the businessman [was] almost always depicted as crass, philistine, corrupt, predatory, domineering, reactionary and amoral'. Only three business novels presented a positive side to him at all. The USA also suffered from 'the agrarian myth', which in the words of Richard Hofstadter, perhaps America's greatest intellectual historian, 'was not a popular, but a literary idea, a preoccupation of the upper classes, of those who enjoyed a classical education, read pastoral poetry, experimented with breeding stocks and owned plantations or country estates'. In Germany, too, the intellectuals shunned industrialism. Professor R. Hinton Thomas has written of a cultural tradition in Germany 'with values derived from a society of a different order [which] acquired such aura and authority that when the new industrial reality materialised towards the end of the nineteenth century, this was not easily absorbed into the intellectual context'. Writers such as Lagarde, Heym, Schlaf, Bölsche, Tucholsky, and Kraus could, as a result, be quoted in the same way as Wiener quotes their English counterparts.

The real conclusion to be drawn then is that industrialism was not particularly welcomed by intellectuals anywhere. This is not, in fact, surprising. It is not an inherently likeable process, and certainly not one which recommends itself to intellectuals who are irrelevant to it. In the wider context, perhaps the last word should be left to that brilliant intellectual historian, Fritz Stern:

> This anti-capitalistic sentiment was of course endemic in the western world; its history has yet to be written and when it is, it most likely will reveal that this anti-capitalistic mood sprang not only from nostalgia for a simple life of

some lost Arcadia, but also from nostalgia for a religious faith that seemed doomed to extinction at the same time.

A second criticism of Wiener is that he is very often naive. It is one thing to quote politicians on the virtue of the countryside; it is another to expect them to say anything else in rural constituencies. Moreover, if politicians retire to farms, it is not a mark of their lack of interest in production – old men rarely retire to factories. Besides, farming nowadays is very often an industry itself and often a highly profitable one. Likewise, legislation concerning 'green belts' is not incompatible with a desire for industrial growth. Konrad Adenauer's Cologne, for example, had designed a green belt years before the British passed their relevant legislation. Yet no one took this to be a sign of anti-industrialism in the Rhineland. Perhaps Wiener is at his most naive when he assumes that landed values necessarily clashed with industrial ones or that the British aristocracy disliked making money. All the most recent research proves him wrong.

Nobles and landowners were involved in the process of industrialisation from the very beginning everywhere in Europe. In the late eighteenth century most forge-owners in France were nobles. In the German lands, Frederick the Great of Prussia described Francis of Lorraine, husband of the Empress Maria Theresa, as the 'greatest factory owner of his age'. Many of the first factories built in nineteenth-century Austria were established by nobles. The idea that the nobility was somehow antagonistic to new sources of wealth is a myth. True, respectability in the nineteenth century demanded the ownership of an estate, and factory-owners everywhere bought land to acquire respectability, if they did not already possess it. But that did not mean that the landowning classes in turn avoided industrial ventures. Far from it. They were often the prime movers in such ventures. As Professor F.M.L. Thomson has written, coal seams and iron ore beds belonged in general to the surface landowners, while transport improvements, canals, docks, harbours and railways, required large amounts of land and capital. Moreover urban and population growth were equally land-hungry. For landowners, coal, iron, slate, gravel, clay, and even railway lines, were 'beautiful crops to grow'. Some landowners took few risks and allowed others to take their chances with these enterprises, yet many landowners themselves became great developers. For example, one only has to think of the importance of the Duke of Bridgewater to the development of Manchester, the Duke of Devonshire to the development of Barrow-in-Furness and Eastbourne, the Marquesses of Bute to the development of Cardiff and the Duke of Northumberland to the development of Newcastle. Thus Thompson has concluded that the landed aristocracy, if it ever had been un-capitalist or anti-capitalist, had certainly gone more than halfway to embrace capitalist methods by the mid-nineteenth century. It is misleading, in his opinion, to think of landed or gentlemanly values as turning hard-headed businessmen into a 'simple landed class'.

This traditional picture has also had to be modified in the light of Rubinstein's findings that most of the newly wealthy did not invest in land, at least as measured in terms of an estate of 2,000 acres or more. If his figures are to be believed, considerably less than 10% of all Britain's greater landowners in 1883 were the products of business and professional wealth created after 1780. From his analysis of 45 individual millionaires who did acquire large estates by 1873, it can be shown that only 11 made their fortunes in manufacturing industry (including two brewers), while 21 were in banking or overseas trade, six in minerals, and four in railway contracting. Hence the whole theory of 'gentrification' may be a myth, although Thompson suggests that by the end of the nineteenth century the mere acquisition of a country house might have been sufficient to ensure respectability. His main point remains, however, that even if some part of the business world moved towards the landed class and its values, they were met half-way by the latter. And in this process there is no need to assume that the entrepreneurial spirit suffered.

Martin Wiener's thesis, therefore, is very difficult to accept. So, too, are many others which have been put forward by critics relying on sociological speculation. And revisions of recently quite standard views not merely of British but also European history are commonplace. For example, it is now clear that the greatest generators of private wealth in France, Britain, Italy, and Austria-Hungary well into the twentieth century were not manufacturing industries but land and finance – often interlinked and intermarried. Of the greatest fortunes bequeathed in Great Britain between 1809 and 1939 only one was made in cotton and railways – supposedly the leading sectors of the economy after the Industrial Revolution. Compared to the wealth of the Duke of Westminster or to fortunes amassed in the City of London, the personal wealth of individual industrialists, as Jose Harris and Pat Thane point out, looked small. These same historians have also reminded us that the political power of the industrialists was limited. In Britain, France and Germany, particularly in the provinces, the landowning classes held the political upper hand. British cabinets and the German civil service were dominated by landowners and nobles right up to 1914. One eminent American historian has even blamed the outbreak of World War I on 'the persistence of the Old Regime'.

Continental comparisons are highly important since they regularly refute commentators, who, although obsesssed with our 'relative decline' are relatively unacquainted with 'relative' or 'comparative' history. Today, it is quite clear that Britain did not suffer economically from any *peculiarly British* resurgence of landed values or influence in the latter half of the nineteenth century. If more subtle social interactions were taking place between the classes than (often Marxist) historians assumed, there is little evidence to suggest that Britain in this respect was out of line with the rest of Europe.

If the British have been accused of cherishing an anti-industrial bias for over a century, they are also held to have been antipathetic to science. In short, 'the decline of the industrial spirit' has been accompanied by the decline of the scientific. As David Edgerton has recently written: 'the first thing we know about *British* science and technology is that it is declining. We have known this for over a hundred years. It is surprising that there is any of it left at all.' The general picture has been one of British higher education dominated by the arts and then the social sciences and of British industry unwilling to invest in research and development (R&D). To quote Edgerton again: 'This picture is more than something we merely know: it is part of the very fabric of British intellectual life. It is a fact beyond dispute that Britain is an anti-scientific, anti-technological and anti-industrial country.' Edgerton, the author of a recent study on *Science, Technology and the British Industrial 'Decline', 1870-1970*, has traced the history of this almost religiously held belief in Britain and has examined it against the scientific evidence. Standing on a mountain of well researched and relevant statistics, he gives short shrift to people like C.P. Snow. The latter, it will be remembered, became something of an intellectual icon in the 1960s with his 'two cultures', the literary and the scientific, and the supposedly dangerous gap between them in Britain. The caricature that Snow was responsible for is deservedly ridiculed as crude and comic. Edgerton quotes the verdict of F.R. Leavis approvingly: Snow was an 'ignoramus'. Other exponents of 'techno-declinism' get equally rough treatment. To quote Edgerton once again:

> Techno-declinism is, intellectually speaking, a mess. It produces explanations which, if taken literally, suggest that British science and technology collapsed around 1870. Oddly, most attention has been given to the years before 1914, when Britain was the most industrialised and richest country in Europe and dominated world trade. The international comparisons declinist historians provide are grossly misleading. They usually seek to explain things which were not the case with explanations that don't work.

Britain, in fact, has been one of the great scientific powers of the twentieth century. Since 1901 it has obtained about the same number of Nobel prizes as Germany and about half as many as the USA. All other countries are way behind. Britain can hardly be seen therefore as a special case of resistance to science.

Myths notwithstanding, in the late Victorian and Edwardian years, British higher education saw the rapid expansion of science and technology so that by 1929, 55% of university students, according to Edgerton, were studying science, technology or medicine. By 1968, the figure was 65%. While in 1929 scientists and technologists alone made up 30% of the student body, the figure rose to more than 50% in 1967. The British higher education system on this reckoning was much more geared to science and technology than that of other European countries. In the mid-1950s, some 44% of British graduates were scientists and technologists; in Germany the figure was 34%, in France 29%, and in Italy 26%. Indeed, Britain during the 1950s and 1960s had more scientists and engineers per capita than any other major capitalist country.

One reason why these facts have been ignored, according to Edgerton, is that historians of 'decline' like Correlli Barnett have made much of the differences before 1914 between British and German education. In their scheme of things, Oxbridge and the British civic universities are compared with German scientific ones. Yet this comparison ignores the traditional German universities. The fact is that traditional British universities embraced science to a far greater extent than traditional German ones. Cambridge, for example, had the largest school of engineering in Britain until the 1940s. Edgerton remarks: 'Those who link the classics to British decline should recall that German universities were citadels of the classics before 1945.'

Another vital part of the declinists' case is that British scientists and engineers have always failed to take up high positions in industry and government. Yet once again, Edgerton refutes this. According to him almost 20% of the leaders of steel firms in the first half of this century had technical qualifications, about half of them acquired at Oxbridge. In the early 1950s, about 20% of members of boards of directors of engineering firms were scientists or technologists, and only about 10% were accountants. There is almost no evience that scientists and technologists were better represented at these levels abroad. At the level of senior civil servants it seems that in the early 1970s the British were much more likely to have had a scientific, mathematical or technical education (26%) than their counterparts in Italy (10%) or Germany (14%). These figures relate to the two highest administrative grades, the equivalent of British permanent and deputy secretaries.

The British record is also much better than popularly supposed if one looks at its record for inventions. Once again, the declinist myth is that Britain gave way to Germany before 1914 and declined in inventiveness thereafter. The truth is that before 1914 Great Britain patented more products per capita in the US than did Germany and that between the wars the two countries were about level. In the post-war period Britain took the lead until the late 1950s. Turning to R&D, which before the 1940s accounted for only a small proportion of inventions, Britain was – like America and everyone else – behind Germany in dyestuffs. But the true picture is that in general most countries were behind America. By the 1920s and 1930s the US was way ahead of the field. Yet there is no evidence that in these decades Britain was behind Germany.

After 1945, it is often claimed, British industry's share of R&D very definitely fell behind that of Germany and Japan as British governments channelled research funds into defence or prestige projects like Concorde. Since Germany and Japan concentrated on civil R&D, their economies grew faster. Even this sort of rigged comparison does not work, however, since, in fact, until the late 1960s, British industry spent more on basic civil R&D than did German or Japanese firms. In the mid-1960s, British firms spent ('with their own money', Edgerton emphasises) 15% of what US firms spent on R&D, with German firms spending 14%, and Japanese and French ones spending merely 10%. In proportion to the output of manufacturing industry, Britain was ahead of Germany and Japan into the early 1970s. In the mid-1960s, remarkably, British industry was spending roughly the same proportion of its output on R&D as was US industry. The trouble is, as the British Ministry of Technology in the 1960s discovered, spending on R&D is neither the only nor the chief determinant of national economic growth.

Still, Britain, as the richest country in Europe until the 1960s, spent the most on invention, innovation and R&D. Its higher education was peculiarly committed to science and technology and its businesses and government had a very high representation of scientists and engineers. This, of course, is Edgerton's conclusion. But it is one that he wisely puts into perspective: 'One should not', he cautions, 'exaggerate contrasts between Britain and other countries. The point is that Britain was not radically different from the main European economies in its attitude to science and technology; such differences as there were suggest British advantages. Nor should we overestimate Britain's place in world technology – this has certainly been the American century. But what is certain is that Britain has been neither particularly anti-science nor anti-industrial.' Edgerton is rightly worried that false interpretations of Britain's scientific past – seeing failure instead of huge success, explaining national decline, when the real historical problem requiring explanation has been our enduring world prominence – will only diminish the reputation of British science and divert potential students from a successful scientific career.

In a quite different way, however, Britain has long been out of step with the rest of Europe: here one enters the realm of psychology rather than that of scientific research or sociology. The main difference between the history of Great Britain and that of nearly all her rivals or competitors between 1850 and 1960, after all, has surely been her enormous success. This has already been touched on. It is also something which rankles, even with many British people, who for one reason or another, are uncomfortable acknowledging it. Nevertheless, it is a factor which cannot be ignored. For the sheer and continued success of British history between 1850 and 1960 – no defeats in major wars, none in world wars, no civil war, no major colonial wars after 1945, no invasions, no territorial disputes or divisions, no collapse of regimes, a high and rising standard of living, world influence on an unequalled scale before 1939 and on a still massive scale after 1945 – can neither be denied nor overlooked. The result was – certainly until the late 1960s – a perhaps not unnatural pride in British institutions, a willingness to take future success for granted, as well as a predisposition not to question British society or institutions. Only in wartime or in the immediate aftermath of war would British governments undertake really radical changes or even contemplate them. Very often, too, changes which had already been introduced in wartime would disappear with the return of peacetime conditions. Elsewhere in the world defeat in war, the collapse of regimes and other national traumas resulted in less complacency. Sometimes, ironically, the situation arose in which the British introduced changes abroad which they might have well have introduced at home: for example, the reform of the trades unions in the British zone of occupied West Germany after 1945; in Britain itself trades unions were allowed to retain their industrial restrictive practices as well as their political influence.

Britain's evident political, economic and international success, therefore, almost certainly promoted the attitude that for the foreseeable future – at least until things went visibly wrong – British institutions should remain the same. It was taken for granted by British policy-makers that British markets would remain unchanged, that British society would stay much the same, and that 'same' would mean 'successful'. Even when, after the 1960s, things seemed to be changing rapidly, there was no strident demand for change. The rise of the Liberal-SPD Alliance represented, if anything, a desire for a quiet life, or in Ralph Dahrendorf's uncharacteristically apposite phrase, 'a better yesterday'. Thatcherism was only popular when it represented traditional values. These did not include innovations like the poll tax, hospital trusts or fundholding GPs – or even at first trade union reforms or privatisation. There was very little gloating over the miners' defeat, despite the cost that a miners' victory would have represented politically and economically. This deeply ingrained conservatism in British life has often had a hugely positive side politically, yet economically it has been one of the causes of our relative decline. The sheer complacency with which we have responded to economic change since 1945 has certainly been a consequence of previous success.

It is now time to turn away from social, sociological or attitudinal factors in assessing Britain's so-called 'relative economic decline' to an examination of the purely economic ones. I plan to do this in two stages, covering the periods 1870-1914, and 1914 to the present. The objective will be to discover whether in either of these periods there were ways in which Britain proved *peculiarly* deficient economically.

Before making a start, however, it is necessary to examine the question whether it was simply 'inevitable' that Britain should be overtaken in terms of production by other, larger nations, once they too had access to the latest technology. Why, for example, should we expect Great Britain to economically outperform the continental United States with a population five times her own? Or a united Germany with a population a third larger or even a Japan with no international defence commitments? Edgerton talks quite straightforwardly about Britain's 'relative decline' as 'inevitable'. Critics who have a problem with this, in his eyes, are 'economically illiterate'. He states:

> They assume that Britain's relative decline was caused by British failures (especially in science and technology). But the bulk of Britain's decline is due to the fact that the rest of the world has become increasingly like Britain; only a small part is due to Britain failing to be as good as other countries. The concept of relative decline is a useful one. If used properly it is a way of saying that in the past Britain carried a much larger weight in the world. So it did, and this past relative success needs explaining. Declinist historians, however, argue that when Britain was at its most successful, it was really failing, and that these failures led to the subsequent decline.

Is this then all that needs to be said? That once other, larger nations acquired the technical knowledge to industrialise, once a skilled (and unskilled) labour force became available to them, they would have access to greater domestic markets than the British (especially if tariff barriers were erected against British goods) and equal access to foreign ones? In fact, did not Britain's 'early start' prove a handicap later on? Her workforce quickly became more unionised, her equipment less modern, her methods and markets more established and therefore less flexible. Did not all these factors mean that after a while Britain's lead in world markets was bound to be challenged? The answer, it seems, has to be yes. Yet this does not in itself dispose of the problem, since some historians have argued that, even so, Britain might have kept her lead longer had she responded to her competitors differently or more vigorously. M.W. Kirby, for example, has written that 'of all possible responses to foreign competition, British industrialists chose the weakest and most conservative course of action, entering new but markedly less prosperous markets, while remaining heavily reliant upon existing product ranges and techniques of production'. He argues that an early start should have meant more technological experience and know-how, and that therefore the lead should have been kept. Besides, in his view, even many of the challengers started with old-fashioned British-type equipment, so that technological change was a problem for them as well. Yet Kirby seems to underestimate the ease with which technology transfers had already taken place and to overestimate the time-lags involved even in the nineteenth century. The German historian, Wolfram Fischer, has pointed out that whereas until 1840 foreign, particularly British firms, supplied German railroads and railway engines, by 1853, 94% of the 729 locomotives used on Prussian railways had been built in Germany. 'It had taken only one decade, from 1842 to 1851, to achieve this dramatic change.' By quickly adapting British technology first in textile machinery and later in mechanical engineering, Germany had by 1850 become an industrial centre in its own right. Or as S.B. Saul has put it: 'Germany was able to use British technology and leap forward where Britain had had to find her way and go up many a blind alley – an inevitable disadvantage of an early start.' It seems therefore that Kirby underestimated the difficulties involved in holding on to a technological lead. What then of his other assertion that the roots of Britain's relative economic decline today are to be found in the period 1875-1900? It has to be admitted that this is a widespread belief in contemporary Britain.

3

Britain's Relative Decline, 1870-1914

The case against British industry in the period 1870-1914 is that it eschewed technological innovation; that it relied far too much on the export of 'staples', i.e. coal, cotton, iron and steel, which accounted for more than 70%; that productivity was falling; that the British share of world markets was declining as exports grew less rapidly than before and more slowly than those of the USA and Germany; while, finally, these exports tended to go to a narrow range of export markets located mainly within the British Empire, South America and Asia. As a result, Germany and the USA could overtake Great Britain by 1914 in terms of industrial production and Germany could take the lead in the 'second industrial revolution' involving chemical products and electrical goods.

Surprisingly, perhaps, given all the clichés about Britain's permanent decline since 1870, there is a counter-case. This is that Great Britain had not lost its entrepreneurial flair; that the British economy was innovating and changing; that its export policies were perfectly 'rational' and that Britain's international financial policies constituted the pivot of an increasingly integrated world economy from which the world as a whole was benefiting. In addition, there is the argument that Germany and the USA were growing more rapidly on account of factors which could not apply to Britain's more mature economy. Finally, the period 1870-1914 cannot be considered one of uniform decline. Between 1900 and 1914, for example, the economy was probably growing less slowly than at any other time since the late eighteenth century. By 1914 there was an export boom; the rate of growth of manufactured exports revived from 1.6% per annum between 1873 and 1899 to 2.7% per annum between 1899 and 1913; the pound was strong and Britain's current account was heavily in surplus.

Let us now look at some of these conflicting arguments in detail, starting with the question of technological innovation or the lack of it. The issue of 'gentrification' has already been dealt with in the previous chapter. The connected argument concerning 'third generation decline', i.e. the hypothesis that the grandsons of the founding fathers of British firms were no longer interested in business, can also be dismissed. It is difficult to find third generation businesses before 1914 for the simple reason that most had only been founded after 1850. Those that did exist, in any case, were not failing. Most British industrialists did manage to adapt to constantly changing market conditions, according to the latest research, and even Kirby has to admit that before 1914 Britain maintained an impressive international lead in a number of industries including heavy armaments, shipbuilding, advanced textile machinery, and heavy machine tools. New industries like pharmaceuticals, soap and confectionary were growing and the period witnessed the rise of the multiple chain store and the expansion of international services such as shipping, banking and insurance.

What about the over-reliance on staples and the lack of technological change there? Economic historians, particularly American cliometricians like L.G. Sandberg, now doubt this. There is no evidence that technological failure in Britain was any greater than in the USA at this time or in Britain at earlier times, certainly no evidence that British 'entrepreneurial failure' or 'technological backwardness' at the time was so much greater than in the USA or Germany that it could have contributed to relative decline.

One reason for this is that economic historians, having developed the tool of 'rationality', now understand that some opportunities which were open to Britain's competitors, were simply not an option at home. Putting themselves in the place of British industrialists of the time, cliometricians (historians working with statistical data) have discovered that these people could not simply have copied techniques being introduced elsewhere. For example, American techniques of cotton-spinning would have been uneconomic in Britain – British wages were too high – and in any case, older techniques were better for the rougher yarns used in Britain. In fact, cotton in the years before 1914 was to report record exports. Another example is coal mining. New American techniques were not introduced before 1914. The reasons for this were partly to do with wages: the sliding scale in British mines meant that it was more rational to employ more labour than use more machinery. Yet geological reasons were also important. To have tried to introduce new machinery into old British shafts would have presented geological difficulties and even risked the collapse of the mines. Finally, with regard to shipyards, Britain was once again in a different position from the Germans and the Americans. The workforce of the latter included large numbers of immigrants from Eastern and South Eastern Europe – cheap labour indeed. In Britain a more stable, skilled labour force was the rule, not unskilled workers. The reluctance of the British industry to move to machine methods, to standardisation and mass production, therefore, was both understandable and justifiable. These, after all, were the appropriate methods for cheap, unskilled labour. But British yards had highly skilled workforces. Hence they were not persuaded of the need to introduce highly expensive new machinery, which could only pay for itself if the yards went in for mass production. This neither the Germans nor anyone else could achieve before 1914. Paradoxically, only the British had sufficient demand to make profits from the new machinery, although they did not need it – and so British yards held on to their competitive lead.

The argument concerning the supposed neglect of science in Britain at this time has already been dealt with. Economic historians now also believe that the British avoided sending workers, foremen and managers to technical schools and colleges because in the British case it was simply more, or at least equally, efficient to train them in the factories themselves through apprenticeship and other schemes. The German historian, Peter Alter, has also stressed official interest in scientific education before 1914 by pointing to the establishment of the National Physical Laboratory (1900), Imperial College (1907), and the Medical Research Committee (1913), as well as to the foundation of new universities at Birmingham (1900), Manchester (1903), Leeds (1904), Sheffield (1905) and Bristol (1909).

It should also be remembered that if comparisons are to be made with German industry it is often not possible to compare like with like. This appears to be the case in matters as diverse as statistics (it is suspected that until 1903 German exports were overestimated by 4% and German imports underestimated by 3%), the trade cycle and the make-up of the national economy. With regard to the latter, we have already seen how cheap immigrant labour was a factor in Germany but not in Britain. Another highly important factor in the German case which did not apply to Britain was Germany's urban boom. Nowhere else in developed Europe, perhaps nowhere else in the world outside the American mid-West, did so many large cities grow up so quickly. There were 48 German towns in 1910 containing over 100,000 people, that is to say with more than a fifth of the total population, and their rate of growth was high because of the skewed pattern of age distribution. Professor S.B. Saul has pointed out that the building of endless miles of stucco dwellings for these people formed a 'constant reinforcement of the process of industrialisation that created them' – a demand for building materials, glass, water and gas and the vast apparatus of trade and transport that allowed them to function. This enabled huge investments to be made in urban electrical works and tramways, but, he points out, there were secondary effects in the production of copper, steel and lead and at the same time electrical generation required more coal and the tramways facilitated more housebuilding. In Britain, by contrast, urbanisation came more slowly, more spread over the century with established horse and steam transport and gaslighting, so that electrification of transport and electric lighting were much slower to come about. Railway building, too, was much more important in Germany at the end of the century than it was in Britain, on account of urbanisation.

The huge urban boom in Germany and the USA, aided as it was by the influx of cheap immigrant labour, also meant that these countries could absorb an influx from the land. In Britain, where there was plenty of spare labour anyway and not much demand from industry for more at this time, the result was higher unemployment, not faster growth. It should be noted in passing that the German boom was not based on chemicals – a common British assumption. True, Germany had taken the technological lead here, but chemicals only employed 2.3% of the German labour force in this period.

In spite of the German boom, however, productivity there remained below the British level. British wages, in fact, remained higher precisely on this account. This was partly because only 7% of Britain's income depended on farming by 1914 compared with Germany's 23%. Moreover, British farming productivity was 30% higher than German. In industry, Britain held the lead, partly because a much higher proportion of her population was employed in mining (a relatively high productivity industry) whereas the Germans had 9% of their industrial workforce in pottery, stone and glass and 10% in wood products, all low productivity industries. The differences between the two countries in metals, engineering and textiles were minimal. But in Germany's high-productivity industry – chemicals – only 2.3% of the workforce were employed. Professor Saul believes it is important to put the German achievement into perspective: the Germans did catch up quickly with the British, but their overall industrial productivity remained lower; they did not match the Americans in terms of specialisation or innovation any more than the British; and a great deal of non-traditional US machinery – typewriters, cash registers, farm machinery – was cheaper and of better quality than the German equivalent. Saul's conclusion is that 'Germany was still a relatively undeveloped country before 1914 measured by the share of her population engaged in farming and did not pass average British income levels till the early 1960s'.

Let us now look at Britain's role in the international economy during this period. Controversy surrounds two aspects of British economic behaviour: the fact that her exports tended to go to traditional markets in the Empire, South America and Asia and that she exported capital on a massive scale. Yet perhaps this was not surprising. Between 1850 and 1914 about 40 million people emigrated from Europe – to North America, Australia, South Africa and New Zealand. Capital was bound to follow. Between 1854 and 1914 the cumulative total of British overseas assets grew from £260 million to £4,107 million, mostly in the form of capital investment for railways, harbours and docks. Thus, from 2% of GNP overseas investment rose to 5.2% of GNP between 1870 and 1913. According to Kirby: 'No country before or since has invested as high a proportion of its resources abroad over such a sustained period.' By 1900 the London capital market was being used primarily for foreign investment and more than 80% of its capital issues were designed for overseas investment. By 1914 Britain owned no less than 43% of the world stock of investment overseas, i.e., in real value, more than all the overseas investments held by the USA today.

Some people have argued that this led to a shortage of capital at home, leading to low investment, productivity and growth and ultimately to a lower share of world markets. Yet the London money market was the most sophisticated in the world and even regional financial facilities were far superior to those abroad. In the 1890s, too, interest rates were very low. So the true picture seems to be that that there was plenty of capital available but little actual demand. Small firms preferred to re-invest their profits rather than rely on the market. There may even have been a paradox involved, namely that whereas the inadequacies of financial provision in the USA would force firms to expand on their own, the adequacy of financial structures in the UK would encourage firms to resist expansion. As Professor Saul has written, 'The efficiency of the capital market inhibited fundamental change.'

One persistent criticism of the British economy during this period has been that its reliance on a limited range of export markets encouraged structural rigidity. In exchange for cheap primary products from Australia, New Zealand, Canada, South America and Asia, Great Britain exported her 'staples' and thus lost any incentive to diversify her economy. Yet British businessmen were in no sense irrational in maintaining their export strategies. Investments in staples were after all *secure* investments with moderate to high yields. Traditional trading links also meant cheap food and hence a higher standard of living. Finally, improvements in transport led to favourable terms of trade. It has even been suggested that 'the close economic relationship between Britain and her principal suppliers means that overseas investment was in a sense tantamount to investing in the primary sector of the British economy'.

Did not these links, on the other hand, tie British traders and manufacturers in the long run to markets which were one day bound to be lost through protection and to goods which were no longer technologically advanced? Did not the export markets comprise countries which (India excepted) were relatively underpopulated and economically semi-developed? Perhaps. Yet who is to say what is to happen in the long term? And how long should the long-term be? And why should good present-day markets be surrendered or compromised in favour of speculative long-term market changes? How were British exporters of staples in 1870 or 1900 to know about conditions after World War I or after the Great Crash of 1929? After all, the Germans, who concentrated on European markets, were to suffer from growing European protectionism. Between 1900 and 1914, in fact, world exports of manufactured goods to semi-industrialised countries such as India, South Africa, Australia and New Zealand rose by 147%, a considerably faster rate than for similar exports to any other group of countries. And since in 1913 Britain supplied 36% of world exports of manufactures and Germany only 9%, she 'obviously positively gained in the structure of her trade'.

Moreover, the 'structure of her trade' should not be confused with 'imperialism'. Here is not the place to enter into a discussion of the defects of the Hobson-Leninist theories of imperialism, yet it should be pointed out that it is by no means clear that Britain benefited from Empire either formally or informally. During this period she was always a free-trading nation with the result that nothing could be imported from her colonies or dominions at a below-world-market price. Imperial preference did not begin until 1897 and even then was so modest as to be of no economic significance. Nor were the consequences of investment in the Empire always directly beneficial. The large sums of money poured into Canada between 1900 and 1914, for example, were mainly used to finance imports from the USA. It must be conceded, on the other hand, that the link with India did help to preserve that particular market for Lancashire cotton. Finally, the costs of Empire were never cheap: men, money, ships, arms and railways all had to be paid for, while other nations were able to trade with the colonies on equal terms and without any of these costs.

Imperialism, like imperial values, therefore, becomes something of a red herring in the history of Britain's 'decline'. The real significance of the trading pattern of late nineteenth-century Britain was that it allowed the City of London to become the centre and pivot for an increasingly integrated world economy from which Britain – and indeed all trading nations – benefited. The system worked as follows: Europe, the USA (and later Japan) imported food from the British Empire and ran up deficits. European countries financed their deficits by running up surpluses on visible account with Britain and on invisible account with the USA; the latter meanwhile financed its deficits by a visible surplus with Great Britain and Canada. Britain for her part was in deficit on her visible account with the USA, Continental Europe and part of her Empire, while running a visible surplus with West Africa, Australia and (particularly) India, and enjoying an invisible surplus with everyone. The system as a whole was financed through the City of London and was based on the gold standard, the latter being based in turn on fixed exchange rates, free convertibility and control of domestic money supplies, controlled at first by the movement of gold and later by the movement of interest rates. The gold standard, however, was in practice a sterling one which meant that sterling as a currency was enormously strong.

The whole system could have faced serious problems due to Britain's constant surplus on current account, yet it proved possible to avoid difficulties partly through Britain's free trade policies and partly through her overseas investments. Free trade in particular allowed debtor countries to finance their debts by exporting to Britain and thus played a key role in promoting multilateral settlements. It therefore restrained international economic trading rivalries of all sorts. On the other hand, it also involved risks: for example, recessions could spread more easily if world markets were closely interconnected. The growing self-sufficiency of the USA was yet another problem, indeed one which was only met by Britain's massive trading surplus with India. The latter financed no less than two-thirds of Britain's balance of payments deficits and could do so because of special free-trading arrangements with the USA and parts of Europe. None the less, Britain was already facing a potential dollar problem as her deficit with the USA on her visible account increased. The question of the future of the Indian market in this respect would therefore be a crucial one.

The answer to Britain's problem was to be found, according to one school of thought, in protection. In the late 1880s, the protectionists rallied under the banner of fair trade and from 1903 under Joseph Chamberlain's banner of tariff reform – the proposal to make the Empire a self-contained commercial unit. This programme, however, conflicted with the booming invisible trade of the City of London (insurance, shipping, banking, investment – worth £340 million per annum by 1914) and the resurgence of the staples in the export markets. Besides, 'Empire trade' was already an anachronism. From 1880 only one-fifth of British imports came from the Empire (despite its expansion), and India too had vital trading links with the USA. Thus the Empire played its part in Britain's well-being only as 'an open dynamic system integrated into the main current of the international economy' and could never have served 'as a defensive mechanism against foreign competition'. Finally, tariff reform might really have overcommitted Britain to traditional markets.

What conclusions should one reach regarding the state of the British economy in the period 1870-1914? An optimist would say that despite the inevitable catching up by other countries, it was still performing well, beginning to diversify and showing no signs of technological failure. He might add that it dominated and sustained an international financial system out of which it benefited enormously and adhered to markets which, however traditional, were booming by 1914. True, there were difficulties on the horizon, which included increasing foreign (particularly American) competition, advancing protectionism, and growing labour unrest at home (a subject which still needs comparative economic research). None the less, the increasing specialisation in shipping, banking, insurance, the build-up of huge overseas investments, the rise of new industries (pharmaceuticals, footwear, food-processing, bicycles) and the development of the multiple chain store all gave grounds for optimism. What really went wrong was not business policies or commercial strategy but the outbreak of World War I, which simply destroyed the international economy of which Britain was the centre.

There is almost certainly a great deal of sense in this viewpoint, although it can easily be exaggerated. It is very difficult indeed to believe that all the apparant technological deficiencies of British industry before 1914 can be explained away by 'rationality'. Even some of the cliometricians are now in revolt against this proposition. Likewise, it is extremely difficult to deny that more diversification was needed. On the whole, however, it would still seem to be wise to resist the argument that the roots of Britain's present-day problems are to be found in the period between 1870 and 1914. If peace had continued, there is every reason to believe that the country would have had time to adjust to new market forces within a favourable international economic environment.

4

Britain's Relative Decline since 1914

World War I killed off not merely the old international economy but Britain's position at its centre. More than that, it made the USA the world's leading economic power; it destroyed the export markets for Britain's staples; and it enhanced the economic significance of the new industries in which Britain was under-represented. At the end of the war America's index of industrial production stood 20% higher; she had no need for economic adjustment. She had provided the wartime requirements of her allies and taken over their traditional markets. Japan had also done very nicely in the Far East – in India, China and the East Indies. And since Japan had concentrated her economic energies on cotton it was Great Britain that she threatened most. However, it was not just the rise of the USA and Japan that threatened British trade. After the war countries like Canada and Australia – not to mention the South American states and China – had become much more industrialised, with the result that there was less demand for British staples in these markets anyway. Perhaps worst of all for British exporters was the fact that India had obtained control of her own tariff policies and had begun raising her tariffs against British goods, particularly cotton. Even demand for coal began to fall once petroleum-based transport became more available. The war, moreover, had brought about a glut in shipping and primary products, causing world prices to fall for commodities produced by countries which had traditionally imported British goods. Britain's trading world had fallen apart and her position regarding invisibles had also weakened. No less than 10% of her overseas assets had had to be sold to help pay for the war; she had accumulated a substantial war debt with the United States; London's position regarding short-term credit had disappeared; while Britain's lack of a surplus on current account in the 1930s (and lack of a trading surplus throughout the period) meant that she could not rebuild her overseas wealth.

Britain's response to these factors was not one of immediate or radical adjustment, however. Her natural desire was for a return to 'normalcy', to employ the Americanism of the time. The re-stocking boom of 1919-20 reinforced this predisposition, bringing a return to the gold standard in 1925 at $4.85 per ounce. This necessitated a policy of deflation, enforced through 'dear money'. The consequence, given the international economic environment, was high unemployment. In the view of some economists and historians, a 10% devaluation might have solved many problems. This view, however, fails to take into account the number of countries which in any case traded in sterling, ignores the possible retaliation of other countries, and overlooks the fact that in certain parts of the world in the inter-war period, British goods were not wanted at any price. Others have suggested that a Keynesian policy of demand management might have been the answer. Yet a growing consensus of economic historians rejects this. Retrospective econometric applications of Keynes's policies suggest that they would merely have scratched the surface of the problem. Moreover, business confidence was absolutely essential to such a policy and neither business nor the Treasury possessed such confidence. Hence deflation prevailed. Even so, the 1920s, despite a million unemployed, could register a sort of boom and an albeit much smaller surplus on current account until the Great Crash of 1929. Industrial production between 1920 and 1929 grew by 2.8% per annum and industrial productivity by 3.8% per annum.

Was the economy adjusting at all? In the view of some economic historians, it was indeed. They argue that the technological advances spurred on by World War I – motor cars, aircraft, advanced machine tools, chemicals, ballbearings, etc. – had led to more applied science and standardisation in new industries such as motor manufacture, electrical engineering, chemicals, paper and printing. Even the staple industries had become more efficient with an 18% rise in productivity recorded in coal mining between 1924 and 1930 and one of 25% in iron and steel production between 1923 and 1930. Other historians, however, have ascribed most of this simply to rising unemployment and increased mechanisation.

We shall return to the controversy concerning the 'new industries' presently. Meanwhile, it is important to understand that growth and current account surpluses were still dependent on the international economy which continued to function since, although the USA lacked experience in running the world economy, dollars nevertheless continued to flow abroad, the USA still imported primary produce from abroad, and Europe continued to enjoy a balance of payments surplus with these primary producers which enabled her to finance her deficit with the USA. But the weaknesses of the new system – short-term American lending to the German banks which in turn lent long; reparations and hot money flows which complicated the trade cycles; and the refusal of the USA to recognise the link between reparations and war debts – were to overwhelm it after 1929. By 1932 it had collapsed and Britain had to face an even more severe problem of adjustment than in the previous decade.

The 1930s were generally a very difficult decade for Britain, but nowhere was this more true than in the field of international economics. Britain's economy, which had been formed within a multilateral trading system, now had to exist in an autarchic world. Extreme protectionism, exchange controls and the bilateral balancing of such controls all indicated trouble for Britain's export trade. If this was not bad enough, the outlook was made even worse by the general contraction of export demand that followed the collapse and slow recovery of world output and employment.

The trouble was that in the conditions of a world slump, British policy alone could not restore the world economy. Britain therefore had to adjust to the new international economic order and did so by a mixture of expedients, including leaving the gold standard, imposing tariff restrictions and expanding imperial preferences. There were various other negotiations involved: with the countries of the Empire at Ottawa in 1932; with the South American and Scandinavian states between 1932 and 1934; and with the USA in 1936-38. These last negotiations confirmed the position of the USA as the leading international economic power. Yet although all these efforts helped exports and and the collection of overseas dividends and interest to some extent, 'their overall effect', to quote a leading economic historian, 'was small.' They certainly failed to revive the export trade, which in terms of value or volume never recovered its 1929 level. By 1938, moreover, Britain's world share of manufactured exports had slightly fallen, while her share of exports to the empire had shrunk substantially. In the 1930s, therefore, the British account was unhealthy. From 1931 to 1938 there were deficits every year except for 1935, and the cumulative current account deficit totalled £375 million. Combined with defaults and the decline in value of many overseas assets, this represented an important fall in Britain's net worth. And 'this dreary performance' according to the same authority, was 'especially striking when we recall that Britain herself had become a protectionist country.'

The same economic historian, however, is correct to point out that this did not 'represent some sort of fundamental failure', partly because an important part of the problem arose from the overseas property account. If overseas property income had flowed into Britain in the 1930s as in the late 1920s, between 1930 and 1938 she would have netted an extra £647 million – nearly twice the accumulated deficit on current account during these years. Moreover, although the export record was fairly feeble (77% of the 1929 volume and 67% of the 1913 volume in 1937), 'Britain did not do so badly in exporting the products of her newer industries, even under the conditions of the 1930s'. In 1929 the old staples produced 42% of export receipts and the new industries only 8.2%; by 1937 the corresponding figures were 37% and 21%. On the other hand, by the same time Canadian-assembled motor cars had developed a certain market in the UK, Japanese and Indian cottons had begun to arrive, while Hong Kong and Singapore were sending some clothes and rubber goods. The 'Third World' had thus begun to industrialise; 'the patterns of the 1960s were already beginning to emerge.'

Britain, therefore, attempted with some success to adjust to the very difficult conditions of the international economy after World War I. Her record was in some ways rather good, leading at least one distinguished economic historian to write of an economic 'recovery' in the 1930s. Not only did industrial production grow faster in the period 1929-37 than in 1901-13, but the rate of growth of output per man-hour per annum was faster throughout the post-1913 period than between 1870 and 1913. International comparisons also showed Britain in a good light (see Tables 1 and 2).

Table 1. Rate of growth of industrial production per annum

	1913-37	1913-29	1929-37
UK	2.0	1.3	3.4
Germany	1.2	0.9	3.0
France	0.8	2.0	−2.8
USA	2.9	4.2	0.4
OECD countries	1.6	1.4	2.2

Table 2. Rate of growth of output per man hour per annum

	1913-38	1913-29	1929-38
UK	2.1	2.1	2.1
Germany	1.2	0.8	2.1
France	2.3	2.8	1.6
USA	3.0	2.8	3.3

Nevertheless, there is much argument concerning the contribution made to this recovery by the 'new industries'. Earlier assessments that these were 'recovery inducing' have been revised for several reasons. For a start, they constituted too small a sector of the economy at the beginning of the 1930s to have been able to exert such an influence. According to one authority, all of them with the exception of motor vehicles were disinvesting by 1932, and in the crucial period of 1932-34 accounted for, at the most in any one year, a mere 3.5% of total net investment undertaken and only 7% of total employment. By the end of the decade, the staple industries continued to bulk just as large in the economy. If three of the most important new industries – motor vehicles, electrical engineering, rayon and silk manufacture – in 1937 accounted for 9.7% of the capital stock of manufacturing industry, cotton textiles alone, after more than two decades of almost continuing decline, still accounted for 8.4%. Finally, if productivity in most new industries rose in the 1930s, it also did so in many of the staples. Thus equally impressive achievements were recorded in agriculture, textiles, iron and steel. It is difficult therefore to assign the new industries more than a contributing role in the recovery of the 1930s, which had, in any case, come to an end by 1938 and was sustained thereafter by rearmament policies.

There is also controversy in the historical literature concerning the role of industrial rationalisation in the recovery. It has been shown that in the

1920s an unprecedented number of mergers took place. However, it would seem that these did not aid growth. Perhaps only two British companies, ICI and Unilever, succeeded in developing a relatively advanced multi-divisional structure, on the American model of General Motors or Du Pont, as an answer to problems posed by large-scale organisation. Even ICI, however, was not much of a model: between 1927 and 1930 it invested £20 million in a fertilizer plant at Billingham (equivalent to nearly one third of total fixed capital formation in manufacturing industry in 1930) all of which had to be written off as a gigantic failure. Detailed studies of Courtaulds and Imperial Tobacco show that these firms also suffered from major deficiencies. Nor did the motor or electrical engineering industries prove highly efficient: mass-produced American radios, vacuum cleaners and batteries flooded the market, while 'in 1939 the six leading British (motor car) producers, making roughly 350,000 private cars, turned out more than forty different engine types, and even greater numbers of chassis and body models, which was considerably more than the number offered by the three leading producers in the United States making perhaps 3,500,000 cars'. It is probable that no close relationship can be established between changes in scale or organisation and productivity increases. A great number of mergers, for example, turn out to have been defensive acts in the face of shrinking markets or intensifying competition. New company names were often just banners under which loose federations of firms tied by mutual financial arrangements operated with a fair measure of individual independence.

Economic historians have thus reached the conclusion that although Britain was not falling behind her main competitors in the 1930s in terms of productivity and was adjusting to the economically altered circumstances of the inter-war international economy, British management was resistant to change and unwilling to adopt US production methods.

One other aspect of British industry during this period which deserves note is its poor industrial relations. After the failure of the General Strike of 1926, the unrest of the immediate post-war years died away. Unemployment brought employers a quieter life as did the fact that falling prices allowed them to reward those in work with reasonable pay rises. However, the bitterness of past disputes, especially in the staple industries, hardened attitudes among organised labour, so that not only their traditional prejudices but their traditional labour practices were transferred to the new industries: these included demarcation disputes, restrictive practices and overmanning. The motor industry, for example, now laid the foundations for all its troubles in the 1960s by agreeing to a multiplicity of unions with all the attendant disadvantages associated with demarcation disputes and wage differentials. In the staple industries meanwhile, due to exactly the same factors, growth in productivity was all too often from a low base, with US competitors achieving productivity rates sometimes 200% greater.

The real upturn in the economy in the 1930s was caused not by the rationalisation of industry or by the growth of new industries but, most probably, by the housing boom encouraged by the government's 'cheap money' policy. British industry, management and labour, still had to come to terms with the challenges of the post-war world and not even World War II would see them put aside their differences. Yet given the world-wide slump, civil wars and political changes of the interwar period, Britain did very well to escape the bloodshed, dictatorships and civil strife of many parts of Europe, not to mention the mass unemployment of the USA. Compared to most places, interwar Britain was a pleasant place to be, and for all her need to adjust, only Fascists or Communists were prepared to write Britain off in terms of economics or politics.

Until fairly recently Britain's domestic record during World War II appeared to confirm the fact that a stable political and economic system served the country well. The traditional Churchillian picture of a nation pulling together, sharing hardship and adversity while taking the lead in resisting the fascist dictators and their New Order in Europe, was taken for granted as the historical truth. Yet the revisionist historian Correlli Barnett, in his book *Audit of War*, has suggested that all this is myth. In his view – and he sees post-war Britain as having been a 'lousy place to live in' (his own words to the author) – Britain during World War II was class-ridden and socially divided with the trades unions, under Communist control, causing strikes in key industries at crucial periods during the struggle. Nazi Germany, by contrast, managed to organise her war effort much better. Barnett's view has not prevailed, however. No doubt his research has provided us with a much needed corrective to the more dewy-eyed accounts of wartime Britain, yet his view has been condemned as unbalanced and historians of Nazi Germany have shown how inefficient wartime production there actually was. Barnett has extended his criticisms of Britain into the post-war period with the publication of his *Lost Victory* arguing that Britain should not have honoured her sterling balances (war debts to India and Egypt, and other countries) after the war, that she should have surrendered her empire, that she should have refused to create a welfare state and that her share of Marshall Plan aid should not have gone into supporting the pound but into modernising her infrastructure. Once again, much of this appears unhistorical and written too obviously under the influence of hindsight. The truth is that, given British victory during the war, certain commitments were unavoidable. These included a world role (although huge parts of the empire were given up or granted independence), the maintenance of sterling as a reserve currency, and the creation of a welfare state, the promise of which played such a large part in Labour's general election victory in 1945. Once again Barnett has written time-and-motion history with human beings and international politics left out.

There can be little doubt that from 1950 to 1980 Britain was in relative economic decline. (This was not true of the immediate post-war period.) In terms of international politics, on the other hand, she was still a world power of considerable influence (see the Introduction, pp. 3-4), decolonising peacefully and successfully, taking part in all key international developments from the Korean War to the NATO twin-track decision to bring Cruise and Pershing missiles into Western Europe. She built up a nuclear deterrent with US help (a sign of her unique relationship with the USA and therefore one of British influence, not decline. Which other power was sold nuclear missiles capable of ending life on the planet?) Nor did she become a US satellite. She vetoed the US plan to allow the French to drop atom bombs on Vietnam in 1954 and despite great pressure on weak Labour governments during the 1960s, refused to become an ally of the USA against North Vietnam. Despite many myths, Suez had no particular symbolism for UK foreign policy or in fact any long-term consequences for the 'special relationship' which certainly existed. And still does. Yet Britain's sensible decision to steer clear of the process of European integration for so long, and her many justified complaints about its deficiencies once she entered, have led Eurofanatics to rewrite her contemporary history in such a way that Britain's huge success in post-war diplomacy has been completely obscured. Should Britain withdraw from the EU, professional historians, those objective and balanced residents of university departments, who follow events, not fashion, will soon redress the balance.

How then do we account for Britain's relative decline between 1950 and 1980? Clearly the impact of World War II had been profound, worse in fact than that of World War I. Between 1939 and 1945 Britain sustained an accumulated deficit on current account of £10,000 million. In order to finance this (not to mention an extra £100 million in foreign and gold reserves) she had received £5,400 million in lend-lease and mutual aid from the USA and Canada, sold £1,000 million of some of her most lucrative pre-war foreign investments, requisitioned £100 million of private gold and dollar balances and increased the volume of short-term overseas liabilities (mainly in sterling) by a massive £3,100 million. Altogether, according to one authority, 'approximate calculations carried out by the Treasury indicated that by the end of 1945 one-quarter of the country's pre-war wealth had been liquidated as a direct consequence of Britain's commitment to the Allied war effort'.

There was a positive side, however. As in 1914-18, World War II also aided the process of modernisation. The amount of electrical power available to the economy increased by 50%, and at the end of the war the Ministry of Supply had made over $100 million worth of machine tools (about twenty years' worth) and 75 million square feet of factory space available. One writer has pointed out:

> The iron and steel, machine tool, vehicle, aircraft, chemical, plastic, electrical and electronic industries had all been expanded. The stimulus afforded

by war needs to the development of radar, radio, even simple computers in anti-aircraft defence, provided an invaluable basis for much post-war civil developments. Chemical substitutes for many raw materials had been known before the war, but the creation of the British petro-chemical industry really dates from 1942 .... Finally, if rail and road transport, the textile and certain other industries had suffered severe disinvestment during the war, the mechanisation of both coal and agriculture had been accelerated.

None the less, the immediate post-war period saw Britain confronted with severe economic problems, mainly on account of the 'dollar gap'. It was only with the implementation of the Marshall Plan, the start of reconstruction and, later on, the world trade boom which accompanied the Korean War that the gap disappeared and the British economy revived – with full employment. By 1950 Britain had a current account surplus of £297 million and by 1951 exports were 75% greater than their 1938 volume.

Yet in the period 1950-1973 Britain failed to take advantage of the booming world economy and fell further behind in the 1970s. Every other country seemed to experience an 'economic miracle' of some sort. Britain's 'economic miracle' was to fail to achieve one. In the words of one expert: 'Surely it must have required a powerful and sustained effort or most unusual circumstances, to prevent the world boom from spilling over into Britain as well.' Instead Britain experienced balance of payments crises every few years after 1947 leading to devaluations in 1949 and 1967. In the years 1953 to 1973 the average growth in GDP for France was 5.3%, for West Germany 5.5%, for Italy 5.3%, for Austria 5.7%, but for the UK only 3%. What factors explain this relative lack of growth on Britain's part?

Several factors have been selected by historians. Popular among them, on the one hand, have been sterling's role as a world reserve currency, Britain's overseas military spending, the concentration of research and development on military-related projects, and the consequent failure to invest in the productive parts of the domestic economy. These factors, taken together, can perhaps be seen as a left-wing model of what went wrong, based on the existence of an imperial, world-power Britain sacrificing domestic prosperity to imperial prestige, the world banking system, outdated military ambitions, all because domestic governments were run by anachronistic elites with out-of-date ideas about Britain's world role. In fact, given Correlli Barnett's books, this is more than just a left-wing critique. But does it hold up?

Barnett quotes a Treasury mandarin who wrote in 1951: 'The existence of the Sterling Area and the widespread use of sterling carry obvious risks for the UK.' Britain had to have balance of payments surpluses to ensure that she could cope with movements of sterling abroad. Thus Marshall Aid was used, not to build up Britain's rickety infrastructure but to finance the Sterling Area's gold and dollar payments. In short it was squandered to keep up the value of the pound. The so-called 'sterling balances' – debts run up to India, Egypt and other countries during the war – exacerbated the problem and Barnett suggests, unrealistically, that Britain should just have repudiated these along with sterling's world role and allowed the Commonwealth – another anachronism – to break up up. Yet the Foreign Office saw the Commonwealth as a basis for world influence and 'the Bank of England strove from 1944 onwards to perpetuate the traditional role of sterling out of much the same kind of nostalgic illusion as inspired the Chiefs of Staff and the Foreign Office to cling on to the world role'.

Sydney Pollard in his devastating study of 1982 entitled *The Wasting of the British Economy* had made the same general point. Yet it was an essential part of his case that sterling was endangered not by any defect in Britain's capacity to trade – the purely private trading account (visibles and invisibles) was invariably in surplus – but by government spending (mainly on defence) overseas. In short, the British domestic economy was sacrificed to please the the international bankers and the military, both of whom showed a contempt for industry and production. This is a case which has been made, with more ideological overtones by others, including both Malcolm Chalmers and Andrew Gamble.

In Pollard's view, government spending overseas tipped the current account surpluses into deficit and caused balance of payments crises which were dealt with by deflation. The means involved, however, always included a cutting-back of investment which meant that the economy was unable to respond to the next period of expansion. Bottlenecks would then arise, imports would flood in and soon another balance of payments crisis would arise. Once again investment would be cut, the economy would once more be unable to respond to the upswing, and a vicious circle or downward spiral of decline would begin. And what was declining in particular was Britain's industrial base. This process, according to Pollard, continued from the balance of payments crisis of 1947 right through to 1972 when at last the pound was floated and sterling abandoned its role as a reserve currency. Yet even this was to make little difference, according to Pollard, since just at the moment when it might have been possible to make some difference, a new set of theories emerged which provided new excuses to cut the country's manufacturing base in an attempt to regulate the money supply. From 1976 onwards, therefore, the result was yet another series of cuts in the real economy leading to a new downward spiral: inflationary pressures leading to cuts, to unemployment relief, to an enlarged public sector borrowing requirement, leading to more cuts, to more unemployment and so on, with the productive base of the economy being so reduced that it could not possibly deliver growth. At the same time, Britain was increasing her defence budget and in 1982 even fighting a war over the Falkland Islands. Pollard was to despair of any long-term economic recovery.

Some of Pollard's key points had already been made in a book by W.A.P. Manser as far back as 1971 entitled *Britain in Balance: the Myth of*

Failure. Manser gave the figures for Britain's balance of payments from 1958 to 1969, reproduced here in Table 3. From these he concluded: 'The plain testimony of the figures, then, is unequivocal. Britain does not run up a commercial deficit. For the cause of her payments imbalance we need look no further than official activity. If there were no Government spending, there would be no deficit and no balance of payments problem.'

Table 3

	Private balance (£million)	Official balance (£million)	Overall balance (£million)
1958	+558	−410	+148
1959	+367	−479	−112
1960	+76	−533	−457
1961	+605	−541	+64
1962	+625	−611	+14
1963	+548	−619	−35
1964	−78	−666	−744
1965	+425	−677	−252
1966	+706	−754	−48
1967	+332	−793	−461
1968	+387	−785	−398
1969	+1326	−924	+384

Manser also pointed out the implications of these figures regarding any comparison of Britain's position with that of Germany or Japan. Had these countries been spending money on overseas defence commitments on the same scale as Britain, Germany in 1966, instead of having a balance of payments surplus of £92 million would have had a deficit of £598 million. Japan's surplus of £120 million would have become a deficit of £300 million. Even taking 'offset costs' for British troops in Germany into consideration, the deficit would still have been £160 million. Manser denied that the British were inefficient or were in any way guilty of 'pricing themselves out of world markets'. The actual prices of world trade were unknown and could not be known, since no statistical service collected them. Nor did it matter, according to Manser, what the British sold. The Swiss did well with clocks, while Britain led Europe in research into aerospace, chemicals, electrical goods and computing. All the relevant data did not point to 'an inert or inadaptable economy'. In reviewing Manser's book, A.J.P. Taylor wrote: 'It is political dynamite, making nonsense of this country's economic policies over the last 40 years. The pundits greeted it with embarrassed silence.'

In 1985, in a book entitled *Paying for Defence: Military Spending and British Decline*, Malcolm Chalmers took Manser's point a great deal further, quoting a 1973 study by Kent W. Rothschild which concluded that 'high military expenditure reduces export availabilities in the machinery and transport equipment sector where chances for export expansion have been above average. This brake on the most expansive sector dampens export growth in general. A slow-down in GNP growth follows from this.' The point was that resources for the modernisation of civilian industry had been lost and that markets had been taken over by others. Britain's share of the world market in manufactured exports had therefore fallen from 25.5% in 1950 to 8% by 1983. Chalmers also enlarged on Manser's arguments concerning the balance of payments for the 1970s looking at the defence element of official balances (Table 4).

Table 4

	Private balance (£m)	Official balance (£m)	Military element (£m)	Overall balance (£m)
1970-81	+11169	−22747	−7021	−11578
1958-81	+16710	−30330	−9790	−13620

Chalmers concluded: 'Even after military withdrawal from most extra-European commitments by the early 1970s military spending abroad remained substantial. In 1984-5 estimated net military spending overseas is £1,369 million, which comfortably exceeded the net government contribution to the EEC (£375 million in 1984-5) over which there has been considerably more controversy.' Chalmers also argued that the higher proportion of GNP spent by Britain on defence compared to other European countries not merely diverted resources from more profitable fields of investment, but positively failed to generate much of a 'spin-off' for civilian industry.

Table 5. Percentage of GDP spent on defence, 1950-1983

	1950	1955	1960	1965	1970	1975	1980	1983
USA	5.1	10.2	9.0	7.6	8.0	5.9	5.6	6.9
UK	6.6	8.2	6.5	5.9	4.8	4.9	5.1	5.6
France	5.5	6.4	6.5	5.2	4.2	3.8	4.0	4.2
West Germany	4.4	4.1	4.0	4.3	3.3	3.6	3.3	3.4
The Netherlands	4.8	5.7	4.1	4.0	3.5	3.4	3.1	3.3
Australia	3.0	3.8	2.7	3.4	3.5	2.8	2.7	2.8
Italy	4.3	3.7	3.3	3.3	2.7	2.5	2.4	2.8
Canada	2.6	6.3	4.2	2.9	2.4	1.9	1.8	2.1
Spain	−	2.2	2.2	1.8	1.6	1.7	1.9	2.1
Japan	−	1.8	1.1	0.9	0.8	1.0	1.0	1.0

According to Chalmers, Britain's high military budget undermined civilian research and development. For example, by 1956 40% of all professionally qualified scientists and engineers engaged in research and development were working on defence projects. Secondly, almost 60% of these projects were financed from defence funds and nearly two-thirds of the research done by private industry were on defence contracts. The result was that the mechanical engineering industry, shipbuilding and steel employed scarcely any graduate engineers before the 1960s, in marked contrast to the prominent place they held in German industry. Ironically, however, Britain still had to look abroad for nuclear weapons and military aircraft, although the proportion of her research and development budget devoted to defence was still extremely high.

Table 6. Percentage of research and development budget devoted to defence

	1963-5	1966-70	1971-5	1976-9	1980
Canada	10.6	7.2	n.a.	3.6	2.7
France	26.2	22.5	18.4	19.6	23.3
W. Germany	10.8	10.3	6.9	6.2	n.a.
Italy	2.6	2.4	2.1	1.9	1.4
Japan	0.9	0.9	0.7	0.6	0.6
Netherlands	1.9	2.3	2.0	1.6	1.5
Spain	2.7	5.1	n.a.	3.3	n.a.
Sweden	34.2	27.3	15.2	14.2	n.a.
UK	34.5	25.6	28.9	29.3	28.0
USA	40.6	31.2	27.7	25.4	23.0

Theoretically, of course, military research could produce benefits for civilian use. Yet in Britain this does not seem to have been the case. Such funds were used, for example, to subsidise Rolls Royce and to produce that 'white elephant', Concorde. Little wonder therefore that N.K. Gardner, according to Chalmers, could report to the Department of Industry in 1976 that since 1945 the total return on £1,500 million (at 1974 prices) invested in the civil aerospace industry had amounted to less than £150 million. As the Germans and Japanese recognised, there was little point in competing in this sphere with the Americans. This was also true of nuclear power generation where the British failed once again to compete successfully. Yet even in 1981-2 the Department of Energy was spending £172 million out of its research and development budget of £216 million on atomic energy, while only £500,000 was going on energy conservation and less than £1 million on solar energy. The case of naval research was equally depressing. Despite subsidised shipyards and concessionary finance, the message had not yet sunk in that naval and merchant ships had to be very differently designed and that 'the community of interest between naval and civil ships research workers can be exaggerated' (Geddes Report).

Finally, according to Chalmers, not even the arms race offered much of an excuse. True, it brought into Britain £2,400 million a year from abroad. But the return was in fact a poor one. Italy, whose defence expenditure was only about 40% of that of the UK, had an equal share of the arms market. And France, with a comparable defence budget, earned two and a half times as much between 1979 and 1983. According to many commentators, therefore, if Britain were to concentrate all her research on defence and related projects, she would lose the chance to enter modern markets like computers, digital technology, and other consumer durables. Once the North Sea oil ran out she would thus face an overwhelming balance of payments crisis. In fact, Chalmers hinted that the state of the UK economy was not that unlike the portrait of the Soviet economy supplied in the Defence White Paper of 1984:

> It has been estimated that (Soviet) military requirements absorb a third of the output of the important machine-building and useful-working sector. The defence industries thus deprive the civil sector of secure resources, particularly skilled management. Unlike the West there is little spin-off from technological advances in the defence sector into the civil economy and this pre-emption of key resources for defence thus inhibits general economic development.

One set of explanations for Britain's relative decline in the period 1950-80, therefore, argues that it was brought about by balance of payments crises caused by government overseas spending, particularly defence spending, and that these crises resulted in the cutting back of investment in the productive side of the economy from which research and development scientists had already been diverted on account of defence policy. This whole situation was made much worse by the fact that the value of the pound had to be upheld in order to maintain the confidence of the other members of the Sterling Area. For this reason, Marshall Aid was used to bolster the currency rather than the real economy and the standard of living of the ordinary citizen was sacrificed to the policy requirements of generals and bankers.

In examining to what extent this case can be upheld, there can certainly be little doubt of the value that ministers ascribed to sterling, particularly before Britain's entry into the EEC. By 1950 Britain's imports from the USA could already be offset by her surplus with the Sterling Area, which was in itself in surplus with America. Meanwhile, the sterling balances were about five times as high as Britain's gold and foreign currency reserves. To risk confidence in these, therefore, meant undermining Britain's currency with ominous and unforeseeable effects. Governments, however, were not always unwilling to cut their defence and overseas commitments, and this happened spectacularly in 1947-8, was meant to happen after 1957, happened in 1967 and again in 1982. However, as one can see, the results were much less radical than were perhaps anticipated. This model, therefore, would seem to fit the facts quite well. Yet other economists and economic historians have cast doubts on its value.

Alex Cairncross, for example, while admitting that investment was consistently lower in the UK during this period than in the USA, France, West Germany or Japan, attached little significance to the fact. His argument was that where output was faster, so too was investment, which merely reflected growth, not caused it. In other words, 'investment seems more likely to be symptomatic, not causal'. Pollard's reply was that perhaps this was so, but that low investment would always preclude growth. Cairncross's main point, however, was that in Britain a given amount of output required twice as much investment. Hence other reasons had to be found to explain relative decline. On arguments about failure to develop new technologies or the devastating results of balance of payments crises, he remained distinctly sceptical. He pointed out, with regard to new technologies, that 'research by the National Institute of Economic and Social Research, covering some of the major innovations of the post-war period from float glass to jet engines, does not bear this out and suggests that the British record was about average in comparison with other countries'. On the balance of payments, Cairncross admitted that it was 'natural' to infer some connection between this and sluggish growth, but it was really rather difficult to explain. Slow growth, after all, might produce low exports. In short, balance of payments crises might be the result of slow growth, not vice versa. The evidence seemed to be that the buoyancy of international markets had made very little difference to British exports, which could fall when world trade rose and rise when world trade fell. Similarly, deflationary policies by British governments had made no obvious difference, according to Cairncross. Hence it was difficult in his view not to conclude that this elasticity should be regarded as a 'symptom of the general sluggishness of the economy'.

In Cairncross's view, the significance of balance of payments crises had been overrated, since in amplitude and frequency they had been no worse than in other countries. France had had such crises constantly in the 1950s and Japan had never enjoyed surpluses on current account until the 1960s. Britain's real problem was the steady decline of her share in world exports of manufactured goods which had accelerated since 1945 despite the expansion of the world economy. British exports were rising, but not nearly fast enough. This had led to calls for 'export-led growth', Cairncross noted, although there was no logical reason to suppose that more exports would lead to more growth. In fact, the opposite was more likely to be true. His conclusion was: 'If exports can be said to have lagged, the lag was not very large and was not obviously decisive. On the contrary, it seems much more in keeping with the evidence to regard exports as held back by the same forces and to roughly the same extent as output itself.' Here, however, he was not thinking of military expenditure, which he clearly regarded as irrelevant to the story. (Others, it should be noted, would agree with him. Defence after all is one of a government's primary obligations and for a long period after 1945, it was clear for political reasons that it could not be entrusted to Britain's former enemies, the Germans and the Japanese. Besides, France managed to achieve an 'economic miracle' in terms of growth with a defence budget comparable to ours and despite balance of payments crises. These critics forget, however, that a huge proportion of the French military budget in the 1950s was underwritten by the USA.) Instead Cairncross believed that the real constraint on growth in Britain was bad industrial relations and that the blame for this was to be assigned primarily to the trade unions.

He was not alone in this view. Almost all the literature shows that British trade unions were perhaps the greatest cause of all of Britain's relative decline. Their traditional legal privileges, their political domination of the Labour Party, their refusal to use modern working practices all meant that they dragged Britain down the international league tables. Alford wrote in 1981 that 'anyone with even the slightest interest in Britain's economy since the Second World War can hardly fail to recognise in this (trade union power) a major, if not the single most important factor in industrial performance – or the lack of it.' There was certainly plenty of evidence to back up such views, much of it summarised by Stanislaw Gomulka in 1978 in his essay on Britain's slow industrial growth. For example, a study carried out by the University of Birmingham's Department of Engineering Production on the working day of workers in 40 engineering and metal-working firms during the years 1968-72 and a series of case studies of 45 firms in the period 1970-74 showed that on average workers spent 16% of their time 'waiting' to use machines, 48% of their time using them, while for about 50% of working time these machines lay idle. R. Bacon and W. Eltis discovered that machine tools used in British manufacturing were on average no older than in the USA, but that output per machine tool and per man was two to three times greater in the USA. Another study discovered that American firms and multinationals all found British labour considerably less productive than that in France, West Germany, the USA or Canada. Finally, the 'Think Tank' report on the British car industry found that British car workers operating the same machines produced only half the output of their West German counterparts. There are many similar studies. And the latest research (C. Bean and N. Crafts) backs them up.

Yet why did these results apply? Were management or workers to blame? Certainly management could not be exonerated: there was far too much evidence of bad design, poor quality and bad performance among a wide range of British products. Yet on the issue of productivity, most of the blame lay with the workforce and their trade union representatives. This was not because of their strike record. Professor Turner of Cambridge demonstrated in 1969 that compared with other countries, Britain was not 'strike prone'. Rather, it was a matter of demarcation disputes and restrictive practices: too many unions inside any given factory, too many men working on any one job, too many arguments over who did what, too many machines lying idle at night or during parts of the working day, too little control of shop stewards by national trade union leaders, and too much political influence on the part of these same leaders who often could not deliver the agreement of their members to nation-wide policies negotiated on their behalf. The result, in Cairncross's words, was as follows:

> The evidence suggests that when British management sought to raise productivity by the use of modern methods and equipment they found themselves obliged to accept conditions as to manning, operation or pay that cancelled out much of the advantage of making changes and were not insisted upon by the employees of their competitors abroad. Managements also had to devote much of their time to dealing with labour disputes and to contend with a heavy weight of government regulation that absorbed scarce managerial time and deflected effort from innovating tasks of prior importance to economic growth.

The reasons behind this situation were well known. Given the rise of unemployment in Britain, which was steady, albeit from a low base after 1945, trade unions never really believed that full employment was possible. Folk memories of the thirties and before also played a part. Innovation was always seen as a threat to jobs, and many shop stewards and union leaders, some of them unrepresentative of their members, simply had no desire to see the capitalist system work successfully. Managers, for their part, with separate canteens, lavatories and other facilities (not to mention different styles of dress and accent) also failed to inculcate in their workforce any sense of identity or loyalty. All this resulted in poor industrial relations and productivity.

Both Gomulka and Cairncross, among many others, added a related factor in their explanations of Britain's relative decline: the lack of what Gomulka called a 'growth culture' or what Cairncross described as an 'environment favourable to business pursuits'. Gomulka stressed that at various times both Western Europe and Japan felt the need to catch up with Britain, and later the USA. This had forged a spirit of innovation which success in achieving growth had sustained. Britain, on the other hand, before the late seventies had never felt the need to catch up, having for so long been a leader in a variety of different ways. If anything, she had become a little relaxed or complacent about the achievements of others. There were also complaints about the low prestige of engineers and managers in British culture: 'If those who have to plan and carry out economic change in industry enjoy little prestige and include few of the ablest (in point of intelligence) of their generation, it is hardly surprising if the rate of change is somewhat slower' (Cairncross).

During the 1960s nothing was done to remedy this situation. In 1969 Labour's attempts to do so as summarised in the White Paper entitled *In Place of Strife* were stifled by internal party dissent led by the then party treasurer, James Callaghan, who recognised the party's financial dependence on the trade unions. When Edward Heath's attempts at industrial reforms failed and the miners came under the syndicalist leadership of Arthur Scargill, the stage was set for further confrontation with the unions. The failure of the Wilson and Callaghan governments in the 1970s to tame them – indeed the surrender to the trade union movement by these governments of their whole political credibility – meant that when the unions went on strike during the 'winter of discontent' of 1978-79, the country demanded that the incoming Thatcher government make union reform a priority. As a result, after eight trade union reform acts, the unions were tamed. Closed shops were outlawed as was secondary picketing; union bosses had to be elected by secret ballots; cooling-off periods had to precede strikes; strikes themselves had to be approved by ballots; and unions were generally encouraged to accept one-union deals in factories. Mass unemployment also undermined union membership, with the Tories presiding over two great recessions. The result was that strikes fell to a historic low and union membership was reduced to about one third of the workforce. The key moment in the destruction of the political power of the unions came with the year-long miners' strike of 1984-5. By the 1990s the unions appeared to be just another pressure group, not the country's hidden masters. What then did all this mean for Britain's relative decline?

Let us recapitulate for a moment. An examination of the various theories explaining Britain's relative decline in the period 1950-80 suggested two groups of contending explanations. The first stressed overseas spending, particularly on defence, and the need to maintain the value of the pound sterling, since the pound, through the Sterling Area, functioned as a world reserve currency. The second stressed the role of the unions in preventing economic growth. These competing explanations raise the question whether both sets are incompatible. In fact, taken together, they represent a sort of chicken and egg problem. Did poor growth cause balance of payments crises and lack of investment or was it the other way round? Were the workers cheated by international capitalism or did they cheat it and themselves in the process? Was the lack of a growth culture the cause or consequence of poor growth? Probably the the answer to these conundrums was that in all cases both explanations were at work at the same time, with cause and effect interacting. It is certainly hard to believe that overseas defence expenditure, military research and cut-backs in investment after balance of payments crises had no effect on growth. Equally it is difficult to accept that appalling industrial relations in no way hindered it. Taking all the wider issues into account, therefore, it would seem that Britain's relative economic decline in the twentieth century, particularly the second half of the twentieth century, can be attributed to a number of factors which taken together seem peculiar to her:

1. The disadvantages of being the 'first industrial nation'.
2. A continuous history of success in politics and foreign policy which encouraged a sense of complacency and discouraged the emergence of a 'growth culture'.

3. The outbreak of two world wars which undermined her position at the centre of the world economic system.
4. An unavoidable world role after 1945 which imposed a heavy defence burden on her economy.
5. A system of industrial relations which undermined her productivity.

The question which must now be asked is whether these factors still plague contemporary Britain and, if not, whether relative economic decline is now definitely behind us? Since it is quite clear that none of these factors still apply, the answer should be yes. Yet the full answer is a little more complicated. It is that, although all these factors have been overcome, the sense of defeatism that was instilled into us while they operated became so pervasive that Britain's political class, in despair of being able to manage the economy themselves, took Britain into the European Union (formerly the EEC and then the EC), membership of which threatens, through European Economic and Monetary Union, to destroy our whole economy and to make the ERM years (1990-92), which gave us the greatest recession since the 1930s, look like a Sunday school picnic. Before examining the issue of Europe, however, let us discover what evidence there is that the UK is no longer in relative economic decline.

It is now perfectly clear that the supply-side reforms of the Thatcher era (the trade union reforms, lower marginal rates of income tax, lower corporation tax, etc.) were instrumental in producing a startling growth in productivity which enabled Britain at long last to reverse its record on productivity and begin to catch up with the Germans. Professor Patrick Minford, for example, has pointed out with regard to productivity gains since 1938 (after which data become available): 'Here the turn-around in relative performance is even more startling. Between 1938 and 1979 German productivity growth was 3.9% per annum, Britain's was 1.8%. Between 1979 and 1990, Germany's was 1.5% per annum while Britain's was 3.1% per annum. In each period growth of one is double the other's but the roles are reversed between periods.' He adds: 'no doubt there is also the mature-economy innovation going on too; we know it is in companies like Unilever, Glaxo, Zeneca and many others. But the largest element in the unusual productivity growth of the UK since 1979 must surely be in catch-up. The combination of rising productivity and the lowest hourly labour costs in developed Europe, with the capacity to hire flexibly at much lower rates, acts as a magnet for foreign investment.' Professor Nicholas Crafts has confirmed Minford's statistics. Whereas in the period 1950-79, Britain lagged behind Europe in terms of growth of real output per head and productivity (% per year), the opposite was true for the decade 1979-89. His figures are:

1979-89	*UK*	*European median*
GDP/head	2.1	1.9
Labour productivity	1.7	1.6
TFP* in business sector	1.5	1.2

*TFP= total factor productivity growth

In Crafts's words: 'The most impressive changes in productivity performance came in manufacturing (where) ... labour productivity grew faster than in West Germany in 26 out of 30 industrial sectors.'

One problem, however, is that manufacturing industry as a proportion of the economy as a whole now represents only 21% as opposed to 26% in 1979, so that its influence on overall productivity has diminished. Hence in terms of GDP per head Britain is still 16th among OECD members today – the same ranking she held in 1980. Since productivity in non-manufacturing industry seems to be about the same as in the rest of Europe, the catch-up in manufacturing industrial productivity (still of course not complete at about two-thirds) still leaves a gap to be filled. Thus between 1989 and 1995, the UK's GDP per head grew a little less than in France, Germany and the USA. Yet for the period 1979-95, GDP per head increased at much the same rates in all these countries.

The changes of the Thatcher years have also meant that both workers and companies have been able to improve their positions. According to the latest OECD data as interpreted by Professor Walter Eltis, in the years 1979 to 1994, the real take-home pay of British production workers increased by almost 26%, while the real take-home pay of German workers grew by less than 3%, the real take-home pay of French workers by less than 2% and the real take-home pay of US workers fell by 7%. Only Japanese workers achieved an increase in real take-home pay in any way comparable to that in Britain. The net-of-tax pay of British workers between 1979 and 1994 has increased by 24% relative to French workers, by 23% in relation to German workers and by 35% in relation to US workers. In fact the differential in favour of British workers has actually been greater, according to Eltis, since OECD figures relate mainly to unskilled workers. On the other hand, since 1992, these differentials have narrowed again. Still, according to the latest OECD data (for 1994), private consumption per head at purchasing power parities, taking the EU average at 100, were 104.5 for the UK, 106.5 for France and 104.5 for Germany – almost all the same.

The share of profits in the national income has also increased since 1979. Then gross trading profits of UK industrial or commercial trading companies represented £23.9 billion while GDP totalled £198.2 billion, i.e. 12.1% of GDP. In 1995, they represented £99.7 billion out of a GDP of £700.9 billion or 14.2% of GDP. If North Sea oil profits are excluded, the increase is still greater, i.e. from 9.3% in 1979 to 12.6% in 1995. This very considerable increase in corporate profits is all the more remarkable, given that 1979 was a cyclical peak year, while 1995 was far from the end of a cyclical recovery. The British economy has therefore been able, for some time now, to generate both real wages and real profits, according to Eltis.

The economy has also recovered in many other ways. There is no longer any talk of 'the two sides of industry' – that weary cliché of 1960s and 1970s corporatism. In most of British industry managers and workers are now on the same side, and unlike their Continental counterparts, British workers have made real gains as a result. 'In Britain *private* sector strikes have virtually ceased,' writes Eltis. In the public sector these have continued and still prevent the order of productivity gains that have been seen in privatised industries. Thus in the electricity industry productivity has grown 15-20% per annum since 1990-91 without a day of strikes, while real prices have fallen. Here, other supply-side reforms apart from trade union reforms have helped, including the privatisation programme itself, the reduction of taxes and the restoration of incentives. Managers who achieve productivity gains now receive large net-of-tax financial rewards. Where such people can be found – Sir Ian MacGregor or Sir Graham Day, for example – they will benefit considerably. It has been possible to find such people as a result of large reductions in the highest marginal rates of taxation, not that this has in any way reduced the tax yield. In 1978-79 the most highly paid 1% of taxpayers contributed 11% of total income tax revenues, while in 1995-96 the most highly paid 1% contributed 15% of total revenues. In 1978-79 the highest paid 1% of taxpayers were paying tax rates of 75% and above (Sean Connery left the country in 1978, complaining that he was 'in the 93% tax bracket'. Labour Chancellor Denis Healey, after all, had boasted that he would tax the rich 'until the pips squeak'), while in 1995-96 they were paying no more than 40%. Yet despite this, they were contributing 4% more of national revenue than before.

Eltis concludes: 'The reductions in the highest rates of tax have led the most highly paid to declare far more income for taxation within the United Kingdom so they pay more at 40% than they had previously paid at 75% and above. In addition, the highest paid are earning more because they are receiving salary in place of the less efficient rewards of more secure job tenure and an acquiescence in incompetence with which those who ran many British companies were more generally rewarded in the 1960s and the 1970s.' One result is that many more of Britain's brightest graduates now opt for a career in industry.

Another feature of Britain's recent reversal of relative decline has been the growth of small businesses and self-employment. This, too, has been a result of lower marginal taxation. The total number of firms in the UK rose from 1,890,000 in 1979 to 3,090,000 in the cyclical peak of 1989. Due to the ERM recession, this number fell to 2,810,000 by 1993. None the less, that still represented a rise of 920,000 from 1979. The number of self-employed also grew from 1,906,000 in 1979 to 3,497,000 a decade later – a rise of 1.5 million people. In 1995, the total was 3,351,000. Income from the self-employed rose from 9.2% of GDP in 1979 to 11.9% in 1989, after which it fell back to 11.2% in 1995. This growth in small businesses and self-employment is one reason why unemployment in the UK is much lower than in the rest of the European Union. There unemployment is rising to twice the British level as unemployment here falls.

Altogether Britain is very well placed to continue her relative economic rebound. Her labour relations are now better than those in France and Germany, her tax rates are lower, and 40% of all inward investment in the EU comes to Britain. She still has problems to face, but those of her European partners regarding public debt (pension debt in particular) and public expenditure seem even greater. The key question is whether she will allow the growing economic and democratic burden of European Union membership to impede her progress. It is to that issue, therefore, that we must now turn, since the prospect of Britain's complete reversal of relative economic decline depends upon it.

5

European Union: Bad for Britain, Bad for Europe

Given Britain's uniquely successful history in modern times, why should she have become mixed up in the experiment to create a European superstate? Why should a free people want to pay billions of pounds each year to unaccountable and unelected foreign bureaucrats? Why should the leaders of all the major parties be willing to transfer all the gold reserves of the Bank of England to Germany under Article 105 of the Maastricht Treaty, with no hope of recovering them when things go wrong? Why such defeatism? Surely it is normal for a free people to want to run its own affairs? So why persist with membership of a system that has proved undemocratic, economically inefficient, immensely corrupt and incredibly costly? It does not make sense. In any case, why should anyone with any knowledge of the rich diversity of European history and culture want to create a united Europe in the first place? Europe is a state-system, not a state. What makes Europeans so fascinating is their differences. To attempt to eradicate these differences in order to construct an unnecessary European superstate is to attack the very essence of European civilisation. None the less, by 1997 the history of European integration is the history of half a century. Its pre-history is even older, yet is really the product of World War I.

The experience of that calamity left politicians inside and outside Europe looking to European unity as a means of achieving their various ambitions. Hitler and the Nazis, like the Kaiser and his generals before them, believed that a united Europe could provide a secure, continental basis for a German *Weltherrschaft*. A German-dominated, European empire could be the centre for world government. The Nazis then came up with schemes for a European Economic Community, a European Single Currency, even a European Exchange Rate Mechanism. European social and other policies were sketched out. Nor were these policies unpopular during World War II, when Nazi propaganda persuaded millions of Europeans that the Nazi New Order represented Christian civilisation. After all, only about 40,000 volunteered to help Republican Spain by joining the International Brigades. Two or three million, on the other hand, volunteered to fight on the Eastern front against the Bolshevik menace in the name of Christian Europe. This despite the fact, or perhaps because of it, that the self-styled leader of the new Europe was murdering – or at least taking care of; not everybody knew of the murders – millions of socially and politically undesirable Jews, communists and homosexuals. In 1943, for example, François Mitterrand – later not just the protector of key French fascists, but the signatory of the Maastricht Treaty – called upon his fellow Frenchmen to form a militia of 300,000 to be sent to the Eastern Front to protect European civilisation from the Soviets. If, after the war, European Union once again became fashionable, there must have been millions of good Europeans who thought that their support of the unsanitised wartime version of that objective should be regarded as more premature than criminal.

Ironically, it was not just the Hitlers and Moseleys of the world who had been in favour of European Union. The Bolsheviks – Lenin, Trotsky and Stalin – had also given it their blessing. For them, nationalism had been a reactionary, bourgeois phenomenon and by the iron laws of Marxist history had to make way for proletarian internationalism. In the first instance this would necessitate European unity, since peoples elsewhere in the world, operating the benighted Asiatic mode of production, would need to enter a bourgeois phase before Communism could be attempted. On a less theoretical level, Communist Russia was in a good position to take over the rest of Europe anyway.

As history would have it, however, it was to be the proponents of another variety of European integration who were to take the initiative. These were the European and Anglo-Saxon supporters of liberal internationalism, who, appalled by the catastrophe of World War I, misinterpreted history and blamed the world anarchy that followed on the evils of nationalism. Their greatest spokesperson was Woodrow Wilson, and Wilsonian moralists in US administrations were to be among the principal architects of European Union (to all intents and purposes they included Jean Monnet, who was as much an American as a Frenchman). Also included were Europeans and Britons who believed in a new world order based on the League of Nations (Monnet had been deputy Secretary-General), some of the British enthusiasts having reached that view via schemes for imperial union. By 1943, not merely Hitler, but Monnet, John Foster Dulles, Harold Macmillan and all sorts of other people were looking to a united Europe as part of the post-war world. By 1945, western intelligence services (SOE in Britain in particular and the OSS, the US forerunner of the CIA) had become infected with the idea, while in the USA the Council for Foreign Relations (a CIA front) saw it as the prime objective of US European policy. Nor, it should be added, was this an anti-Soviet policy, since there was not much fear of the Soviets immediately after the war. Indeed, global management – for which European unity was a necessary preparation – would inevitably require close cooperation with the Soviets. So, too, would nuclear cooperation and world economic management. Harold Macmillan and others took all this for granted. He saw the IMF as a future world central bank and the UNO as the beginning of a new era of world global management. Indeed, a whole generation of leaders who had cooperated against Hitler (condemned as a German nationalist rather than an internationalist; the Soviets could never be tarred with this brush) believed that the real threat after 1945 would still be nationalism, not communism. By 1946-47, it is true, the story had become more complicated.

None the less, it was taken for granted by US administrators and politicians that the European *quid pro quo* for Marshall Aid would be European Union – nothing less than a United States of Europe. And in order to achieve this they had already created and funded the European Movement – yet another CIA front. Winston Churchill lost its leadership when he let the Americans know he did not favour British membership of a federal Europe. However, there were plenty of politicians in Britain and Europe who took CIA funds and Paul-Henri Spaak, the Belgian prime minister, replaced Churchill as the repository of American hopes. Other reasons why America became the greatest proponent of post-war European union included the fact that it would simply be more convenient for the State Department to deal with a single European government rather than sixteen or twenty. Besides, imitation being the sincerest form of flattery, Americans flattered themselves that since American union had worked so well, so too must a United States of Europe. Working hand in hand with Monnet, who had been Roosevelt's de facto personal emmissary to the Free French during the war, the American diplomats took a direct hand in all the negotiations leading to the construction of the European Union, actually drafting key clauses of the key treaties.

Under the Attlee and Churchill governments, however, Britain stood back from these developments. World War II had confirmed her faith in her national institutions, just as it had undermined faith in national institutions elsewhere in Europe. Britain had been a victor in World War II and had a victor's mentality. Only later would she be infected by the moral defeatism that characterised continental Europe in 1945. Besides, Britain, if not a superpower, was still indubitably a world power with a Commonwealth and Empire that straddled the globe and defence commitments in the Middle and Far East. She could not think of herself as a minor regional actor, for the simple reason that she was not one. Churchill therefore took the view that she was 'with Europe but not of it'. And far from isolating herself from Europe at this time, Britain was in the forefront of developments leading to European reconstruction. She began the process of building up European defences against the Soviet threat with the Dunkirk Treaty with France of 1947 and the Brussels Treaty Organisation of 1948. It was British intervention in Greece that saved the Greeks from Stalinism. It was Bevin's diplomacy that helped secure Marshall Aid in 1947 and the establishment of OEEC which led in turn to the economic reconstruction of Western Europe. British pressure was also vital in persuading the Americans to establish NATO in 1949. Those who argue that Britain neglected Europe after World War II are thus either Euro-fanatics or simply people who don't know their history.

The British, however, were not going to be bounced into American plans for a United States of Europe. If Americans thought of all Europeans as the same, the British were well aware of the differences between them. Besides, it was crazy to expect a people with a parliamentary history going back centuries to amalgamate themselves with nations of limited demo-cratic experience, whose most recent acts of statesmanship included the Holocaust, the bombing of British cities or collaboration with the national enemy. The British were also well aware that ideology was rife in Conti-nental Europe after the war, and that Communism, Christian Democracy and Socialism were the successors of Nazism and Fascism, which them-selves were still not dead. In every way, therefore, the British people felt – and were absolutely right to feel – closer to their democratic relatives in the English-speaking world who had taken arms with them against a united Europe between 1939 and 1945. After all, the democratic creden-tials of Canadians, New Zealanders, Australians and Americans were not in doubt.

Still, there was a minority of zealots who wanted Britain to merge itself in a United Europe. Most of them were to be found in the Tory and Liberal Parties and their most ardent spokesman was Harold Macmillan, who from the very start supported European federalism. As the process of European integration got under way in the 1950s, he became its main proponent in the British cabinet. This process was ideologically driven and not the result, as some historians have attempted to argue, of pragmatic adjustments made in order to 'save the nation state'. Nation states had no need of salvation by pragmatic adjustments to federalism; they simply were not under threat. The integrationists, in any case, had shown their hand when in 1948 the Congress of the Hague – and lots of other pro-fed-eralist bodies – had drafted schemes for political union. Ideally, for the federalists, political union should always have come first. The truth was that, with the failure of political union, a step by step or 'functionalist' approach had had to be adopted by Monnet and his collaborators, and that during the negotiations over coal and steel, or atomic energy, or whatever, different states had protected their national interests. Yet there was never any contradiction between day-to-day negotiating objectives and long-term federalist ambitions. (Monnet, by the way, always made it clear – and Macmillan accepted this – that European federation was only a staging post on the route to world federation.)

Macmillan, who had advocated a European coal and steel community in a speech to the House of Commons before the Schuman Plan had been announced, attempted to nudge British policy under Churchill and Eden in the direction of European federalism. He did not succeed, yet did not quite fail either. He arranged for a Treaty of Association to be signed with the European Coal and Steel Community and ensured that a British representative was sent to the Brussels negotiations following the Messina Conference of 1955 on the creation of a European Economic Community. In the late 1950s he pushed negotiations concerning a European Free Trade Association in the direction of membership of the EEC and when faced with the prospect of General de Gaulle turning the EEC into a less federalist body, took the risk of submitting a British application for full membership in the hope of frustrating Gaullist ambitions. His aim was, in alliance with US and European proponents of an Atlanticist and federalist world order, to frustrate the emerging Franco-German alliance which, in his view, represented an alliance of French and German nationalism. Monnet met secretly with Heath and Macmillan on innumerable occasions in order to facilitate British entry. Indeed Monnet was informed before the British parliament of the terms in which the approach to Europe would be announced. Despite advice from the Lord Chancellor, Lord Kilmuir, that membership would mean the end of parliamentary sovereignty, Macmillan deliberately misled the House of Commons, the cabinet, the Commonwealth and the public over the significance of his démarche, arguing that was happening was simply the opening of negotiations about negotiations over commercial policy. He also attempted to mislead General de Gaulle in a bid to facilitate entry. The President of France was spun a line that suggested that Macmillan was not only an anti-federalist but a friend who would arrange for France, like Britain, to receive Polaris missiles from the USA on terms which would allow the French to use them independently. De Gaulle, who was a real nationalist and European (the two are not incompatible) saw through this and vetoed British entry at a press conference in January 1963. It was on that memorable occasion that he asked the British why, when they had secure access to cheap food from the Commonwealth as well as strong democratic, parliamentary institutions, they should want to enter the EEC. This supremely rational question was never to be answered. Instead, Macmillan left his party to Heath, a committed federalist, who with the help of Douglas Hurd paid a substantial sum of money in 1968 to make the Tory party a corporate member of Jean Monnet's Action Committee for a United States of Europe. The Liberal and Labour parties also became corporate members, according to Monnet's biographer and aide, François Duchene.

In 1972, afraid of the resurgence of West Germany under Willy Brandt, President Pompidou finally allowed Great Britain to enter the EEC. As a result, English and Scots law became subordinate to European law, British fish became a common European resource and Britain accepted the common policies and institutions of the customs union – not free trade area – known as the Common Market. Many justifications were given for this irrational act, which, predictably, turned out to be an economic and democratic disaster.

So why had Great Britain entered in the first place? The real reason was that the Tory Party had been captured by the internationalists – people like Macmillan, Heath and Hurd – who believed in global management of economic and political affairs. These were not internationalists in the old-fashioned sense, men who believed in cooperation, free-trade and peace between individual nations. Indeed, they thought of sovereign nation-states as positively dangerous political anachronisms. By the 1970s they had also given up any hope of reversing Britain's relative decline through domestic reform. In short, they had become defeatists. Not they, but others, they believed, would have to sort Britain out. The gentlemen in Brussels would know what was best. The federalists, of course, never admitted to defeatism as their motive. Their case was that 'Europe', as they pleased to call the set of institutions which oversaw the common policies on which they had agreed, should be supported on a variety of grounds, all of which were superficially attractive. Yet it is instructive to examine these claims in detail.

Their basic claim remains 'that in order to trade with Europe we have to be part of it'. Yet this is economic nonsense. Countries as diverse as the USA and South Korea do a roaring trade with the EU and have no intention of becoming part of it. Great Britain is the largest foreign investor in the United States, and the City of London, which trades largely in dollars, has boomed on Eurodollars for the last thirty years. Yet no one in their right mind suggests that on this account we have to have the dollar as our currency or that we must become the fifty-first state of the USA. Likewise, the largest and fastest growing market in the world today is Communist China, which for the past ten years has been experiencing growth rates of 10-15% a year. The European Union, meanwhile, has been stagnating with growth rates of 1-2%. Within a few decades Communist China will have five times as many customers as the EU with standards of living which will mean a huge demand for high-class Western goods. Yet even John Major does not say that 'our future lies at the heart of China' or that we must be represented 'at the top table' in Beijing in order to ensure that we influence the regulations for China's enormous internal market. So far, not even Kenneth Clarke has advocated a common currency with China and not even Chris Patten has advocated following Hong Kong into political union. Perhaps he has learned something about neighbouring monoliths.

Britain today is again one of the world's leading international economic actors with no less than £1.7 trillion invested around the globe (70% of it outside Europe) bringing in an annual dividend of £100 billion. We trade with the whole world. So too do the USA and Japan. If the argument holds water that 'in order to trade with country A we have to be part of country A', then the world should have a single government and a single currency. The reason it does not, as any economist will explain, is that currencies have to operate in areas which react to external stimuli in the same way.

The reason that the world does not have a uniform system of government is really the same: different peoples in different parts of the world have different political traditions, philosophies, standards and expectations. Thus it is no more realistic to expect China and the USA to share a government than to expect the United Kingdom and continental Europe to share a currency. Britain, for example, language and political traditions apart, has far too few characteristics in common with the Continent to form a natural currency zone or 'optimum currency area' in the jargon of economists. To quote the top city financier, Rodney Leach:

> We have a much lower level of unfunded pensions, something which threatens to double French, German and Italian national debt by the year 2025; high technology exports are 75% more significant to Britain than they are to Germany, and in general our business is more service and finance oriented; corporate funding in Britain is based on the stock market (on the Continent it is essentially provided by banks); investment overseas plays an exceptionally large role in Britain's economy; by comparison with other major countries we are light on agriculture and long on oil and gas; our system of floating rate finance makes the British house-owner uniquely sensitive to swings in short-term interest rates; and the City has more links with Wall Street, Singapore and Hong Kong than with Frankfurt or Paris. Less tangibly, after centuries of maritime commerce the British outlook on a number of key issues, from deregulation to free trade, is more Atlanticist than European.

If Britain therefore were to be wise enough to refuse to join the European single currency, the supposed threat to the City or to the country's economy, to quote the Governor of the Bank of England, would be 'trivial'.

The second ground for supporting European Union is often given as 'European integration has preserved the peace of Europe since 1945'. Once again, the slightest review of the evidence will refute the proposition. The only threat to Europe since 1945 has come from the Soviet Union. That threat in turn was met by NATO, chiefly by the Americans, the British and the Canadians – those whom General de Gaulle used to denounce as the Anglo-Saxons. Certainly at the height of the Cold War, neither the French nor the Germans had anything to do with defending the Continent. The French army was fighting a losing war in Vietnam from 1946 to 1954; between 1954 and 1962 it was losing another one in Algeria. By this time General de Gaulle had returned to power and in 1966 he expelled all NATO forces from France and withdrew the French armed forces from the military wing of NATO altogether. They have not yet returned. The Germans were not allowed to have an army until 1955, after the collapse of a ludicrous scheme for a European Army. That they were allowed to rearm by the French (who laid down extraordinarily strict conditions – so much for Franco-German cooperation helping peace!) was due entirely to the fact that the British agreed to establish the British Army of the Rhine and station 77,000 troops and a tactical airforce in Germany. Even so, the *Bundeswehr* did not become a functioning fighting force till the 1960s.

The fact is that large parts of Western Europe remained neutral during the Cold War – Sweden, Finland, Ireland, Switzerland, Austria – and that other parts contributed little. The truth is, therefore, quite irrefutable: that peace in Europe after 1945 was kept mainly by the Americans (not to mention US nuclear weapons), aided by the British and the Canadians.

It is sometimes argued that the European Coal and Steel Community was important in keeping the peace by removing from Germany the means of building up the material for war. This argument, unfortunately, is both anti-German and silly. In the first place, there was no desire on the part of Germans after 1945 to start another war. The devastation of the war had been simply too overwhelming. In fact, the majority of Germans were opposed to rearmament in the 1950s, which was forced on them by Adenauer and the allies. Their slogan was *'ohne mich'* or 'without me'. Even if they had been foaming at the mouth for revenge, with 500,000 NATO troops stationed in West Germany and 500,000 Warsaw Pact troops in East Germany, there was nothing they could have done. Thus the ECSC was really of little importance with regard to peace and those who bring up the argument are really only insulting the Germans, who since 1949 have been peaceful, democratic, law-abiding and pacifist (witness German attitudes and policy during the Gulf War of 1991). To a certain extent, however, the Germans have only themselves to blame for lingering suspicions of German ambitions. For decades now tedious German politicians have been using the argument that European unity is necessary to contain the slumbering Teutonic psychopath. Chancellor Kohl with his recent boast that 'the future belongs to the Germans' is in danger of sounding like one. Yet nobody today really believes that ordinary Germans are a threat to peace or even that their leaders need to be contained by European unity. What baffles ordinary British people is that Germans repeat this old slur and that they still cannot get used to the fact that they are an ordinary democratic people, who, like all ordinary democratic people, should run their own affairs and be happy to inhabit an ordinary, prosperous and democratic nation-state. Besides, German diplomatic leadership may not prove to be a blessing. Inexperienced German blundering over Balkan policy, with the premature recognition of breakaway republics from Yugoslavia, undoubtedly helped precipitate the dreadful conflict in Bosnia.

The third reason often given for supporting European unity is that it 'has increased democracy'. Once again, this is hard to sustain. It is well known, for example, that the right of initiative in the EU rests with the Commission and that the whole process of thrashing out regulations and directives is secret, bureaucratic and undemocratic. There is, of course, a European Parliament, yet everyone recognises it for the farce it is. Members of the European Parliament, according to a talk given at the LSE a couple of years ago by the Principal Administrator of that body, have had to invent a pseudo-science called 'commitologie' (or committee-ology, analogous to Sovietology) meaning that they indulge in pseudo-scientific guesswork to try to discover which committees of the Commission are responsible for taking which decisions. MEPs do not know and are not told. The *Financial Times* in 1992 ran a story that the Commission's new 'openness policy' was being scrapped because it contradicted its 'secrecy rules'. The result is that very few people bother about the European Parliament, which is seen as toothless and irrelevant. In fact, 70% of voters stay at home during elections to it. (At the Mersey East Euro-by-election in December 1996 only 11.2% of the electorate bothered to vote, the figure in Liverpool itself being a mere 8.2%.) On the other hand, over 70% make sure that they vote in elections to the British Parliament.

According to the Principal Administrator of the European Parliament, 'the only people who listen to MEPs are the interpreters'. 'The Council's attitude to Parliament,' he added, 'is still one of disdain.' Ministers and Commissioners still occasionally address it, but of their speeches he said: 'When distilled to their essence you might find a small stain at the bottom of the test tube, but everything else has vanished.' This view is understandable when one realises how few MEPs bother to do anything. For example, they are so rarely to be found in their Parliament that Caroline Jackson, the Tory MEP for Wiltshire, had an official motion accepted by the Speaker of the Parliament, Egon Klepsch, in 1993, asking how many of her colleagues were still alive. She was particularly worried about a neighbour, a Neapolitan MEP, who had not been seen for ages. According to her own words as reported in the *Swindon Evening Advertiser* of 17 December 1993: 'He has not been there for more than a year. Is he possibly dead? In which case, I am very sorry but maybe he should not be paid his salary .... Some MEPs have not been there for years and I wonder how many other dead souls there may be .... There are about 100 who never show their faces.' One of them turned out to have been shot by the Mafia. Today, there is still the same absenteeism. In fact, a recent Channel Four documentary showed footage of MEPs signing on for their daily allowance of £175 and then going straight to the airport having done no work at all that day. Despite their journey home by air they were also eligible without receipts for a generous car-mileage allowance, half of which was tax-free. A parliamentary motion calling for receipts was voted down by 626 votes to 32. Each MEP also receives an extra £85,000 a year for 'assistance'. This is paid direct to the assistants, who are usually wives or daughters. The average cost of an MEP is £190,000 (grand total £125 million). The television programme which so upset British viewers was justly entitled *Fat Cats* and was shown on 18 October 1996.

If MEPs are a democratic embarrassment, the Commission is a positive danger to British parliamentary democracy. Parliament now passes about 40 Acts per year, but passes up to 4,000 pieces of delegated legislation, half of which rubber-stamp Brussels regulations or directives. MPs have little idea of what goes on. Some government ministries (Agriculture and Fisheries, Trade and Industry) spend half their time or more simply implementing this Euro-legislation. Nor is there any hope of resisting it. When a sub-committee of 14 MPs debated the metrication directives of 1995, for example, they gave up after 14 minutes instead of wasting their breath. Opinion polls had shown that 70-90% of the population wanted to retain traditional imperial weights and measures, but it made no difference. Britain became the only country in the EU – apart from Eire – to be deprived of the choice of using imperial or metric units. The choice remained legal everywhere else in Europe (as it had been in the UK since 1897). Now, however, it became illegal to ask for a pint of lager shandy in a British pub and butchers were forced to weigh their meat in kilos. Nobody wanted this except our bureaucratic European masters. (The excuse is sometimes trotted out that the numbers of civil servants actually employed by the Commission are very few. Quite right. But this entirely misses the point, since it is their *power* which is objectionable, not their size. In any case they simply use national bureaucrats to do their bidding for them – and British bureaucrats, unfortunately, are particularly zealous.)

The sheer stupidity of Brussels has been demonstrated many times in relation to a myriad of weird and wonderful directives. My own favourite stems from the summer of 1992 when the Commission decreed that henceforth the dung and slurry of all farm animals throughout Europe should smell the same. Teams of 'olifactromotists' or sniffers were set up to enforce this by smelling air-tight sachets of evidence from all corners of the European Union. Whether animals who failed the test were despatched to the abattoir, we do not know. However, the Commission has become the first legislative body in history to have legislated literally for the harmonisation of bullshit. The whole episode would be funny if it were not so tragic. For all stories concerning ludicrous directives are simultaneously evidence of the emasculation of the British Parliament and therefore of British democracy. But it is happening all the time. For example, *all* British parties at the end of 1995 passed a parliamentary resolution supporting British fishermen against the Spaniards. It made no difference. Our European partners simply supported the Spanish and the Minister concerned, William Waldegrave, did not even vote against them, but merely abstained. Perhaps he had drawn the lesson from the 1988 Merchant Shipping Act, which in an attempt to execute the Common Fisheries Policy fairly, outlawed the practice of Spanish ships registering in British ports in order to fish the British fishing quota. This Act was suspended and later declared illegal by the European Court of Justice, and the Spanish fishermen who had been fishing the British quota were granted compensation. So much for European 'justice' – or the sovereignty of the British Parliament!

Yet British democracy is undermined by Europe in two other ways.

First, the EU will not obey its own laws when federalist advances are at stake; secondly, the European political system is endemically corrupt.

The last clause of the first Title (part) of the Maastricht Treaty, for example, states that its signatories will take all steps necessary to fulfil the aims of the treaty. This became clear when the Danes, in their first referendum on the Treaty, voted 'No'. The Danish referendum, never mind the result, came as a great shock to Europe's leaders, since it meant that the Maastricht Treaty had to be published. In the words of the French Foreign Minister, 'it was meant to be secret'. Worse still, once it had been published in Danish (and had become, within hours, a best seller) it could be translated into English. The real debate over the Treaty in the UK, where in the 1992 general election the main parties had seen no need to make Maastricht an election issue, could only then begin.

Did the Maastricht Treaty come into force legally? Officially it was an amendment to the 1957 Treaty of Rome, article 236 of which provides that if one signatory votes against, any amendment fails. Yet when the Danes voted against, Chancellor Kohl of Germany told them that they were just a little people who could not hope to block the Treaty. To try to do so would be as futile as an attempt to dam the Rhine. The Danes, he said, would simply be swept away by the tide of history. In short, if they did not change their vote, he would expel them from the European Community. After this highly democratic discourse, with its totally illegal threat, enormous pressure was put on the Danes by both their government, which was pro-Maastricht, and their European 'partners'. A hastily patched-up summit offered them some concessions and a second referendum was held in which a cowed electorate, which had been told to expect all sorts of calamities if it voted 'No' again, reversed its decision and gave the Treaty a small majority. The Treaty was then ratified by the other states, although the concessions made to Denmark were never incorporated into it. Thus, despite article 236, an amendment was passed to the Treaty of Rome, even though one country had indeed voted against the text of the amendment that was incorporated into the Treaty. This might have been challenged in the European Court of Justice, but since that body itself believes that its duty is to extend federalism, there was really no point. (The whole Common Agricultural Policy may also be in breach of the Treaty of Rome, but, once again, there is no point in arguing this case before the European Court. See below.)

The real threat to democracy, however, comes less from the inability of the European Union to obey its own laws than from the endemic political corruption in Europe, both within the individual states and within the institutions of the European Union itself. Sad as it may seem, the factor which the member states have most in common is the, by British standards, extraordinarily high level of political corruption. Take Belgium, for example. Recently a former minister has been charged with the assassination of a former deputy prime minister. Another deputy prime minister had to endure a parliamentary debate to discover whether his parliamentary immunity would be removed to enable him to face charges of procuring twelve-year-old boys for his sexual gratification. (In the end the charges were dropped.) In 1996 the Belgian Secretary General of NATO was forced to resign after corruption charges, after the resignation of the Belgian Foreign Minister on similar grounds. And that was after two suicides aand one murder. The whole population of the country has recently taken to the streets to protest at the suspected high level of corruption in the judiciary and police force in the aftermath of the country's worst ever paedophile scandal involving the murder of young girls.

Or take Italy, where Giulio Andreotti, the prime minister who signed the Maastricht Treaty, is now on trial accused of being head of the Mafia and having arranged the murder of an Italian journalist who was about to point this out. There are witnesses who state that they saw him kissing the *capo di capi*, and it is an open secret that his party's votes were organised in Sicily by a henchman who was a leading Mafioso. Andreotti's predecessor as premier, Bettino Craxi, meanwhile languishes in permanent exile in Tunisia, unwilling to face the eight charges of corruption of which he has been found guilty. He declares that his treatment was unfair and that all Italian politicians had their hands in the national till right up to their armpits. There is evidence to suggest that they still do. This high level of corruption has been equally widespread among Italian civil servants. A top man in the health service whose house was raided by the police was found to have 250 gold ingots under his bed and five Swiss bank accounts. When asked to explain, he said he was saving for his old age. (He need not have worried, he will now be spending it in jail.) The so-called 'Italian revolution' of the 1990s has unfortunately been unable to clear up the mess. The Mafia still collects votes in Sicily for the Italian Right. One of the 'clean' prime ministers brought in to try to change things believed that only a national amnesty would succeed, corruption being so widespread. Perhaps this will still have to happen. But that will mean that all those who were corrupt will be free to spread their corruption again, and not just around Italy but around the new Europe, with the Mafia, which has been perhaps the main beneficiary of European Union, prominent among them. According to one authority (John Follain, *A Dishonoured Society: The Sicilian Mafia's Threat to Europe*, 1995), Mafia defrauding of the EU through the Common Agricultural Policy now amounts to between 150-300 billion lire annually. It is already reckoned to skim off 3-4% of Italian GDP per annum. Yet Judge Giovanni Falcone, the Mafia's most distinguished victim, warned before he died that the Mafia hoped to organise crime not merely on a European scale, but globally. Its main aid is the dismantling of internal borders in Europe. And more than any other organisation in Europe, it is looking forward to the entry of Eastern European countries into the EU with their own huge criminal networks and corrupt politicians. Dismantling Europe's internal borders and making way for the entry of East European states are now the main objectives of the European Commission.

Italy, however, is hardly unique in its levels of corruption inside the EU. According to one recent report in the *Sunday Times*, Spain is even worse for insider dealing, graft and corruption. The President of the Bank of Spain had to resign as a result of a scandal. The Interior Minister of Felipe Gonzales's government stands accused of running death squads in the Basque country and Gonzales himself is suspected of having given him his orders. The head of the internal security services was prevented from leaving the country with billions of pesetas in a suitcase. No one in Spain doubts that corruption there is at least on the same level as in Italy.

The history of post-war Greece offers sufficient examples of corruption, but under Georges Papandreou this recently reached scandalous proportions. Having just escaped a guilty verdict on corruption charges as a result of his own conduct as prime minister (his co-accused, a more expendable political figure, was found guilty but died of a heart attack), Papandreou proceeded to have his main opponent arrested on similar charges. The Greek political saga became even more hilarious when Papandreou divorced his wife and attempted to make his voluptuous ex-mistress, Mimi, the Evita Peron of Greece, an attempt which almost succeeded and indeed was frustrated only thanks to his ill health and subsequent death plus the publication of a stream of pornographic photos of the lady in the Greek press.

Yet it is not simply the Mediterranean countries with their lax political habits that shame European democracy. The dominant countries of the EU, France and Germany, are scarcely any better. France's leading European is ex-President Valery Giscard d'Estaing. Yet his presidency came to a rather sour end in 1981 over the Bokassa affair. This involved gifts of diamonds by the corrupt dictator of the Central African Republic whom the French agreed to crown as Emperor in a mock-Napoleonic ceremony. The ruler of the Central African Empire was later tried for murder and cannibalism by his own people but before then let it be known that trayfuls of diamonds had been offered as 'presents' to Giscard (and accepted). The President claimed to have received only one diamond which was subsequently sold for charity, but he was not widely believed. Perhaps the memory of the de Broglie affair had had an effect. As a result of this, Giscard's Interior Minister, Prince Poniatowski, was compelled to resign for having failed to warn an embarrassing party colleague, the Duc de Broglie, who was involved in gun-running, that a contract had been taken out on his life by leading French mobsters. The Duc, as a result, was shot down in a Paris street.

Under President Mitterrand, Giscard's successor, the French security services were used to tap the phones of literally thousands of people who might know the secret of the President's officially maintained mistress and illegitimate daughter. One of those involved committed suicide in the

Elysée Palace. But that was only the tip of the iceberg. One prime minister committed suicide after he was accused of corruption while a second was committed for trial before the French Senate on charges of manslaughter. Mitterrand himself was discovered to have aided leading French fascists from the Vichy era and to have presided over all sorts of shady deals. One of his ministers ended up in jail on corruption charges including the rigging of football matches. Yet under Chirac the system continues, with the President's record as Mayor of Paris itself coming under fire and with several of his closest colleagues facing arrest.

In its edition of 13-19 July 1996, The *Economist* magazine, having reported that the head of France's railways had been placed under investigation for the possible misuse of corporate assets, commented that he was

> only the latest of an extraordinarily long line of luminaries among France's business, financial and political elite to have been caught in a tidal wave of sleaze allegations that have swept across France in the past few years. Hundreds of prominent people have been *mis en examen*. They include eight former government ministers, two former party leaders, dozens of mayors and past and present members of parliament, and one in four of the bosses of France's biggest 40 companies as well as scores of other businessmen. Several have already been convicted. Some like Alain Carignon, former Gaullist communications minister and once mayor of Grenoble, who began serving a four year sentence a few days ago, have been sent to prison. Some cases have been dropped, but few who have been placed *mis en examen* have emerged unbruised.

Those convicted have included some of France's most prominent politicians such as Bernard Tapie, Henri Emmanuelli and Michel Noir.

Germany, although less prone to corruption scandals than France, Italy, Spain, Greece or Belgium, is by no means a stranger to them. In 1996 alone, Dieter Vogel, the chief executive of the German steel and engineering group, Thyssen (with a £17 billion turnover in 1990) was arrested with nine other executives on charges of widespread fraud. Fourteen other executives are now also being investigated. According to Wolfgang Schaupensteiner, the Frankfurt lawyer who is seen as Germany's top anti-corruption prosecutor: 'Economic crime has spiralled to levels never seen possible until a few years ago. We are witnessing a loss of values in Germany. Moral and ethical principles in German boardrooms are going to the dogs. Crimes are committed daily and the only thing that seems to matter is profits and selfish materialism.' Since 1987, Schaupensteiner has started proceedings for 1,624 cases of bribery alone and secured more than 300 convictions. In a recent fraud report compiled by the auditors KPMG, 60% of German managers said they had been victims of white collar crime. Police recorded more than 700,000 cases of fraud and embezzlement last year alone, a rise of 40% between 1993 and 1996. In one of the largest corruption scandals ever, Schaupensteiner is investigating more than twenty companies and a group of Frankfurt officials suspected of defrauding Frankfurt airport of millions of D-marks during the building of a new terminal. The case follows the arrest in 1996 of Friedrich Hennemann, former chief executive of the bankrupt Bremer Vulkan shipping group, who was accused of diverting £300 million of government subsidies meant for the modernisation of East German shipyards. Investigations were also under way in 1996 into Daimler Benz and Volkswagen.

Nor have German politicians escaped charges of corruption on a large scale. The Flick Scandal of the 1980s even touched Helmut Kohl, although only the Federal Economics Minister, Count Lambsdorff, and the Speaker of the Federal Parliament and former Christian Democrat Chairman, Rainer Barzel, were forced to resign after admitting accepting 0.5 million and 1.7 million D-marks respectively from the Flick Corporation for their political parties. They had done so in return for tax exemptions worth 800 million D-marks. Kohl admitted before a Bundestag investigating committee that as prime minister of Rhineland-Palatinate he had accepted 140,000 D-marks from the company for the local Christian Democrats, but claiamed that these contributions had been purely political, i.e. there had been no conditions attached and that he was unaware of any deliberate tax evasion on the part of his local party.

Individual member states aside, the various institutions and programmes of the European Union itself are notoriously corrupt. This is confirmed every year by the Court of Auditors' Report, which gives chapter and verse on the waste and fraud that it manages to uncover. The real trouble is that this amounts to 'only the tip of the iceberg', to quote former British Treasury official, John Wiggins, who sits on the Court. In fact, nothing is ever done to carry out its recommendations. The 1994 Report, for example, complained: 'Many of the criticisms that have been brought up since 1983 can again be found in the 1993 Report.' The Court itself, however, can hardly be said to give the impression of having divorced itself from the political culture it condemns. In 1994 it released its Report to the press at a party at which journalists were served the best champagne to accompany a lunch of the finest caviar, pâté de foie gras, smoked salmon and asparagus canapés wrapped in gold leaf. The Report itself suggested that 'the tip of the iceberg' amounted to some £6 billion or no less than 10% of the EU budget – and all this was lost in just one year. Such sums could buy space stations, Channel Tunnels, keep charities for ever, buy hospitals by the dozen, educate Third World countries, buy a few African states or a few European political parties. But this is no cause for fun. If a public company lost money on this scale to fraud, it would simply be closed down.

According to the 1994 Report a plan to reduce the European wine lake cost £1 billion to operate and increased wine production by 21%; £16 million of grants were awarded to non-existent South African students; £480 million were spent on a palatial debating chamber in Brussels for

MEPs despite the fact they only go there for ten days a year and already have two identical palatial debating chambers in Strasbourg (in the words of the Report: 'A more suitable and less expensive solution was possible'); olive oil producers received £27 million for oil they never bottled; Italian crooks received £8.8 million for airline training courses which never took off; £16 million was paid to EU officials who stayed at home for holiday expenses; Italian beef exporters received £16 million in export subsidies for herding the same cattle back and forth across the same border; while Greek tobacco farmers were paid hundreds of millions of pounds to export unsmokeable tobacco to Albanians who dumped the stuff but who were later paid by the farmers out of their export subsidies. (One official commented: 'It would be cheaper to give the farmers money directly and cut out the tobacco. You could save £300 million a year that way.')

One could go on, but the point to note is that nothing is ever done to stop these things. For example, when Norman Lamont, as Chancellor of the Exchequer, put the subject at the top of the agenda for EU Finance Ministers during the 1992 British Presidency of the Council, and read selected extracts from the Court's annual report to his colleagues, 'they ostentatiously read their newspapers'. Lamont's successor as Chancellor, Kenneth Clarke, reported to the House of Lords European Communities Committee that several distinguished Greeks had been caught passing off Yugoslav maize as home produce in order to attract EU export subsidies, but had been pardoned or released from jail by the Papandreou government. In Clarke's words: 'Some of them have been reinstated quite prominently in public office and one of them I think has now become the head of a state bank.' Yet he concluded: 'I think that we should deplore what the Greeks have done but there is absolutely nothing whatever that anybody can do about it.' (Hand over the pound to such bankers, perhaps?) Shortly afterwards, the British government – no doubt on Clarke's advice – voted not to take the Italian government to the European Court to force it to repay billions of pounds of illegal milk subsidies.

It should be fairly clear, therefore, that if the arguments from trade and peace do not carry conviction, the argument that European Union enhances democracy fails just as resoundingly.

The fourth argument that is often held to justify British membership of the European Union is that Britain is just too small to survive on her own. Given that she has the fifth largest economy in the world, is one of the world's eight large island states, that only seventeen other countries have a larger population, that she has the most professional fighting forces in Europe, not to mention the most advanced nuclear weapons, this is a bit of a non-starter. She also sits on the Security Council of the UN, is a member of the G7 Group, is a leading member of NATO, is at the centre of the Commonwealth, and is a member of the IMF and World Bank. Frankly, it is only those who are anti-British who make this claim, because they never argue that states such as Japan, Canada, Israel, Australia,

New Zealand, Norway or Switzerland are too small to survive, far less such Asian tigers such as Singapore, Taiwan or South Korea. One fails to understand how they can explain the continued existence of Albania, Chad, Nigeria or Peru. Paddy Ashdown MP, the leader of the Liberal Democratic Party, for example, who believes that it is impossible to talk of 'an independent Britain in an interdependent world' was highly vocal in 1995 in urging British and other troops to risk their lives for an independent Bosnia. Perhaps he just cannot think logically; perhaps he has double standards.

When pressed, some of these people are reduced to clichés such as 'there is no such thing as independence' or 'sovereignty does not exist any more'. Occasionally they mutter 'you just want the empire back'. All such arguments are based on simple confusion. The proponents of such a view seem to believe that to be sovereign a state must possess the power to do whatever it likes in world affairs, although this has never been the prerogative of any state in history. Roman emperors, Charles V, Louis XIV, Napoleon, Hitler and Stalin were all just as aware as Saddam Hussein is today that they cannot just do what they please. Yet nobody doubted that Augustus Caesar, Louis XIV or Napoleon were absolute rulers. Even Jesus Christ said: 'Render unto Caesar the things that are Caesar's.' Today, Saddam Hussein still rules over an independent state and no one inside Iraq has the slightest doubt that to disobey his sovereign will, would entail the severest consequences, despite the hostility of the outside world. Similarly, at the 1995 Commonwealth Heads of Government Conference in Australia, a whole array of world leaders pleaded with the tin-pot military dictator of Nigeria not to execute fifteen opponents. But he executed them all the same. He, too, had no doubt about his sovereignty or independence. Yet Euro-enthusiasts still insist that Britain cannot be called independent.

At a recent debate at the University of Aberdeen, the resident Jean Monnet Professor of European Integration argued that since Britain had required the help of the USA to beat Germany in two world wars and even to beat Argentina in the Falklands War, she could not be described as independent, as she was merely a puppet of the USA. When it was pointed out that with equal 'logic' it could be argued that since the USA had required British help to defeat Germany in two world wars but had failed to beat North Vietnam when that help was denied, the USA could be described as a puppet of the UK, he was strangely silent. And little wonder. For since when has the need for allies constituted evidence that sovereignty does not exist? And since when has economic or commercial interdependence proved the same proposition either? Human beings have inhabited an interdependent world since the dawn of time. The Jews needed God to escape from Egypt; the Greek city states formed alliances to fight their wars; the emperors of imperial Rome needed allies. Yet the world has always respected the sovereignty and independence of states.

And trade treaties between them have been regarded not as infringements of that sovereignty but as affirmations of it – so long as these treaties can be revoked.

The sovereignty or independence of a state does not give it the power to do whatever it likes. It means rather that it has the supreme legal authority to take final decisions on its own behalf or on behalf of its citizens. In other words, in a world that has always been interdependent, the government or ruler of an independent state decides how that state will run its internal affairs and how it will react to the external challenges of interdependence. That is why the world today remains full of sovereign and independent states of various descriptions, big and small, tin-pot and superpower. Thus not only is Britain big enough to remain independent but so too are Singapore and Norway. The latter, of course, has remained outside the EU for as long a period of time as we have been inside. Logically, therefore, Norway, as a much smaller nation – despite its oil wealth – should have suffered all the woes of isolation, falling living standards, investment withdrawal and lack of influence with which an independent Britain outside the EU would supposedly be threatened. However, the facts speak for themselves. Outside the EU, Norway is experiencing 5% growth, 1% inflation and has no budget deficit. She still does 70% of her trade with the EU and a third of the companies quoted on the Oslo stock market are foreign-owned. In fact, after her second 'No' to Europe in 1995, she experienced an inward-investment boom. Nor is she diplomatically isolated. After all, it was 'little Norway' who brokered the peace agreement (the 'Oslo Accords') between the Israelis and the Arabs, when nobody bothered consulting the EU, given that body's stunning lack of influence in world affairs.

Finally, those who mutter that a desire for independence equals a desire to have the Empire back, should be told that exactly the opposite is true. The point of membership of the EU for Eurofanatics was that *Europe* would be the substitute for Empire, that Britain's prestige would be sustained by swapping imperial leadership for European leadership. That is precisely what Dean Acheson meant in 1962 when he famously opined that 'Britain had lost an empire but had not yet found a role'. That, perhaps more ominously, is what some of Chancellor Kohl's more dizzy foreign affairs advisers mean when (like Horst Teltschik) they talk of a superpower Europe keeping America and Japan in line or (like Karl Lammers) they demand equal control of British and French nuclear weapons and their targetting – in their case, meaning of course that Europe should be a substitute not for the British but the German Empire.

The final excuse sometimes proferred for British membership of the EU is that Britain's economic record inside the EU has been wonderful. Alas, no plausible case can be made out in support of such a proposition. When Roy Jenkins, that quintessential British pro-European, edited a book of essays on the effects of British membership after ten years inside the EEC, the chapter on economics concluded: 'there is no evidence of any benefits being generated'. Today, after the disaster of ERM membership between 1990 and 1992, when it cost us between £6 and £15 billion just to be thrown out, the situation is much worse. A list of costs would have to include an accumulated trade deficit of £146 billion at current prices, an accumulated net membership subscription of £30 billion, an ERM cost of £80 billion (the result of record unemployment, record interest rates, record bankruptcies, record home repossessions, record public debt and record tax increases – not bad for just two years in the preliminary stage of monetary union, with the real thing threatening even greater disasters), £40 billion for implementing European regulations and directives, and another £40 billion for participating in the CAP. There is nothing to offset this on the credit side. The cost has to be financed from exports to the rest of the world (54% of which, including 65% of invisible exports, go outside Europe) and higher taxes. All food imports from outside Europe have to be taxed, so that the average family of four pays about £28 extra on its weekly food bill.

In fact, after more than thirty years of existence, the Common Agricultural Policy, which pays rich landowners hundreds of thousands of pounds for doing nothing (according to the *Sunday Times*, the Tory Leader of the House of Lords, Lord Cranbourne, receives £400,000 a year for *not* planting conifers on his Dorset estates etc., although even that newspaper has been unable to name Britain's fifteen set-aside millionaires) leaves 53% of farmers, among whom the suicide rate is rising fast, with living incomes of under £20,000 per year. It also encourages highly intensive, high-yield farming which pollutes the countryside with phosphates and other chemicals which put the nation's health at risk. In short, it is an insane system by which poor urban dwellers subsidise only the richest rural ones, whose farming methods threaten everybody. Yet the CAP still accounts for 55% of the EU budget. If this is an improvement on the 91% it represented in 1973, it is simply because other areas have come under EU control. The actual budget of the CAP itself in money terms has increased by no less than 973% since 1973.

It should be pointed out that the CAP is not only an ecological disaster on a European scale; its effects are felt world-wide since the agricultural products it exports are dumped on third world countries, thus destroying their hopes for development. Often the EU export subsidies are larger than the entire GDP of the developing countries which are victimised. Curiously, according to a memorandum from the Ministry of Agriculture, Fisheries and Food of 1995 to the House of Lords European Communities Committee, 'The huge costs of the policy to taxpayers and consumers far outweigh any benefit to them … such large transfers into agriculture represent a major misallocation of resources and thus damage the economy as a whole … the policy is extremely complex in detail, hence difficult to administer and giving scope to fraud.' Another section condemns its 'unnecessary trade disputes with third countries', but its most amusing section includes a devastating analysis of how several of the CAP's central pillars are unauthorised by the Treaty of Rome. These include the central-ised payment of subsidies through Brussels; the intervention system giving producers guaranteed payments; and the erection of tariff barriers against food imported from the outside world. All three main pillars of the CAP are thus, strictly speaking, illegal. The document then shows in an equally devastating manner how the CAP has failed to honour or be guided by any of the five central objectives laid down in Treaty Article 39. Yet the memorandum concludes that any attempt to move the CAP in the right or legal direction would be unlikely to win any support from the other EU states who profit from it. In short, to quote the words of Dr Richard North, 'the British Government makes three simple points: firstly, the CAP is a complete and utter disaster; secondly, its implementation is probably illegal within the context of the Treaty of Rome; and thirdly, there is no hope whatever that anything could be done about it. Apart from that, as they say, there is no problem.'

The Common Fisheries Policy has been little more of a success. It began just hours before the start of negotiations on UK membership with the Heath government, when the Council of Ministers hastily agreed that such a policy would guarantee 'equal access for all' in Community waters. In this way all fish became a 'common European resource'. Geoffrey Rippon, Heath's main negotiator, had meanwhile informed parliament that the government would resist the CFP. Instead, Heath ordered him to capitulate during the negotiations and simply accept a derogation allow-ing the UK to retain control over waters out to 12 miles 'until December 31, 1982'. On 13 December 1971 Rippon, none the less, told the House of Commons that Britain had retained full control of her territorial waters and that none of the arrangements made were to be merely transitional. MPs were not given the terms of the concessions made over fishing rights until after the Treaty of Accession had been voted on and signed. It is interesting to note, however, that although Heath managed to persuade the Norwegians to accept similar terms, this contributed to EEC member-ship being rejected by Norway in a referendum.

Since she joined the EEC, Britain, perhaps predictably given the above, has suffered outrageously from the CFP. The main problems have been the policy of quotas introduced in 1983 and that of decommissioning intro-duced in 1992, both of which have been exacerbated by the size and practices of the Spanish fleet. Eighty per cent of EU fish come from British waters, but thanks to the quota system, British boats have been allowed to catch only 30-50% of many species. Moreover, since 1983 the tonnage of fish landed in British ports has declined by a third. There have been several reasons for this. First, the quota sustem has destroyed fish stocks by forcing fishermen to dump dead fish back into the sea to pollute it if these fish are of the wrong type or if they take a vessel over its quota. Secondly, the Spanish pay little attention to the rules. The huge Spanish fleet (18,000 vessels compared with 1,000 British) is known as 'the whore of the sea' and is not policed by Spain whose inspectors are in land-locked Madrid. Consequently it breaks all the rules and takes what it likes. It also registers its vessels in British ports and then fishes the British quota with EU approval. These 150 Anglo-Spanish (and Anglo-Dutch) vessels take about a third of British fish quotas by tonnage (including about half of our plaice and hake quotas); worse still, they are aided by British taxpayers who, through our EU contribution, help pay both for the sums given to African states to allow the Spanish to fish their waters and for the grants paid to subsidise the Spanish in building a new generation of trawlers. They are also aided by renegade British skippers who are now in such despair that they sell their fishing licences to Spaniards.

Since quotas have not worked, a policy was introduced in 1992 of decommissioning boats. Fishermen were to be encouraged to leave the industry since (to a large extent) the quota system and the Spaniards were destroying fish stocks. The aim was to reduce our national fleet to 209,370 tonnes by the end of 1996. Since it stood in 1996 at almost 250,000 tonnes, another 167 boats became due to be scrapped. Since 1993 the UK has scrapped 436 boats at a cost of £26.2 million. The 1996 cull was due to cost a further £12.8 million. However, in 1996 the European Commission announced that it wanted a further 40% cut in the British fishing fleet and proposed changes in mesh sizes and netting use that would further discriminate against British and in favour of Spanish fishermen. The result has been that British fishermen now commonly fly *Canadian* flags since, unlike the British government, the – totally independent – Canadian government in 1995 resorted to armed protection of its fishing vessels against predatory Spanish trawlers off Newfoundland. In the so-called Tuna War of the same year in the Bay of Biscay, the British authorities forced British boats to return to port at the behest of their Spanish colleagues. Today, the once proud British fishing industry is totally demoralised and expects to disappear. So long as EU policy is to put British waters at the disposal of a mainly Spanish EU fleet, who can blame it?

The prime minister, John Major, has said that he will never lead Britain into a federal Europe. Yet Britain is already inside a federal Europe. The Common Agricultural and Common Fisheries Policies are federal policies. The European Court of Justice, which overrides national law, is a federal Supreme Court. The system of majority voting in the Council of Ministers is federal law-making. European citizenship, established by the Maastricht Treaty, is federal citizenship. The European flag ('like a clock without any hands and just as useful', in the words of one critic) is a federal flag. European Union ambassadors are federal ambassadors. The European anthem is a federal anthem. The proposed euro is a federal currency. All that Europe lacks as a federal state is a federal army and a federal constitution. That is what the Maastricht review conferences will try to establish by the end of the century. The pressure from Chancellor Kohl and his European allies will be relentless, yet it is quite clear from this review of Britain's twenty-five year membership of the European Union that it has been responsible for neither enhanced peace nor democracy and that its policies and institutions have been borne at enormous cost.

This is why British business is now turning against the whole experiment. The experience of ERM membership between 1990 and 1992; the huge amounts of red tape; the higher social overheads and taxation that are causing so much unemployment on the Continent; not to mention the greater profits to be found in Britain and elsewhere in the world, are turning British business off the European nightmare.

At its 1995 annual conference, the Federation of Small Businesses voted by a large margin to pull out of the European Union altogether. The FSB represents more companies in the UK than any other business organisation. The *Sunday Times* in a report by David Smith and Simon Reeve in its edition of 31 March 1996, entitled 'Top industry chiefs turn against the euro', stated: 'Britain's top businessmen, long thought to be the strongest backers of a single currency, have moved decisively against it .... By two to one they are opposed to the euro.' The report continued: 'The survey was of the chairmen and chief executives of nearly 90 of Britain's biggest companies, including BP, Rolls-Royce, GKN, Trafalgar House and BAT. It shows that faced with the prospect of a fully integrated Europe, with a single currency and central political decisions, most preferred an independent Britain, outside the EC. Given a straight choice, 52% wanted an independent Britain against 48% who favoured full integration.' The November 1995 edition of the magazine *Overseas Trade* (the official Department of Trade and Industry/ Foreign Office 'magazine for exporters') also reported a survey and concluded that 'exporters oppose a single currency': 75% believed that a single currency would mean a loss of competitiveness. *Commerce* magazine in February 1995 reported on its own poll. Asked whether they wanted their businesses to be part of a united Europe, 83% of companies did not. Asked if they wanted their businesses to be 'exclusively British trading with Europe', 60% said 'Yes'. When asked whether they wanted their businesses to be 'British and part of Europe', 57% said 'No'. 87% were against further European centralisation; 88% against the Social Chapter; and 78% were against a single currency.

The only organisation that claims that British business supports European federalism is the Confederation of British Industry (CBI). On 15 November 1993 a majority of its members were reported to be in favour of a single currency. Two days later it was revealed in *The Times* that of the 485 questionnaires sent out only 179 had been returned and that of these only 49 had said that that a single currency might be required in the long term. Only 12 respondents had expected to see a single currency by the year 2000 and only nine out of the 485 polled had actually wanted Britain to join one.

It thus seems clear that British membership of the EU has brought no benefits after twenty-five years; indeed that the EU simply has not lived up to the claims made on its behalf. If Britain does stand on the brink of renewed prosperity it is because, first, the purely British problems which brought about relative decline this century have been solved, and secondly, because lower taxes, greater productivity, political stability, the English language and all the other factors which make Britain different from the other member states of the European Union have made Great Britain an attractive place to invest in. Britain meanwhile has built up a huge portfolio of overseas investments around the world – overwhelmingly outside the stagnating, unemployment-ridden economic black-spot of the European Union. If she is to be able to enjoy the great prosperity and good fortune which awaits her, she can surely best guarantee this by withdrawing from the European Union altogether.

Such a course, in fact, would hardly be un-European, since European Union, despite the hype, is totally against the grain of European history. Thus if European integration is bad for Britain, it is also bad for Europe. A United States of Europe, after all, could hardly be like the United States of America. The latter prospered because it was peopled by immigrants who wanted to forget their European pasts and begin anew as citizens of a new world. We Europeans, on the other hand, have no desire to surrender those pasts which make us so different from one other. The truth is that we are not the same. We have separate histories, political traditions, languages and literatures. The essential and fascinating thing about Europe is precisely this diversity.

The Eurofanatics, predictably, are actively attempting to overcome traditional distinctions by inventing a new European history which entwines all the differences into a seamless whole. Under this new dispensation, the history of Europe becomes an historic odyssey from ancient Athens (not Sparta of course) to modern Brussels. This is in fact a voyage from the sublime to the ridiculous, but it is necessary to spell out the objections. Most obviously it is such a selective way of interpreting Europe's past that it ends up as propaganda rather than history. There really is little point in treating Europe's past as if the Greeks existed only in ancient times; as if Fascism and National Socialism were not an integral part of it; or as if Christianity did not divide Europeans as much as it united them. Yet nineteenth-century historians served their nation-states well as propagandists. And if today's European historians are the servants of an emerging superstate, it is simply a nation-state on a bigger scale. (The Europhiles are not genuine internationalists. Their aim is merely to create a nation-state for Europeans with imperial ambitions. They have no new ideas to offer on political organisation.)

Curiously, it is in fact not very plausible to claim Greece, Rome and Christianity as essentially European civilisations. Greece and Rome were Mediterranean cultures with major centres in Asia Minor, Africa and the

Near East. Alexander the Great chose to conquer the civilised world in Egypt, Persia and India. He was unaware that he was doing so in the name of European civilisation. Greece and Rome were followed by other Mediterranean civilisations – Byzantium and the Turks. Byzantium, like the Western Roman Empire after Constantine, was a Christian power. Yet Christianity, it should be recalled, arose in Palestine from Jewish roots and was thus a Mediterranean religion. Although Christianity spread, it did so in a way that divided as much as united Europe. The Eastern Church refused to recognise the leadership of Rome, which leadership was also rejected by much of Western Europe after the Reformation. The result was that Russia and other parts of Eastern Europe developed a different culture from that of Western and Central Europe, while for centuries religious wars and rivalries divided the Continent. Meanwhile, the Mediterranean tradition survived. The Turks were only slowly driven out of Europe (the battle of Lepanto in 1571; the siege of Vienna in 1683; the Balkan Wars of 1912-13), although even today they are members of NATO and candidates for full membership of the European Union. When the great French historian, Fernand Braudel, came to write on the age of Philip II, he chose the title of *La Méditerranée et le monde méditerranéen a l'époque de Philippe II*: He did not write about the *European* civilisation of that era.

Finally, despite the pretensions of Mitterrand's France, the legacy of the French Revolution cannot be claimed as a unifying force in European history either. Mrs Thatcher in Paris in 1989 was quite correct to point out that its legacy was less one of liberty, democracy and human rights than the opening of a Pandora's box of passionate ideologies which caused as much division as unity.

Europe, in truth, has been the home of many civilisations, often at the same time, with mixed results for the human race. It is facile and unhistorical to pretend that they have been a cumulative or a unifying force. To quote a historian who gave much thought to this matter: 'Civilisations do not add up. The extraordinarily impressive portrait head of Yarim-Lun, King of Alalakh in the eighteenth century BC, the Hermes of Praxiteles and Raphael's Sistine Madonna, are not stages in a continuous development towards artistic perfection; each is the expression of a distinct civilisation.' The same is true of Egyptian pyramids, Doric temples and Gothic cathedrals as far as architecture is concerned. And it is true of literature: Aristophanes, Virgil, Shakespeare, Goethe, and Dostoevsky are not links in a chain. They do not add up to 'European culture', but reflect different European cultures.

Today it is difficult to talk of a contemporary European culture. Europeans read their national newspapers and watch national television programmes. They may dine at Indian restaurants (not to mention McDonald's) or watch American films, Australian soap-operas and American videos. They belong both to national cultures and to a cosmopolitan

Western culture based on jeans and junk food. To state that they belong to a specifically European culture is to indulge an act of faith.

This essential European diversity, moreover, should not be regarded merely as a cultural or intellectual curiosity. It has, according to one of the world's most eminent economic historians, Professor E.L. Jones of Canberra, been at the very heart of Europe's success over the past five centuries. In his book *The European Miracle*, he asks the question why was it that after the fourteenth century Europe sped ahead of China, India and the Middle East, while during the fourteenth century itself all these areas of the world had been at the same stage of intellectual and technological development? His answer is that Europe never became united. All these other parts of the world became empires – the Ming, Moghul and Ottoman – but in Europe neither the Emperor nor the Pope could unify the Continent. The Reformation split the Church, while the Empire disintegrated into nation states. But, according to Jones, it was precisely on this account that freedom and progress could survive in Europe. When tyranny or orthodoxy threatened one part of Europe, the torch of freedom passed to another. In short, the existence of a kind of market in competing polities and economies drove Europe forward. Or in other words, *disunity not unity has been the secret of Europe's progress*.

Historically, this model seems to fit the facts. For example, when Philip II suppressed Antwerp, he caused the rise of Amsterdam; when Louis XIV expelled the Huguenots, he politically and economically enriched both England and Prussia. In a similar vein, the diversity of Europe encouraged reforms. Peter the Great of Russia, for example, could make a grand tour of the Continent to discover which economic and political structures were best suited to his homeland. The European Enlightenment in turn was essentially a debate over the merits of various forms of government among academicians, intellectuals and rulers who tried to reform their own and other countries in the light of their knowledge. Finally, when Bismarck introduced social welfare into imperial Germany at the end of the nineteenth century, his work was studied by other governments which introduced their own laws in the light of local circumstances. No one would have dreamt of applying a social chapter to the whole of Europe. Thus diversity and disunity have always been at the heart of Europe's progress.

Elsewhere in the world, empires have stagnated thanks to the bureaucratisation, centralisation and regulation that stifled their ability to adapt both intellectually and technologically. Europe is now heading along that same fateful route. It in turn is now centralised, regulated and bureaucratised to such a degree that it cannot adapt to the global economy of the late twentieth century. It is no surprise, therefore, that it should be suffering from high unemployment, low growth, social unrest and political turmoil. Yet none of this is necessary. The cure for Europe's problems is for her leaders to be satisfied with a continent of free-trading, politically independent, democratic states. European Union, on the other hand, is the wrong future, not merely for Britain, but for Europe – and indeed the world, which does not need and does not want a European superstate.

Part II

6

The Domestic Background

It looks entirely certain that the major parties in Britain will put an end to the country's independence before the next millennium. So let us take a brief look at these parties and at the society and political system they intend to kill off.

The UK has three so-called 'major parties'. These are the Conservative Party (otherwise known as the Tory Party), the Labour Party (now calling itself New Labour in order to shed its past record and principles) and the Liberal Democratic Party (formerly known as the Liberal Party, before its merger with the ephemeral Social Democratic Party). Only the Tories can claim to have been successful as a political machine designed for government.

The Liberals date from the 1860s and have not formed a government since 1916. They have not really had any chance of forming one since 1923, and after World War II seemed set for oblivion. This was postponed, largely due to the inspired leadership of Jo Grimond, who began a tradition of 'Liberal revivals', although these have become rather rare recently and the Liberal Democratic vote is now down to almost single figures. The Liberals do have a core of activists, but in reality they depend on protest votes from people who cannot bear to vote for either the Labour or Conservative Parties. These people have little idea of what the Liberal Democrats actually stand for. For example, opinion polls suggest that 55% of them oppose UK membership of the European Union, yet the Liberal Democratic Party has been the strongest and most consistent advocate of European unity. Indeed, its present leader, 'Paddy' Ashdown (his real name is Jeremy) is on record as saying that those who oppose European Union are either 'xenophobes' or 'false patriots'. Perhaps this explains the standard Westminster joke that when you call his answering machine, you are asked to leave a message after 'the high moral tone'. On the other hand, Mr. Gladstone he most certainly is not. Basically, no one bothers about Liberal Democratic views on matters such as economics, education or defence. They are only treated seriously as advocates of 'a federal Britain in a federal Europe', i.e. as potential allies of a Labour government which might seek to break up Britain. For many commentators, even these policies are less important than the sheer desperation of the party to receive one or two cabinet posts in a Labour government. Memories have not yet died of the Liberals' role under Sir David Steel of maintaining James Callaghan's abysmal government in office during 'the winter of discontent' of 1978-79. Despite Labour's desperation to cling on to power, the feckless Liberals could not even secure a single cabinet post in their negotiations. But they supported Labour anyway. Lord Callaghan, by the way, now shares with Sir Edward Heath and John Major a claim to be possibly the worst prime minister since 1945. (But note the fairness of the British honours system: historical failure is no bar to titles. Mr Major's still awaits him.) There is little more of any importance to say about the Liberal Democrats, save that they are good for party games like trivial pursuit. Naming ten famous Liberal Democrats is like naming ten famous Belgians or ten famous Albanians. One always gets one or two.

The Labour Party takes us into more serious history, since there can be no doubt that the rise of Labour has changed the political history of Britain this century, especially since 1945. However, it has done so less profoundly than one might think. In a sense, just as the Jacobins preserved European monarchy for over a century, the Labour Party has saved the Conservative Party for just as long. It will be interesting to see if New Labour achieves anything better.

The two key facts to remember about the Labour Party are, first, that it practically takes a world war to propel it into power and, secondly, that it has an historical fear of being betrayed by its leaders. These factors have meant that it has not developed into an election-winning machine, having achieved an overall parliamentary majority for only about fifteen years in almost a century. First-time voters in the general election of 1997, for example, will have no memory of the last Labour government. This fact, not his looks, will be Mr Blair's greatest asset.

Long periods out of power have meant that Labour has often been deeply divided. Its experience of 'the great betrayal' by its first prime minister, Ramsay MacDonald, has much to answer for in this respect. Since then Labour has spent three long periods in opposition: 1931-39; 1951-64; and 1979-97. Each period has been longer than the one before and each has been marked by leadership challenges, policy disputes and battles over the party's constitution. In 1939 it was rescued by the war; in 1964 by the political genius of Harold Wilson, highlighted by the shortcomings of Sir Alec Douglas-Home; in 1997 it hopes to be rescued by stealing the clothes of a Tory Party that, quite ironically, has become well nigh unelectable. Tony Blair intends to enter 10 Downing Street as an updated version of Mrs Thatcher, not Lord Callaghan. Who can blame him? Yet, if he succeeds he will have brought about a greater betrayal than Ramsay MacDonald was ever guilty of and he will have done it quite deliberately. But then the Liberals are not the only party to practise the politics of desperation. New Labour has made it an art form.

It is usual for the Labour Party in its long periods in opposition to have disputes over both its constitution and its policies, disputes which fuel leadership challenges. In the 1930s, for example, it was felt necessary to ensure that the party leadership would never again betray the membership as Ramsay MacDonald was held to have done by agreeing to head a National Government in 1931. The subsequent general election saw Labour reduced to a rump of about 50 MPs, facing what was effectively a Tory government with a majority of over 500. The result was that the 1933 Labour Party conference laid down that the party might only take office after all its affiliated bodies had been consulted, that a Labour cabinet could be chosen by the Labour leader only in consultation with three representatives of the Parliamentary Labour Party plus the party secretary, that cabinet decisions had to be taken by majority votes, that dissolutions of the House of Commons had to have cabinet backing, that cabinet members and and backbenchers should liaise between the government and the parliamentary party, that only party policy as established by conference should provide the programme of government, that the TUC should always be consulted, and that any Labour government should begin its period in office with a symbolic act of socialism (e.g. the abolition of the House of Lords).

Socialism, too, was now put unequivocally on the party's agenda, although in 1929 MacDonald's government had not had the faintest idea what to do about the world economic crisis. Later on, despite all its talk of socialism, Labour would still have little idea of what it meant in practice. Still, in its programme of 1934, entitled *For Socialism and Peace*, the party advocated the nationalisation of banking and credit, transport, fuel and power, agriculture, iron and steel, shipping, textiles, chemicals and insurance. If that did not sound socialist enough, it promised employees 'the right acknowledged in law to an effective share in control and direction of industry'. Parliament was to be reformed and made efficient. The House of Lords was to be abolished and any internal crises were to be dealt with by emergency powers. By 1937, after more moderate MPs had been returned in the 1935 general election, the programme had been modified. Now nationalisation was to be restricted to the Bank of England, mines, electricity and gas, and railways – although land was to belong to the people as well and certain dud transport services were also to be brought under public ownership if necessary.

In reality, Labour was not nearly so radical as it appeared and – just as in the 1980s – did nothing to mobilise the three million unemployed. They were left to Communist-dominated organisations like the National Unemployed Workers Movement and the Plebs League. Yet the NUWM managed to attract only 50,000 members and fizzled out after 1934. The Communists themselves only had about 18,000 members in 1939 and most of them were middle class. Given all this, it is little wonder that Fascism never took root in Britain. The National Government not only had a huge parliamentary majority but a decent record on housing, economic recovery and health. Since most people were also enjoying unprecedented prosper-

ity, there was simply no reason for voters to shift to the Left to a degree
that might have worried the middle classes. Besides, Labour, if not radical
in practice, had an extreme economic policy and did not trust its own
leaders. It was hardly electorally attractive.

Still, it did find things to quarrel about, particularly foreign policy,
where it split four ways on the question of how to deal with the dictators.
Out of power, Labour in future would usually find foreign policy a good
issue to argue over. In the 1930s this brought about a change of leadership
when Ernie Bevin humiliated the pacifist, George Lansbury, into resigning
in 1935. Lansbury represented the Christian, pacifist streak of the Labour
movement, a current of thought which relied on the abhorrence of war that
was a legacy of 1914-18. Yet, by 1935, this was simply not a basis on which
to formulate a defence policy. Nor indeed was the second position to be
found in Labour's ranks, namely support for international disarmament
and collective security through the League of Nations. True, there was
support for rearmament on the part of people like Bevin and Dalton, but
the Labour Party only supported it after 1937. Before then, it opposed the
defence estimates and the party conference voted to abolish the RAF. Even
afterwards a fourth faction in the party believed that rearmament could
only be supported under a Labour government. Ironically, in spite of its
lack of credibility over defence, it was to be Labour's participation in a
wartime national government led by its quintessential political enemy,
Winston Churchill, that brought it political salvation. For Churchill gave
it wartime control of the home front and allowed it to become associated
in the public mind with plans for a post-war welfare state. The popular
demand for better homes and health care as a reward for defeating the
enemy meant that Churchill was bound to lose. He was not interested in
social reform and did not believe the money would be available, although
by the time he returned to office in 1951 he had learned his lesson. Labour,
therefore, was to establish the basis for Britain's post-war consensus, a
consensus in fact which was anything but radical.

Clement Attlee's governments between 1945 and 1951 were to provide
Labour with the only political credibility the party has ever obtained.
Insofar as voters credit Labour with anything it is with the establishment
of the National Health Service and the welfare state after 1945. Even
today, Labour lives on this political credit, for nobody remembers any
achievements of Harold Wilson's (1964-66; 1966-70; 1974-76) or James
Callaghan's (1976-79) governments. Wilson's, it is true, presided over the
'moral revolution' of the 1960s, but the reforms of that period – the
abolition of censorship and capital punishment, homosexual law reform,
legal abortions, easier divorce – although aided by Roy Jenkins's tenure of
the Home Office, were really the work of individual MPs. Wilson and
Callaghan spent most of their time managing economic crises and trades
union bosses and patching up internal party feuds. Wilson himself was
absolutely paranoid about party management and threats from colleagues

or the intelligence services to unseat him as party leader. Callaghan, who had held all the great offices of state – Foreign Secretary, Home Secretary, Chancellor and Prime Minister – exuded an air of statesmanship, but in practice failed in all these positions. His own premiership was marked by an economic crisis which left Britain in the grip of a series of strikes when his special relationship with the trade union bosses fell apart. Even before then it had been necessary to transfer the management of the economy to the IMF in order to save the pound. His final flawed legacy was to saddle Labour with a policy of supporting devolution for Scotland and Wales in one of the most cynical manoeuvres yet witnessed in British politics. In 1979, however, he got his just deserts when both the Scots and the Welsh, just like the trade unions, rebuffed him and voted against his hastily invented proposals in a referendum When, on their retirement, both men were questioned on TV about their greatest achievements, Wilson chose the establishment of the Open University, Callaghan the installation of cats' eyes in the roads when he was Under Secretary in the Departmant of Transport in 1947. Their answers spoke volumes about the record of the Labour Party in power in the 1960s and 1970s.

The real hallmark of the Labour governments of these years, however, had been their close relationship with the trade union barons whose agreement was needed for every prices and incomes policy or social contract – the names then given to the corporatist, Keynesian demand-management initiatives resorted to in an attempt to contain inflation. Denis Healey, Callaghan's ebullient if unsuccessful Chancellor, even offered publicly to make tax changes dependent upon prior union agreement to one of these corporatist arrangements. The thing that Labour could not do, however, was to reform the unions themselves. Not only did the latter control Labour's income, they also dominated the voting at Labour Party conferences, sponsored many MPs and dominated Labour's national executive. When in 1969, Harold Wilson and Barbara Castle attempted to bring in reforms, Callaghan, who as Labour Party treasurer knew precisely how dependent Labour was on the unions, frustrated their attempts. If, as a result, he became Labour's most eminent victim of union hostility during the 'winter of discontent', he had no one but himself to blame.

Callaghan's defeat in the 1979 general election was to send Labour on its longest journey into the political wilderness, yet in the years between 1951 and 1964, Labour had been there already. In a sense this had been bad luck, because, although Labour's policies under Attlee had enjoyed popular support reflected in increased votes in 1950 and 1951 (until 1992, the highest ever recorded for a political party in power), the collapse of the Liberal vote in 1951 (as again in 1970) helped return the Tories to power. Labour was to leave office until 1964.

During this period, the party was at first content to wait upon the Tories making mistakes or appearing extreme. Given the increased votes it had attracted there seemed no need to reassess policy or to criticise its recent record. Indeed, during Labour's period in power between 1945 and 1951, a post-war consensus had been established in both home and foreign affairs. The National Health Service based on national insurance had established a basic welfare state that the Tories did not in principle. oppose. The mixed economy of nationalised and private industry – with the exception of the nationalisation of the steel industry – had been accepted as well. So, too, had been the basic commitment to full employment and to Keynesian economics. No less than the Labour Party did the Tories avoid trade union reform, so that the basic economic structure of the country appeared to be settled. In foreign and defence policy, the consensus prevailed. Both parties accepted the need for decolonisation, both wanted a British bomb, both supported NATO and both resisted British participation in European integration. Both were also anti-Soviet and happy to support the Americans in the Korean War, despite the huge financial cost involved. The Tories had attacked Labour, therefore, less on principles than on practicalities – the long wait before wartime rationing and restrictions could be dismantled, the position of doctors in the new NHS, the conduct of certain foreign policy questions. Churchill knew that his stridency in the 1945 general election had struck the wrong note and like the rest of his party was impressed by Labour's rising vote. Attlee also never lost a by-election.

Still, in 1951 Labour were out of office. After waiting in vain for Churchill to upset the consensus or to start a war (in fact, Labour had almost got involved in one with Persia in 1950 and had, of course, entered the Korean War that same year), Labour eventually resorted to the habits of opposition – disputes over policy and the constitution and challenges to the party leadership.

The new hero of the disaffected was Aneurin Bevan, the ex-miner from South Wales, whose rhetorical skills had been honed by attacks on Churchill and Lloyd George. He had created the NHS almost single-handed and had proved almost as effective as Housing Minister under Attlee as he had been brilliant as Health Secretary (the two posts had been combined). However, he had resigned along with Harold Wilson and John Freeman when Hugh Gaitskell as Chancellor had imposed charges on spectacles and teeth to help pay for the Korean War. Thereafter, he was to be the main thorn in the Labour leadership's side and during the early 1950s, along with his supporters on the Left, who were organised by Michael Foot around the newspaper, *Tribune*, Bevan led a campaign against German rearmament, SEATO and the bomb. He also stood unsuccessfully for the party's deputy leadership (1952) and treasurership (1954) before resigning from the Shadow Cabinet in 1955 and losing the party whip in 1957. Then came a stunning turn-about when he decided that the British H-bomb was necessary after all (Khrushchev told him that unilateral nuclear disarmament by Britain would achieve nothing), declaring to the Labour Party conference that no Labour Foreign Secretary should be 'sent naked into the conference chamber' and condemning the unilateralists for indulging in an 'emotional spasm'. By now, he had been reconciled to Gaitskell, who, backed by the then right-wing trade union bosses, succeeded Attlee in 1955 as party leader.

Gaitskell was to suffer two main challenges as party leader before he died in 1962. The first was from the unilateralists, the nuclear disarmers who founded CND (the Campaign for Nuclear Disarmament) in 1958 as a moral crusade. They were not interested in nuclear strategy; nuclear weapons were intrinsically immoral and all politicians who had anything to do with them were more evil than Hitler since they risked destroying the planet. CND decided that the only way to achieve their aims was to capture the Labour Party. By capturing the leading trade unions and many constituency parties, they won the vote in 1960 at the party conference. Yet Gaitskell, who approved of nuclear weapons and had been in favour of rearmament in the 1930s, fought back with the help of the Campaign for Democratic Socialism and had the vote reversed the following year. Thereafter CND split and became a kind of home for rent-a-mob, an all-purpose protest movement. It resorted to direct action (sit-ins and sit-downs mainly) under the ageing Bertrand Russell and soon lost political credibility. The Cuban missile crisis of 1962 helped undermine it as did the approach of the 1964 general election and Labour's leadership after 1962 under Harold Wilson, who was wise enough never to mention defence or nuclear weapons if he could help it. Instead, with the Nassau Agreement of 1962, he evaded the entire issue, maintaining that since the British nuclear deterrent was now American, CND's attack was really against NATO.

Before then, Gaitskell had lost the 1959 general election, an unexpected result for Labour after Eden's 1956 Suez disaster, and so he had begun to rethink party strategy. Unadvisedly, he proposed to abolish Clause IV of the Labour party's constitution, believing that its commitment to the public ownership of the means of production, distribution and exchange, made Labour look like a party of the extreme Left. (Labour manifestos after 1951, it is true, included merely 'token' industries for nationalisation, but they were still industries.) The result was huge internal division and Gaitskell's defeat. Pragmatists (why bother?), idealogues (we believe) and sentimentalists (it's part of our tradition) outnumbered realists (it doesn't work), so that in the end a mere national executive motion in 1960 recorded Gaitskell's view as party policy. The party was not interested in fundamental change.

None the less, the intellectual vacuum of the early fifties was being filled for various reasons. First, it was absolutely plain that nationalised industries did nothing for productivity, workers, industrial accountability, profits or the taxpayer. The real achievements of Labour in office had been full employment and the welfare state. As a policy, therefore, nationalisation was clearly a vote-loser. Moreover, it seemed to go against the grain of social trends. Rising incomes and hire purchase meant that in the 1950s disposable income per head had risen some 20%. Workers were becoming more mobile and more bourgeois. Hence they were no longer attracted by state socialism. The intellectual backlash came in the form of revisionism, represented by people like Douglas Jay, Roy Jenkins, Denis Healey, Hugh Gaitskell and Tony Crosland, who in 1956 published *The Future of Socialism* which declared nationalisation irrelevant. Socialism, he wrote, was about equality or moral solidarity in the community, which required primarily educational reforms (comprehensive schools) and fiscal changes (progressive taxation). Like the American economist, J.K. Galbraith, Crosland differentiated between ownership and management and argued that since managers were now in control of companies, the public ownership of these had become irrelevant. None the less, government regulation was still essential to protect the economic and social infrastructure, although the basis of everything was growth. This was possible through demand management, the basis of Keynesian economics.

By the time he reached Downing Street, therefore, Harold Wilson led a party which was more consensual than ever. The trouble was that, despite his undoubted brilliance as a speaker, TV performer and party manager, he was overwhelmed by events – primarily sterling crises – and achieved very little. The disaster of the Heath government allowed him to return, only to retire unexpectedly in 1976 while still the dominant political figure in the land. Perhaps he realised that Labour had no solutions to the country's problems., given its total dependence on the unions, who had brought down Heath and would bring down the hapless Callaghan. Certainly, Callaghan's government – like every British government after 1964 – represented a desperate attempt to entice the unions to acquiesce in government policy to stave off economic ruin.

After Labour's defeat in 1979 it entered its latest and longest sojourn in the wilderness. At first it lurched to the Left, first under veteran Tribunite, Michael Foot, and then under his protégé, Neil Kinnock. Both men were unilateral disarmers, both believed in quitting the EEC, and both were acknowledged to possess certain oratorical skills. But whereas Foot was seen to be educated, literate and, rather perversely, a member of the establishment, Kinnock was soon condemned as a 'Welsh windbag' whose verbosity outran his intellectual gifts, which were commonly assessed as rather limited. Foot, whose election was a monument to sentimentality within the party, soon proved an unmitigated disaster. Under him, Labour not only became identified with CND and opposition to Europe, but with a general sort of socialist isolationism encapsulated in the so-called Alternative Economic Strategy. This envisaged Britain leaving the EEC and enacting a programme of reflation and substantial public ownership (with minimum compensation) behind a wall of tariff barriers and currency controls. When it was incorporated into Labour's 1983 manifesto, the latter became known as 'the longest suicide note in history'.

Before then, however, the party had already split. The Left had become so alienated from the leadership as a result of Callaghan's fiascos that immediately after the 1979 election it had demanded and secured important constitutional reforms, in particular a new system of electing the leader which placed 40% of the vote in the hands of the trade unions, and the right of constituency associations to reselect (or deselect) MPs between elections. These developments, coming on top of Foot's election as leader, provoked four leading right-wing figures in the party to quit it altogether and to set up a Social Democratic Party in 1981. The almost simultaneous near-defeat of Denis Healey as deputy leader by left-winger Tony Benn encouraged millions of supporters to transfer their allegiances to the SDP. In the 1983 election, Labour trailed the Tories by 14.8%.

Kinnock at first made little attempt to alter matters. In a sense there was little he could do, since his natural allies in any attack on the Left had quit the party. On the other hand, as a protégé of Foot's, he was a left-winger himself, albeit from the 'soft' or moderate rather than from the 'hard' or extreme Left. His troubles multiplied as his party became ever more dominated by the Left. Three things in particular went wrong. First, local councils were captured by the so-called 'looney left' (in particular the Greater London Council under Ken Livingstone, but also many London boroughs and several town councils) who used them to implement policies favouring gays and lesbians, blacks and other minorities; secondly, the Militant Tendency, a hard-line Trotskyist faction, infiltrated the party and under Derek Hatton took control of Liverpool, the finances of which were manipulated as a means of confronting Tory local government policy; finally, for a whole year, 1984-5, the miners' leader Arthur Scargill led a strike, one aim of which was to overthrow the government by destroying its credibility to manage the economy. All of these factors meant that Kinnock was seen as leading a party of extremists. Given his own beliefs, his inability to condemn the violence of the miners during their strike and his inability to rid the party of its extremists (Mrs Thatcher did him the favour of abolishing the GLC and Hatton eventually over-reached himself in Liverpool), not to mention a revived British economy, Labour entered the 1987 election on weak ground. Then in an interview on a TV show, Kinnock made it clear that he would not even threaten a nuclear response should the Soviet army be approaching the Channel. The result was a Tory election poster showing a British soldier with his hands up. The caption read: 'Labour's defence policy'. This time Labour trailed the Tories by 11.5%.

The loss of three elections in a row concentrated Labour's political mind. In 1988 a process of policy reviews was initiated which meant that by 1992 the party had moved considerably to the right. The failures of Mrs Thatcher's final years in office also improved morale. The key steps in Labour's reinvention of itself under Kinnock included a rejection of state interventionist economics, a commitment to competition between companies, and an adoption of supply-side reforms to the economy; the acceptance of privatisation; the zeal of a convert for ERM membership; fiscal prudence; the acceptance of most of the Tharcherite union reforms; and the acceptance of nuclear weapons as a national defence. Policy differences between Labour and the Tories had almost disappeared. Electoral success seemed assured.

The party itself was also modernised. Off-the-record press briefings were used to undermine the Left within the party in order to ensure change. In any case, change did come about, with the end of reselection of MPs by constituency parties, the introduction of one man one vote as the procedure for elections to constituency bodies and the constituency section of the NEC, while the NEC itself lost most of its influence to the parliamentary leadership and became a reflection of that leadership rather than the centre of opposition to it.

None the less, Kinnock still lost the 1992 election, with Labour still achieving only 34.4%, less than Callaghan in 1979. One reason was the Shadow Chancellor John Smith's proposals to raise income tax; another was Kinnock's unrestrained enthusiasm at a key election rally which revived memories of his Welsh windbag image; while too many people still suspected that Labour was really a party of the Left. Crucially, many of them still voted for the SDP.

Immediately after the election, Kinnock resigned and was replaced by Smith, a solid, Scottish lawyer. He presided over further party reforms – the reduction of the union vote to 33% in leadership elections, the introduction of something like one man one vote in parliamentary selections and the real thing within trade unions in party leadership elections. However, in the summer of 1994 Smith died suddenly from heart failure and was replaced as party leader by the youthful Tony Blair. Under Blair, Clause IV was replaced in 1995 by a new commitment to a dynamic market economy; Keynesian economics were dropped in favour of monetarist, supply-side nostrums, and the name New Labour was adopted to differentiate the party's present stance from its past. No longer directing its appeal primarily at the working class, the party now saw itself as the vehicle for the upwardly mobile, still aspiring, if insecure middle classes, especially those who affected to retain some sense of social responsibility. In practice, however, it had simply accommodated itself to the Thatcher revolution and stolen all the clothes of its Tory opponents. Only on constitutional reform (see below) did it seek to differentiate itself from the Conservatives, although, ironically, given its new zealous commitment to Europe, it might have aligned itself with that party precisely at a time when the Conservative policy package began to seem irrelevant and when opposition to European integration and other constitutional changes began to make itself felt on a massive scale.

The Conservatives were able to watch the transformation of the Labour party with a certain patronising disdain. It had come about, after all, largely due to their own electoral success. The great paradox of British politics was that the Labour Party had exchanged its principles for Conservative ones at the very time when the Tories had abandoned theirs altogether.

The exact meaning of 'conservatism' in the British or any other context has been the subject of many boring books and articles. The extent to whether it is essentially an authoritarian or libertarian philosophy has consumed much ink. Yet, like liberalism, the term is obviously a relative one, since what is to be conserved will vary over place and time. Surviving Stalinists in Russia, for example, are now referred to as 'conservatives', as are those in the Labour Party who wish to retain socialism. Conservatives, in other words, are those who feel uncomfortable with change, although they usually concede that some change is necessary. Those who positively want to turn back the clock are usually referred to as reactionaries. With all this in mind, let us approach the recent history of the Conservative Party.

Twice in the modern history of the Tory Party, there have been tremendous splits: once in 1846, over the repeal of the Corn Laws, a split that kept the party out of power for thirty years; then a split over free trade that kept the party out of power from 1905 until 1922 (although it had been the senior partner in Lloyd George's coalition governments from 1916 to 1922). Between the wars, however, the party dominated British government and provided the country with moderate reforming policies. The depression affected the country much less badly than it did either Germany or America and most British people enjoyed higher living standards as well as new-fangled devices such as radios, talking films, nylons and hoovers. The real weakness for the Tories was defence. The rise of Hitler and his axis with Mussolini and the Japanese posed problems which were well nigh insoluble: the chiefs of staff predicted defeat if war broke out on three fronts around the world simultaneously; the Treasury predicted bankruptcy within a year and a half once war began, not to mention inflation, labour unrest and a deteriorating economy in the run-up to war if a large rearmament programme were needed; the Foreign Office, for its part, could point to the lack of any probable allies (saving the French, who did not want to fight) and the unreliability of even the Empire. Churchill did not seem to acknowledge any of these problems in his speeches. Still, rearmament got under way (without Labour support) and in 1939, with no possible prospect of success, war was declared on Germany.

When Churchill became premier in 1940, he also became leader of the Tory party, thus causing pain, as he put it, to many honourable gentlemen. Yet, precisely because he provided such superb wartime leadership, he had little time for domestic problems and politics, leaving Labour as the champions of a post-war welfare state. Churchill never really believed that the money would be available to build one. The electorate saw this and in 1945 voted in Attlee, after an election campaign in which Churchill was at his worst, sinking even to the extent of saying that Labour would introduce a Gestapo.

In opposition, the Tories learned their lesson. They accepted the welfare state and the mixed economy and supported Labour's foreign and defence policies. They were surprised to win in 1951 (they had fewer votes than Labour) and it took them a couple of years to feel the confidence of a government party. Churchill, therefore, had no intention of rocking boats and presided over a government that extended the welfare state (Macmillan made his reputation by building over 300,000 council houses a year) and consolidated the NHS. He himself, along with Eden, provided strong leadership on the international stage (refusing to intervene in Vietnam, organising German rearmament, allowing the French to exit peacefully from Indo-China, attempting a reconciliation with the Soviets after Stalin's death, rebuffing schemes for European integration), leadership which Eden provided in overdose during the Suez crisis of 1956.

Yet the Tories after Suez were to fall into the hands of Macmillan, a political wizard in many ways, but one whose leadership was eventually to change the course of the party. Macmillan was a consensus man – welfare state, mixed economy, corporatist economics – but was obsessed with European integration and wanted rid of the Empire. He was a Wilsonian internationalist and believed that a federalised Western Europe in tandem with America could cooperate closely with the USSR and its satellites to manage global economic and political challenges. He loathed Adenauer and de Gaulle as European nationalists; for their part, they saw right through him. Hence all his secret cooperation with Monnet could not stop de Gaulle from vetoing his Common Market application of 1961. Yet Macmillan so altered the leadership of the Tory Party that for ever afterwards the Europhiles kept control, until Mrs. Thatcher – quite by accident – was voted in as leader in 1979.

The party meanwhile had come under the leadership of Heath, Macmillan's key Europhile protégé. Heath was a strong personality who, after the disasters of the Wilson governments in the 1960s, determined to reform the trade unions and to deregulate the economy. The trouble was that the trade unions simply boycotted his industrial courts and ignored his Industrial Relations Act. In the meantime, his promises of a return to free-market capitalism were swept away as world economic problems forced him to intervene on an unprecedented scale to save major firms from going under. Since he had promised not to save these 'lame ducks', his U-turns on this and other matters soon made him a political lame duck himself. Unprecedented levels of inflation – 27% no less – then forced him into freezing prices and wages with the introduction of a Price Commission and a Pay Board. This brought more confrontations with the workers and strikes increased by a factor of four. In 1972 the miners were bought off with increases three times the size of the Coal Board's offer, but in 1974 they went on strike again. When eventually Heath went to the country on the issue 'Who governs Britain?', the voters decided that it had better not be him. Even Harold Wilson was preferable. However, by this time Heath himself had decided that Britain was ungovernable and had secured entry into the Common Market in 1972. The terms included a transition period, during which Wilson, in 1975, arranged a referendum on cosmetically renegotiated ones. The voters were given three official documents, two in favour, one against. They were told that Britain would always have a veto on everything affecting her national interests and that there was no possibility of monetary union. None of this was true, but since nothing much had changed during the two years of the transition period which had elapsed and since the media and the establishment were in favour of entry, two-thirds gave their approval.

After the disasters of Heath's government, the party leadership, instead of going to his right-hand man Willy Whitelaw, passed unpredictably to Margaret Thatcher, an entirely unremarkable figure until then, but one who, under the influence of Sir Keith Joseph, had repudiated Heath's legacy in favour of the free-market economics of von Hayek and the monetarism of Friedman. Most of all, she was determined to tame the unions and had a mandate to do so after the 'winter of discontent'. The miners, who had acquired a taste for bringing down governments, would inevitably mount a challenge, but Nicholas Ridley, one of Thatcher's friends, had worked out how to deal with them.

In power between 1979 and 1990, Thatcher changed the face of British politics and economics, not merely by winning three general elections in a row with huge majorities, but by breaking the trade unions and placing them within the law, privatising almost all nationalised industries, reducing the marginal rate of income tax and corporation tax, restoring Britain's international prestige by winning the Falklands War and working with Reagan and Gorbachev to end the Cold War, and finally by changing the intellectual climate of Britain. Corporatism was out; free-market capitalism was in. Incentives replaced subsidies. Competition became the ethic, not state support. The individual became the centre of discourse, not society. Thatcher even opined: 'There is no such thing as society.' Instead of enjoying the opportunity to win a fourth general election, however, she was assassinated by her own party over Europe in what was without doubt the most ruthless act of political ingratitude in modern political history. By 1990, it is true, she was highly unpopular. The ERM recession, presided over by Chancellor John Major, the return of inflation, and popular hatred of the poll-tax (a piece of local government 'reform') had undermined her position. It was also being said that she had broken with the post-war consensus and had destroyed the welfare state. In fact, welfare spending had risen to historic highs and she had only succeeded in winning three elections in a row by partly creating, partly following a new consensus that had demanded a rejection of trade union privileges, corporatism as a means of government, and high taxes and welfare as a way of life. Nor had the overall tax burden or the state's share of national income been reduced. In this sense she had failed to achieve her own aims. None the less, she was the most important prime minister since 1945.

Her successor was John Major, whose disastrous decision as Chancellor, along with Foreign Secretary Douglas Hurd, to force ERM membership on Thatcher was to overshadow his entire premiership. The history of the Thatcher years in economic terms was one of recession under Geoffrey Howe until 1983 (which squeezed out inflation but killed off 18% of the country's industrial base and caused huge unemployment), followed by the golden years under Lawson until 1987 when fiscal laxity plus his determination to shadow the D-mark saw the economy go out of control. This disaster was compounded when Major, as Chancellor, forced Thatcher to agree to British entry into the ERM (an exchange rate system whereby several currencies floated within fixed bands alongside the D-mark on the international currency markets). The result was the greatest recession since the 1930s with unemployment, interest rates, home repossessions, bankruptcies, public debt and tax increases all at record levels. By the time the markets forced the pound out in September 1992 at a cost of £8-15 billion in a single day John Major had become prime minister. No one knew much about him, save that he had had little education and was the son of a circus performer who later made garden gnomes.

Major's main act as premier was to repudiate Thatcher's European policy by signing the Maastricht Treaty. This made all British subjects citizens of an embryonic superstate called the European Union with obligations of citizenship that Hurd, still Foreign Secretary, could not define. It extended majority voting in many areas of European decision-making, brought defence, foreign affairs, policing and home affairs within the aegis of the European institutions, and laid down a timetable for Economic and Monetary Union (EMU) which would culminate in the creation of a single currency (the euro) by 1999 at the latest. This would be managed by a central bank which would take over the gold reserves of member states. Major negotiated an opt-out on both the single currency and the so-called social chapter, which became a kind of taboo for Tories to rally against, but was of no significance compared to EMU.

Major, with Liberal Democrat and Labour compliance, avoided all discussion of Maastricht at the 1992 general election, which he won largely as a result of public hostility to Kinnock, but then faced a tough struggle in Parliament over its ratification after the Danes said 'No'. In the end, thanks to unprecedentedly ruthless whipping, the Treaty went through with a majority of three. Not a single Tory MP voted against the government in the confidence vote at the end of the parliamentary debate. One alone abstained, perhaps by accident.

Maastricht and the ERM, however, would not go away. Britain's ejection from the ERM in September 1992 confirmed Major's reputation for economic incompetence and although the economy recovered afterwards, everyone knew that this was despite Major's policies, not because of them. They were also aware that entry into EMU would mean entering a permanently rigid version of the ERM with prospects much more dire than even the recession of 1990-92. The result was a Tory Party totally split on the subject and Major reduced (along with Tony Blair) to reiterating inanities, the main one being that he would 'wait and see' how the 'technicalities' were arranged – most conveniently and undemocratically – after the 1997 general election. Like Tony Blair he simply professed to have no view on the most important issue of the day, out of fear of splitting his party. Clearly the Tory plan was to avoid any discussion of EMU during that election in the hope that entry could take place with all-party support afterwards. In the meantime, a minority of Tory 'Eurosceptics' were allowed their say in the hope that their voices would keep traditional voters from defecting to the newly established UK Independence Party, the only mainstream party that advocated withdrawal from the EU and the replacement of membership by a free trade agreement. In fact, these 'Eurosceptics', like Sir James Goldsmith, the French MEP who campaigned for a referendum on different kinds of European union (but not withdrawal) simply confused the issue, which soon became startlingly clear: Britain would either have to be inside or outside a federal Europe since nothing else was on offer. John Major, whose Eurosceptic credentials were non-existent given Maastricht and the ERM, meanwhile pretended that he was battling with Brussels and opposing federalism, an act which wore incredibly thin, given his failure to win any battles with Brussels and his approval in Dublin of the timetable for EMU. His Chancellor of the Exchequer, Kenneth Clarke, on the other hand, made no bones about his support for EMU.

The result was that under Major the Tories became very unpopular. And little wonder. Everything they were supposed to stand for had been sacrificed. They no longer wanted to conserve British national independence, since they signed the Maastricht Treaty. They failed to conserve law and order, since during the previous twenty years crime rates were allowed to double. They no longer believed in conserving the Union since the Downing Street Declaration Mr Major signed with his Irish counterpart in 1993 proclaimed that Britain had 'no selfish, strategic or economic interest in Northern Ireland'. Why not? It was surely the prime duty of any British government to have precisely such an interest in each and every part of the United Kingdom. The prime interest of the Major government was to reach a deal with the IRA, whose terrorism was the curse of Northern Ireland. This was called a 'peace process', although no other Western government had ever pursued a 'peace process' with terrorists. The Italians even sacrificed their prime minister (Aldo Morro) in 1976 rather than negotiate with the Red Brigades. The Tories also maintained they were the party of low taxation, but gave Britain the greatest tax increases in history. They claimed to be the party of high standards, yet presided over the near destruction of the education system with levels of innumeracy and illiteracy at an all time high. Finally, despite their supposed hostility to the state, they smothered universities, hospitals, schools and town halls in more red tape than ever before. Perhaps, therefore, it was because they no longer conserved any of their principles that it proved so easy for the Labour Party to imitate them. Certainly, by 1997 the two major parties had become almost identical.

Was there any difference between them? The answer is that like the Liberal Democrats, the Labour Party believed in giving Scotland and Wales home rule. But even here there were doubts about how committed Labour really was. And doubts there should have been. However, before examining these, let us take a look at Scotland's position within the Union.

Quite clearly, Scotland could exist as an independent state. She has a gross domestic product of £50 billion, making her the 21st richest country in the world, with a per capita gross national product similar to that of Sweden. (This, of course, is another argument against those who say that Britain is too small to go it alone. If Scotland could survive by herself, why are there arguments about Britain?) Scotland weathered the 1990-92 ERM recession better than the UK as a whole; her production and construction index has outperformed that of the UK since 1990; unemployment is now lower than the UK average; and average wages are among the highest outside the South of England. Thus on 2 June 1996, the *Sunday Times* could carry a story headlined 'Scots better off than English' which began: 'It's official: the Scots are better off than the English. Income per head after tax in Scotland averages £8,210 per year, according to the most recent edition of the government's Economic Trends, compared with £8,160 in England.' During the three years to March 1995, inward investment topped more than £2 billion, spread over 257 projects, many of them in high tech sectors. (This is all recorded by the author as a proud Scot!)

The financial and business sector deserves special attention. It employs 206,000, more than one in ten of Scotland's working population. The value of funds under management is £135.8 billion, a figure that has almost doubled since 1989. Skills in fund management and banking in Scotland are recognised and respected the world over. One might take all this as evidence that the present constitutional position has worked, so why is there so much talk of Scottish independence?

The real reason has been the rise of the Scottish National Party, whose fortunes have worried its Labour rival. This was demonstrated most clearly when in 1975 a reluctant Scottish Labour Party was force-fed a diet of Scottish devolution by James Callaghan after the SNP gained 22% of the vote in the general election of October 1974, winning seven seats and coming second in about thirty others, thus opening up the prospect of them obtaining a majority of Scottish seats in 1979 and seceding from the Union. Until then, the Scottish Labour Party's line had been one of proletarian internationalism – Scots and English workers had more in common with one another than Scottish Labour supporters had with Scottish national-ists – but since Labour's overall majority in the UK depended on its Scottish base, Callaghan wanted to ensure that the nationalist threat was disposed of by devolution. The result was a weak scheme for a Scottish 'assembly' (not a parliament) under the leadership of a Scottish 'chief executive' (not a prime minister). The 'assembly' was not to be given powers to raise taxes. The proposals were put to the Scottish people in 1979 in a referendum which required the approval of 40% of the Scottish electorate. (This very sensible provision, given the magnitude of the constitutional change proposed, was the work of George Cunningham, a Scot who represented a London seat in Parliament.) This meant in effect that 55% of those actually voting would have to approve and that absten-tions would amount to a vote against. Everybody in Scotland knew this and the result was that roughly one third of the electorate voted for, one third voted against, and one third abstained. The 52% recorded for the proposals meant that they failed the test. (Somewhat weaker devolution proposals for Wales were rejected by the Welsh by four to one on the same day.)

Why then had Scottish nationalism become an issue and why do com-mentators still believe that most Scots want independence when they clearly do not? Until the 1970s the SNP had never managed to achieve more than 10% of the vote; until 1966 it had never secured even 5%. So why did Scottish nationalism emerge in the 1970s as a major force in Scottish politics and why does it still represent a major one today (attract-ing up to 25% of the Scottish vote in opinion polls)? Many explanations have been offered.

Certainly the nationalist vote cannot simply be written off as a protest. It has been much more permanent than such an explanation would imply. The reaction of the Labour Party also suggests this. In reality, the vitality of SNP organisation has demonstrated that it represents an alternative political system and one which one day could become the dominant one in Scotland, although this is highly unlikely. Yet why did it have to wait until the 1970s before making itself felt? To some observers the answer lay in the discovery and exploitation of North Sea oil – 'Scottish oil' as the SNP called it. Yet most Scots did not believe it was Scottish oil. Besides, the SNP had taken off (in the 1960s) before oil had been discovered and in any case that discovery says nothing about the lack of nationalism in Scottish politics between 1750 and 1950. It seems more probable that the discovery of the oil only added confidence to the opinions of those who were con-vinced nationalists already. Others have suggested that the SNP rose because the Scots had become fed up with being treated as an English colony. (The recent Scottish film, *Trainspotting*, has its leading character complain that while the English are wankers, Scotland has been colonised by wankers.) Yet, this, too, is difficult to accept, since by the 1970s the Scots economy was beginning to catch up with that of England, while politically it was plain that Scots were well represented at all levels of public life in Britain. Politically, too, the Scottish vote had often been decisive in imposing Labour governments on England (as Callaghan knew only too well). Besides, it was a strange colonial system that subsidised the colony and not the metropolis. There was, finally, the argument put forward by the neo-Marxists that Scotland had only joined the Union in order to exploit the British Empire and that with the decolonisation of the Empire the break-up of Britain would inevitably follow. Yet the Union had never come about primarily to allow the Scots to build up the Empire, which, in any case, had hardly smothered Irish nationalism at the height of its influence. The Scots economy, like that of Britain as a whole, had expanded more rapidly after the Empire had been dismantled. Its dismantling, therefore, did not create an argument for Scottish independence. Again, it does not explain the fact that Scottish Home Rule had been conceded by Asquith in 1913, only to be permanently postponed by World War I.

The most convincing explanation for the rise of the SNP in the 1970s and periodically since (although they lost influence after the 1979 referendum defeat) seems to be that, whereas in England the Liberals proved unable to capitalise on the failures of Conservative and Labour governments (and they did fail), the SNP, with new methods, fresh faces, and young enthusiasts, were able to create a more efficient party organisation, aided by lack of class identification (nationalism crosses class boundaries) and wide support in the Scottish media (which saw the SNP as a great news story.) As it happened, however, the nationalists were to suffer from the ambiguity of Scottish patriotism. For, given that the Union had left the Scots their own system of law, their own Church and their own education system, given too that they have their own currency, read their own newspapers and watch their own television programmes, they do not feel it necessary to have a separate state to protect their sense of nationhood. Thus in 1979 most Scots were proud to be British and many outside the Central Lowlands actually preferred 'London-dominated government' to domination by Glasgow or Edinburgh.

In any case, one must question whether Scotland is actually run from England at all. Since 1892 Scotland has always been represented in the cabinet by a Scottish representative (Secretary of State since 1926) and since 1939 the principal base of the Scottish Office has always been in Edinburgh. Over the years the functions and importance of the Scottish Office have increased. Today, the Secretary of State, with four junior ministers and a Scottish Office organised into five departments, is responsible for agriculture and fisheries, the arts, crofting, education, the environment, the fire service, forestry, health, housing, industrial assistance, some legal matters (with other functions falling to the Lord Advocate's department), local government, police, prisons, roads, rural and urban development, social work, sport, transport, tourism, and town planning, as well as some minor departments and public corporations in so far as they operate in Scotland. In some other matters the minister is jointly responsible with another minister (who has the relevant functional responsibility). More generally, as one parliamentary committee put it, 'there is a wide and undefined area in which he is expected to be the mouthpiece of Scottish opinion in the cabinet and elsewhere'.

Scotland's representation in the House of Commons is, it should be added, a generous one (as is that of Wales). There is a 'Celtic preference' built into the rules concerning parliamentary constituencies, which are found in the Parliamentary Constituencies Act of 1986. Instead of providing (as might be the case) that all constituencies should consist of equal numbers of electors, the legislation prescribes minimum numbers of constituencies for Scotland, Wales and Northern Ireland (but not for England) within the total, and establishes four Boundary Commissions to review and report for their respective national territories.

Under this legislation, Scotland must have no fewer than 71 constituencies. In 1991 the average size of the electorate in Scottish constituencies was 54,369, the average size in English constituencies being 69,279. It has been calculated that on a basis of arithmetical equality throughout the UK, Scotland's share of seats would be only 58 or 59. Thus the Celtic preference is quite significant and, in the words of Colin Munro, Professor of Constitutional Law at Edinburgh, must be seen 'as a concession to Scottish nationhood within the Union'. He adds: 'one may doubt whether Scotland's over-representation at Westminster would survive, if a Scottish Parliament should ever be created without corresponding institutions in England.' (Northern Irish seats, it may be recalled, were reduced from 17 to 12 when a Parliament sat at Stormont.)

Inside the House of Commons parliamentary procedure is different for exclusively Scottish Bills. The rules allow for such proposals to be debated by the Scottish Grand Committee (all 72 Scottish MPs) at the Second Reading stage instead of in the House itself, if fewer than ten members object. For the Committee stage, where matters of detail are debated and resolved, Scottish Bills are sent to one of two Scottish Standing Committees, composed of upwards of sixteen members, mostly Scottish. Since 1980 the Scottish Grand Committee has been able to meet in Scotland and since 1995 has been able to question senior ministers in Scotland. On 5 July 1996 John Major became the first prime minister to be questioned by it in Dumfries. During that week, too, he announced that the Stone of Scone would be returned to Scotland, a political gesture which was carried out in late 1996. Most Scots, however, were unimpressed at what was clearly a manoeuvre to contain Tory vote losses north of the Border, while many were disturbed at the brusqueness with which the reliquary was removed from the Chair of St Edward at Westminster Abbey. Since the reign of James VI and I, it had come to symbolise the union of the crowns.

The political advantages to Scotland of remaining in the Union are thus fairly obvious: de facto control of her own affairs, a separate cultural identity, a separate currency, a separate legal system, a separate Church and a separate education system, all within the confines of a Union where everyone speaks the same language and shares a long and successful common history. The Union also allows Scots to help determine the foreign and defence affairs of the UK, not to mention the domestic policy of England.

In economic affairs, too, Scotland has obviously not been discriminated against by England. Polemics over which country 'subsidises' which to one side, it is clear that today Scotland's economy is flourishing within the Union. As one distinguished Scottish economist has put it, 'anyone who is tempted to regard Scotland as a depressed region of the UK is quite wide of the mark'. We have already noted the figures which prove this.

So why would anyone want to change this situation? The SNP say they are in favour of Scottish independence, yet this is quite untrue. Their programme is actually for 'an independent Scotland in a united Europe'. The logic behind this is so faulty – how can Scotland be independent in a united Europe if it cannot be independent in the United Kingdom? – that as a Scot one begins to feel embarrassed about Scottish education. It is quite clear that inside a united Europe, Scotland could be at most only a separate province of a European superstate – the equivalent of Rhode Island within the USA. Moreover, she would only have three votes (perhaps five) to dispose of in a Council of Ministers which would vote in hundreds. Scots Law would give way to European Law (within the UK it is the equal of English Law and is supreme in Scotland), Scottish pound notes would disappear, and young Scots would become liable to conscription in a future European super-army. Real independence on the Norwegian or Swiss model would appear to represent a much better option. Yet the SNP seems to have climbed on the EU gravy train, and Brussels, full of people who used to refer to Scotland as England or Angleterre, is content to use these so-called nationalists as the means with which to divide and rule the UK.

Some Scots see SNP acquiescence in this as nothing less than a betrayal of Scotland and the UK. Nor are they affected by half-educated responses by SNP supporters that Scotland is more continental than England, with allusions to close links with France. This is historical codswallop. Mary Queen of Scots may have come to the Scottish throne via the French one, but her real interest was the throne of England. In the meantime no less than five kings of England had died on French soil pursuing their own claims to the throne of France. Shakespeare and Chaucer were just as aware of European history, geography and literature as any figure of the Scottish Reformation or Enlightenment. However, the main point to note is that England and Scotland have exerted much more cultural influence on each other than they have on Europe or Europe has on them. Today, 750,000 Scots live in England and almost 400,000 English live in Scotland.

Scots, therefore, are much more likely to stick with the Union than to demand independence.

But what of devolution? Would it make any difference? The Labour Party's plans do not seem to offer very much, save more politicians, more taxes, more bureaucrats and more lawyers. True, they would allow the new Scottish Parliament to raise or lower the basic rate of income tax by three pence in the pound, but is that worth voting for? The highly respected Institute for Fiscal Studies has costed Labour's plans and concluded that they would require a basic Scottish income tax of 37% and a higher band of 58.5%. Three extra pence in the pound would be only the beginning. Such tax increases would drive the financial sector of the Scottish economy down to London extraordinarily quickly. Scotland would soon lose all financial credibility with inward investors.

Suppose that a Scottish parliament were to raise current rates by 3%. This would raise less than £500 million in Scotland, or 3% of the Scottish Parliament's revenues. Most of its money would still come from the grant currently made to the Scottish Office by Westminster (£14.5 billion) So much for accountability. Moreover, the parliament's ability to tax earned income at the standard rate by an extra 3% would still depend on Westminster. Any decision by the Chancellor to narrow that band (e.g. by increasing tax thresholds) would automatically cut the Scottish parliament's revenues. Finally, the power of a Scottish parliament to reduce taxes would seem fictional even at best. Since government spending per head is higher in Scotland than in England (21% higher in 1993-94) and Labour does not intend to alter the spending formula, 'there would inevitably be irresistible pressure to eliminate this differential if a Scottish Parliament attempted to use the extra money to reduce income tax'. The *Economist* has therefore concluded that under Labour's proposals, the Scottish parliament's powers 'to reduce taxes would be a fiction, and its powers to raise them severely restricted'. Yet that is a best-case scenario; the worst-case scenario, represented by the analysis of the Institute for Fiscal Studies, is probably more realistic. Devolution as proposed by the Labour Party, would therefore seem to offer as flawed and fruitless a future for Scotland as the SNP's impossible plan for an independent Scotland in a united Europe.

Wales, on the other hand, has never been as nationalist as Scotland, voting by four to one against devolution in the 1979 referendum. There are probably several reasons for this. For a start, almost three times as many people in Wales were born in England – almost 20%. In the 1980s there was a considerable migration to Wales, particularly to Welsh-speaking regions.

Secondly, although less than 20% of the Welsh population speak Welsh (down 10% since 1950), and although they are concentrated into areas in the north-west such as Gwynedd and Dyfed, the non-Welsh-speaking areas are generally suspicious of the Welsh nationalism connected with these areas. There is a fear that Plaid Cymru in power would discriminate against non-Welsh speakers even under a devolved government. Thus, although the comparatively healthy state of the Welsh language gives Welsh nationalism its cultural strength (in contrast, Gaelic is spoken by only about 1% of the Scottish population and according to some recent research is actually being artificially stimulated by the children of English immigrants), it divides the nation politically. Many of those who consider themselves nationalists thus vote Labour or Liberal Democrat.

Nor can Plaid escape the language issue. The Welsh Language Society, Cymdeithas Yr Iaith Gymraeg, in the 1980s kept up the pressure on the party to stick to its commitment to Welsh as the only language of the country by a campaign of civil disobedience that involved burning the holiday homes of English people in Wales. The SNP, incidentally, has no plans to foist Gaelic on Scotland as her official language.

The third reason why Welsh nationalism has been weaker than Scottish is perhaps that Wales has had an entirely different history. Thus, while Scotland remained an independent monarchy until the Scottish king James VI inherited the English throne in 1603 and kept its own parliament until 1707, Wales lost what statehood it possessed in 1536 and did not retain separate institutions thereafter. Scotland, by contrast, kept a separate legal system, a separate Church, a separate educational system and separate political institutions and cultural representations (the significance of separate national football and rugby teams should not be underestimated in this respect – although these were also maintained by the Welsh). Welsh cultural nationalism, on the other hand, has chalked up some notable recent successes with education in Welsh now firmly established in certain areas, street signs in both languages, and since 1982 the establishment of a Welsh TV channel (largely as the result of a threatened hunger strike by the Plaid Cymru president, Gwynfor Evans).

It is necessary at this point to say a few words about the Irish problem. Since 1921 the island has been politically divided, with the British, who first united it politically – myths notwithstanding, there was never any independent united Ireland before British rule – withdrawing from most of it after that date. They remained only in Northern Ireland, where the vast majority of the population supported the Union with Great Britain. That vast majority were Protestants who remembered the victory of William III over the Catholic James II in 1690 at the battle of the Boyne and the triumph of parliamentary government over European-style Catholic absolutism. (The twenty-first century may yet resemble the seventeenth in British history more than any other.) Given that the Irish Republic refused to recognise the legitimacy of Northern Ireland as part of the United Kingdom and that there were many on the Left in the UK who advocated a united Ireland, the Protestants of Ulster soon adopted a siege mentality and discriminated against the Catholic minority – many, but certainly not all of whom looked to the South for political protection and leadership. Not that Eire was a model democracy; given its civil war, political violence, Catholic political domination, etc., it was anything but. It did not even declare war on the Nazis, who, had Britain lost World War II, would have taken it over in twenty-four hours. Yet tens of thousands of ordinary Irishmen volunteered to fight in the British forces, demonstrating the most fundamental aspect of Anglo-Irish relations, which is all too often forgotten, namely that in spite of all the political antagonisms, the two peoples – who are really the same – get on extremely well. Thus to this day, for example, citizens of Eire living anywhere in the UK receive the same welfare benefits as British subjects and can vote in UK elections; again, opinion polls in the Republic show that the most favoured foreigners among the Irish are the British. Even in Northern Ireland, half of the Catholic population wish to remain under British rule.

Yet the discrimination against Catholics by the Stormont regime (Northern Ireland had its own Parliament at Stormont until 1973) meant that civil rights abuses led to riots by 1968, which in turn brought intervention by British troops to protect the Catholic minority. The British government then abolished Stormont and ruled directly from London, introducing reforms to end the discrimination. These might have worked had not the IRA also intervened to radicalise the situation by shooting at troops who then had to enter Catholic areas on search and seize missions which alienated nationalist locals. The IRA, a Marxist terrorist organisation, also meted swift punishment to anyone who stood in its way. Gradually, in fact rather swiftly, the British troops found their welcome coming only from the Protestant population. In short, the IRA succeeded in manipulating the situation to keep the two communities polarised.

They were aided in this objective by two factors. First, their own intervention gave Protestant die-hards the excuse that reforms would only be seen as concessions to violence and would make terrorist activity all the easier. This created much resistance to them – especially since they were being imposed from London – which in turn made the argument for greater reforms all the more plausible. Eventually a ratchet effect was produced, whereby more and more radical solutions were called for to solve the problem once and for all. This ratchet was driven all the time by increasing violence on the part of the terrorists (they, of course, spawned Protestant or 'loyalist' opposite numbers) who at one point even descended to killing themselves in an attempt to blackmail the British into concessions (Mrs Thatcher was not deceived). But no solution came, because in the end no British government could be seen to desert an overwhelming democratic majority which wanted to remain part of the UK – this despite the probably correct belief on the part of the people of Northern Ireland that the British government would like nothing better than to dispose of them in order to win the support of foreign governments like those of the USA and Europe who have a romantic attachment to the Irish nationalist cause, not to mention the billions that would be saved in subsidising and protecting the province.

Some commentators argue that there has been no solution because the so-called 'moderate' parties on both sides of the divide – the Ulster Unionists and the SDLP (Social Democratic and Labour Party) have to compete with more extremist parties for votes (the Democratic Unionists or Sinn Fein), or because in the various negotiations, the British have been too reluctant to make concessions to nationalist opinion. The first point has some force, but the second seems absurd. British governments have abolished Stormont, attempted to force the two sides to govern together (power-sharing), brought in all sorts of reforms to end discrimination, pretended that Sinn Fein is not the political wing of the IRA in order to let it contest elections, given Dublin almost joint rule of the province, while pretending it can only give advice, and have made a public – and humiliating – declaration that the United Kingdom has no economic, strategic or selfish interest in the province (the primary duty of governments everywhere to their national territories). The government of John Major even allowed talks on Northern Ireland to be chaired by a former US Senator in an incredible display of neutrality towards its own country, so sensitive – or servile – had it become to foreign pressure. Major's renowned servility failed to produce peace, however, for one simple reason. The IRA – his would-be partners in the 'peace process' – were less interested in peace (democracy didn't come into it) than in victory. Peace, in their eyes, could only come with the withdrawal of British troops from Northern Ireland and the unification of the island, albeit with the prospect of another civil war. Even Major could not be seen to concede that, although after every IRA bomb and atrocity he still pathetically maintained that 'the peace process must go on'.

But why? No other western government has had a 'peace process' with terrorists. The Italians did not have a 'peace process' with the Red Brigades (they even refused to negotiate when their prime minister was kidnapped, allowing him to die); the Germans did not have a 'peace process' with the Baader-Meinhof Gang; the Spanish have not had a 'peace process' with ETA; the Japanese did not have a 'peace process' with the Red Army Faction. So why should there be one in Northern Ireland? Northern Irish Catholics have always had the vote. For the last thirty years they have had reform after reform. They have never given majority support to Sinn Fein, the political arm of the IRA, which in the Republic of Ireland itself attracts only 2% of the vote. There is simply no moral justification for violence in Northern Ireland, where over two-thirds of the population repeatedly demonstrate their desire to remain British in free elections and in opinion polls. The only conditions necessary for peace are the renunciation of violence by the IRA and its agreement to abide by the results of democratic elections. Until then British governments should deal with IRA violence merely as a security problem.

Northern Ireland, for its part, should be treated as an integral part of the UK, just like Scotland or Wales, with a Secretary of State for Northern Ireland, free local government, a Northern Irish Grand Committee, and a civil service at Stormont implementing particular legislation for the province. Naturally, the special problem would remain of a minority of the population whose loyalties would be to the Irish Republic. Yet there should be no intent to supress these. Rather, some arrangement should be sought whereby their representatives could be elected to the Diall (the Irish Parliament) without threatening the Union between Great Britain and Northern Ireland.

Let us now return to the issue of constitutional reforms. Devolution has hardly been the only reform demanded by the British Left. The liberal chattering classes have for years now been demanding a whole array of changes based largely on European models. The idea seems to have originated with the liberal false logic of the 1960s that German-type political institutions would provide German-type economic growth. Today, Liberals and Socialists are still completely hung-up on the idea that constitutional change will produce economic growth. The basic fact of life, however, is that constitutional change has nothing to do with economic growth, which would be just as likely (or unlikely) to occur if half the population dyed their hair red.

Other people advocate change simply for the sake of change, for 'keeping up with the times', or for 'modernising' our system of government. Usually they want the same things: devolution, proportional representation, a written constitution, a 'reformed' monarchy or better still, a republic. They usually also support a united Ireland. Needless to say, they all believe that a Britain 'reformed' in this way would fit in better in a united Europe. In fact, these people have transferred their loyalties from Britain to Brussels. They oppose the continued independence of the United Kingdom, reminding one of Canning's universalists: 'steady citizens of the world alone, the friends of every country but their own'. They want less to reform Britain than to put an end to it. They appear to loathe its past, resent its success, and hate its distictiveness. They want to make it a made-to-measure, plastic province of a tacky, artificially-created superstate.

A united Europe, it is assumed, would be a republic. The advocates of this particular future therefore have had little incentive to support the monarchy. Instead, knowing its continued popularity, they have sought to undermine it by arguing that monarchy is out of date and socially privileged and by calling for 'democratic reforms' and the abolition of remaining royal prerogatives. They have been aided in this work, it must be conceded, by the unfortunate behaviour of some of the younger royals, particularly the Duchess of York and the Prince of Wales. Yet the remaining prerogatives are very few and the Queen takes great care to exercise them uncontroversially on the advice of ministers. In fact, the 'royal prerogative' today has no greater significance than the royal mail. None the less, there have been calls for the Speaker of the House of Commons to assume the task of granting dissolutions and appointing ministers of the crown. This reform was introduced in Sweden in 1974 but served merely to politicise the role of Speaker there and thus to undermine that office. In Britain, the same thing would happen; not only that, but the little glamour that still attaches to parliament as a result of the royal connection would be undermined as professional politicians, who remain much less popular than the monarchy, demanded even more of the limelight.

Constitutional monarchy, in any case, is hardly incompatible with social and political egalitarianism or with advanced technological society. The most egalitarian countries in Europe – Norway, Denmark and Sweden – are all constitutional monarchies; the most advanced technological society in the world, Japan, is also presided over by a constitutional monarchy. When Spain returned to democracy after the death of Franco, it succeeded only because of its new, constitutional monarch, Juan Carlos, whom left-wing, academic commentators wrote off as a political joke. They do not laugh now. In fact, the emerging democracies of Russia and Eastern Europe are highly interested in the Spanish example and are toying with reintroducing monarchies themselves. The key to their interest is the same factor which makes the monarchy so popular in Britain – the knowledge that a constitutional monarch operates above party politics. Thus British subjects can give their emotional loyalty to the Queen as the embodiment of Britain's national history and pride without any constraint of political loyalty. In this respect they have the advantage over the citizens of America or France, whose executive presidents can be guilty of political corruption. Even the citizens of countries such as Germany and Italy, whose presidents are mere figureheads, have seen them resign on account of corruption. Here the Queen is not involved in politics and is too rich to be tempted into corruption. (Not that she is subsidised by her subjects. In fact, since she agreed to pay income tax and limit the civil list to herself, her husband and her mother, arguments about her 'paying her way' have settled down. In 1996 the total cost of the monarchy was £55 million, the income from the crown estates £90 million.) Perhaps that is why in January 1997, even after several years of scandal surrounding the younger members of the royal family, a majority of two to one out of over two million people who participated in a television phone-in, supported the proposition that the British monarchy should continue.

What then of the House of Lords? Can this undemocratic, unelected body be defended as part of the constitution? Perhaps it can.

The case for retaining the House of Lords cannot be made on democratic grounds; it exists because no better alternative has yet been devised. The House of Commons, which apparently does not mind surrendering large amounts of real power to unelected foreign bureaucrats, shies away from creating an elected second chamber in Britain because such a chamber would have a democratic mandate to equal its own. Were this to be the case, it could demand just as many powers as the House of Commons. It could also demand the right to veto all legislation it disagreed with that emerged from the House of Commons. The House of Commons, of course, would be equally justified in claiming the right to veto all legislation it disagreed with that emerged from an elected House of Lords. The result would therefore be deadlock. Governments, not surprisingly, have found it simpler to retain the House of Lords as it is. It has only a suspensive veto over non-financial legislation and can only delay such legislation by a year. It thus provides the House of Commons with time to rethink hasty proposals. Given that the House of Lords has a membership of distinguished experts and former ministers, as well as the variety of types created by the British aristocracy, some commentators believe that it is actually a more distinguished chamber than the House of Commons.

The most likely thing to happen to the House of Lords is 'gesture democracy': the exclusion of hereditary peers on the grounds that they are not elected but the retention of life peers who are not elected either and who may well be failed politicians long past their sell-by date. This, of course, would be a non-solution to a non-problem – the House of Lords has no power to do any constitutional harm – but it would suit the politically correct prejudices of the Left. In fact, the only real reform needed as far as the House of Lords is concerned is the introduction of an oath requiring all peers to defend the independence of the United Kingdom. The least one expects of aristocrats, even pseudo-aristocrats, is that they should swear an oath to defend the sovereignty of their monarch. Given the deplorable record of their lordships over Maastricht, this reform should be introduced as soon as possible. Needless to say, all MPs should be made to swear a similar oath.

If 'democratic' reform of the monarchy or of the House of Lords would only make constitutional matters worse, what of these other touted reforms, proportional representation and a written constitution? Proportional representation would certainly enable a fairer distribution of MPs to enter parliament. But that is hardly a deciding argument. Elections, after all, serve two purposes. The first is to allow the voters to have their say. The second is to provide a government. The present system unarguably makes for much more stable government than PR and given that it is based on single member constituencies, representation is eminently fair: the candidate who wins most votes in any constituency gets elected. Football games are hardly unfair when the team that scores the most goals wins. Nor are league championships which depend on the total number of individual matches won. PR, on the other hand, far too often provides weak governments in which small parties, who hold the balance of power, dictate to larger ones. Even in Germany, which is often held out as an example of a PR system which overcomes this handicap, the formation of governments since the war has been dependent not on the votes of

the electorate but on the post-election manoeuvres of the small Free
Democratic Party which makes and unmakes chancellors. Little wonder
the British Liberal Democrats are so keen to emulate the Germans.

The Liberals insist that the British system leads merely to 'adversarial
politics', a point which is simultaneously naive and dishonest. Since
political argument is about political alternatives, it is bound to be adversarial, although it can still be conducted in a perfectly civilised way. It is
dishonest to deny this; besides, if one wants to conduct the argument in a
non-adversarial way, and the alternative policies are sufficiently close as
not really to constitute alternatives at all, the better course of action would
simply be for parties to merge. This might well soon happen between the
Labour and Liberal Democrats with perhaps some Conservatives joining
in.

What then of a written constitution? What advantages would it bring?
We are already signatories to the European Convention on Human Rights,
which might indeed be better served if entrenched in Scots and English
Law. But what is the point of a written constitution? The present constitutional structure gives us a framework of law based on statutes and the
common law. We are perfectly aware of how parliament works. Judges are
being daily more robust in bringing ministers to heel, without claiming
any general right of judicial review that would undermine the sovereignty
of parliament. This is yet another sign of the flexibility and pragmatism
which the British political system represents. A written constitution would
guarantee no rights: Stalin and Ho Chi Minh had admirable ones that
made no difference to their dictatorships. Perhaps Pol Pot had one too. In
the end, only popular vigilance ensures the triumph of democracy.

A written constitution also requires a Supreme Court to interpret it.
And any such Court would have to have the right to judicial review. This
means that it could override the will of parliament – the people's elected
representatives – while at the same time it could prevent parliament from
deciding controversial matters by making its own judgements legally
binding. The US Supreme Court regularly decides the law on abortion or
positive discrimination without caring what Congress may desire. It may
declare any law to be illegal no matter how large the democratic majorities
it secured. That is why there is such a political battle every time a US
Supreme Court justice is appointed – senators are less interested in how
good a lawyer the candidate is, than whether he is a liberal or a conservative. In short, they are interested in his political, not his legal
qualifications, because under a written constitution powers of political
decision-making are transferred from elected representatives to unelected
judges.

The European Court of Justice provides an even more horrific spectacle
of judges (many professionally unqualified) playing politics to further the
ideology of European federalism. Little wonder, therefore, that just as
Liberal Democrats are the greatest proponents of PR, lawyers are the

greatest advocates of a written constitution. Yet why should we surrender our democratic rights to lawyers of all people? No doubt in some countries, where corruption is endemic, a Supreme Court and a written constitution might provide some measure of protection against public dishonesty, but Britain has not yet reached that stage. Her own flexible, adaptable legal system remains a better alternative. In the last resort, however, the will of the people must prevail.

Taken together, the package of constitutional reforms recommended by Charter 88 and the Labour and Liberal Democratic parties could soon reduce this country to constitutional gridlock. Just imagine the situation: a parliament deadlocked between two elected legislatures both claiming equal powers but different mandates; both houses locked into semi-permanent immobility on account of proportional representation; both involved in endless disputes with new parliaments in Scotland and Wales demanding more powers; both involved in disputes over the rulings of politically biased Speakers; both bringing down the reputation of democracy. Ironically, the only person who would emerge unscathed would be the Queen. Alas, even she would not remain so for very long since the European Union, the new superstate, would soon push her aside, just as it would all these other, much less dignified institutions. All the new politicians, the new bureaucrats, not to mention the army of lawyers created by the reforms, would soon discover that they had bought first-class tickets on a sinking ship.

All this is not to say that the British constitution is perfect. Far from it. It requires a Freedom of Information Act, freedom of local government, freedom from the hundreds of quangos established by Tory governments, the regulation of those strange, constitutionally anomalous persons called official regulators of privatised industries. The bureaucracy that smothers the NHS, the universities and schools, not to mention the small businesses of this country, also needs to be tackled. The sad thing is that the so-called constitutional reforms advocated by the chattering classes would make this task more difficult by creating hugely expensive, bureaucratic and inherently unworkable structures that would bog down the work of reform. None of Europe's republics are noted for their lack of bureaucracy or corruption, and their political systems have fallen into disrepute time and time again despite proportional representation and written constitution after written constitution. One should never forget the reply given by the librarian to the small boy who asked for a copy of the French constitution: 'I am terribly sorry,' he said, 'but we don't stock periodicals.'

Unwritten constitutions save a huge amount of politics, bureaucracy, litigation and taxes. After all, politicians need to be staffed and paid for. The rule of thumb should be: the fewer the better. The same goes for laws and lawyers.

The Social and Cultural Background

A number of factors have conditioned British social structures and behaviour since 1945, the most important of which may will have been the development of the welfare state.

The welfare state was first established by the Liberals before 1914, with the introduction of old age pensions in 1908 and limited national insurance against illness and unemployment in 1911. Destitute school children were given free meals and the unemployed encouraged to use new labour exchanges. Between the wars governments undertook to build council houses for the working class and local authorities were given further responsibilities in the field of public health. In 1942 came the Beveridge Report, advocating, on a sound actuarial basis, the provision of a safety net for all by the introduction of a comprehensive system of national insurance against sickness and unemployment. This was carried out – more or less as Beveridge had intended – by the 1946 National Insurance Act and the National Health Service Act of the same year. Thereafter Britons enjoyed health care free at the point of use and an ever growing array of social benefits and services.

Today, contributory benefits include old age pensions, invalidity and unemployment benefit, with a cost to the taxpayer of £40 billion annually; income-related benefits include income support, housing/council tax benefit, family credit and others and now cost £27 billion annually; while non-contributory benefits include child benefit, disability, attendance and care allowances and cost £13 billion annually.

Until well into the 1960s there was little questioning of the welfare state. Even after the start of the debate on Britain's 'relative decline' few people saw welfare as a relevant factor since our European competitors, who were then doing better in terms of economic growth than we were, were also spending larger proportions of their national wealth on welfare. In 1960 the British share of GDP devoted to social expenditure was 13.9%; in 1970 it was 18.6%; and in 1980, 22.1%. The equivalent figures for OECD (Europe) were 16.9%, 20.5%, and 28.3%. Moreover, social spending seemed to work for Britain. In the mid-1970s the percentage of households below a poverty line defined as 50% of average disposable household income was

6.3% compared with 13% in Denmark, 14.8% in France, 6.6% in France and 21% in Italy. Only the Netherlands could boast a better figure of 4.8%. Again, European countries required higher taxes. Even in 1979 tax revenue as a percentage of GDP amounted to 33.8% in the UK, but 52.9% in Sweden, 47.2% in the Netherlands, 46.7% in Norway, 45% in Denmark, 44.5% in Belgium, 41% in France and 37.2% in West Germany.

Most people believed, therefore, not merely that the welfare state represented the hallmark of a civilised nation, but that it was a success. Before 1979, for example, more homeless people were being housed than ever before; the percentage of overcrowded households was falling; between 1950 and 1980 the percentage increases in numbers of hospital doctors, consultants, nurses, midwives, general practitioners and health visitors were 146, 218, 116, 88, 26 and 238 respectively. During the same period life expectancy for men and women rose, there was increasing literacy and numeracy and greater care for the elderly and handicapped.

People also assumed that public welfare was economically useful: better educated people were more likely to perform well in industry than ill educated ones; education would reduce resistance to new ideas and improve information and choice; increased education would lead to a more rational labour market and would allow workers to master more complicated technology. The case for a healthy workforce seemed self-evident.

There were also arguments that by taking care of the very old and the very young, the sick and others, public services, by replacing the extended family, would make adults more available for employment, particularly women who had traditionally been limited to household work and bringing up children. By providing minimum standards of living, it was also argued that social services reduced public apathy and dejection and thus maintained the will to work. In a more positive way, by raising public expectations, social services might reinforce, for better or worse, the general belief that economic growth was and must remain a paramount objective of any government.

For a long time, therefore, the welfare state was an object of considerable veneration. Nor was it considered in any way a challenge to the work ethic. Reviews in 1951, 1956, 1958, 1961 and 1964 by the National Assistance Board found no evidence of work-shyness. A report by the Supplementary Benefits Commission in 1978 concluded: 'the proportion of unemployed who actually get more money in benefit than in work is very small. They are mainly men in the early months of unemployment for whom higher unemployment benefits have been deliberately designed and when the disincentive effect seems very small anyway; or men on supplementary benefit with low earnings potential and large families.' In November 1979 the Labour MP Frank Field claimed that benefit fraud amounted to only 0.273 % of all claims and 0.027% of all expenditure. Research on earnings-related benefits and family income supplements during the 1980s also failed to find any disincentive effects.

Of the welfare state in the post-war period, Julian Le Grand has written: 'For many people it was the crowning achievement of the post-war consensus: a public edifice constructed through the efforts of altruistic people to help the disadvantaged and promote social justice.' Run by public-spirited politicians and civil servants and staffed by caring professionals, its free services provided a healthy and educated workforce and aid for the disadvantaged and disabled.

However, even before 1914 the welfare state had had its critics. John Burns wrote to H.G. Wells in 1910: 'The new helotry in the Servile State run by the archivists of the School of Economics means a race of paupers in a grovelling community ruled by uniformed prigs.' Yet memories of the 1920s and 1930s meant that after 1945 the welfare state was seen as a higher stage of civilisation. Criticism in the 1950s was very muted, and this remained the position for another decade and a half. Social security costs, on the other hand, rose all the time – in real terms by an average 4.6% a year until very recently when the figure dropped to 3.5% – so that by 1975 even Tony Crosland, the leading ideologist of social democracy, could warn local councils that 'the party [was] over'. By then public spending as a share of national income had reached a peak of more than 47%. (It was to reach 45% in the early 1980s, then fall to 38% in the boom of the late 1980s and rise again to 43% in the early 1990s, where it remains today.)

There were several schemes put forward in the 1960s and 1970s to deal with these rising social security costs – the integration of taxes and benefits, tax credits etc. – but nothing came of them. Under Mrs Thatcher child benefit was frozen for three years, but was unfrozen again by her successor. Welfare spending under Thatcher rose to historic highs despite continuous talk of 'cuts' which never represented anything more than revisions of planned expenditure increases. The real differences under Mrs Thatcher were twofold: first the cut-back in council housing as it became government policy – and a very popular one – to sell off council houses; but secondly and more importantly, the decision in 1980 by Patrick Jenkin, then Health and Social Security Secretary, to raise state pensions in line with prices rather than, as before, with average earnings. Since prices usually lag behind average earnings by 1 or 2%, the effect was not an absolute reduction in the welfare bill, of course, but a saving of £7.5 billion per year in what would otherwise have been needed. This also meant that old age pensioners would be the main victims of Tory welfare reform – indeed the only real ones, if one disregards the much more marginal cases of students with grants or welfare cheats (who have been hardly touched.) Thus in 1981 the average state pension was worth 22% of male average earnings. In 1996 it was worth 15% and projections by the Institute for Fiscal Studies show that within a generation it will be worth only 7 or 8% of average male earnings – or absolutely worthless. We shall return to pensions in a minute.

In the meantime, it is important to note that attitudes towards the welfare state have changed in recent years – and not just because the total social security bill threatens to top £100 billion by the year 2000 (i.e. four times the defence budget). To quote Julian Le Grand once again:

> From being a saintly, even a heroic enterprise, the welfare state has become the villain of the piece. For many thinkers on both right and left, it has become an incubus, sapping the spirit of the nation, draining the life-blood of the economy and corrupting the citizenry. The attacks have come from every corner. Social historians now believe that the origins of the modern welfare state do not lie in the collective interests of the working class. Rather, it is the product of pressure from the middle classes, anxious to secure state insurance following their experience of the inter-war years.

Some commentators believe that the 'well of middle class self-interest' has now run dry and that better-off taxpayers have reached the limits of their social altruism. Some politicians suspect that many of these middle-class voters would prefer private health, education and pension schemes, particularly since the Tories have cut back on student grants and mortgage interest tax relief. At the same time, Le Grand points out, the influential 'public choice' school of economists has challenged the belief that defenders of the welfare state have acted out of a spirit of public interest. In their view, politicians have merely been concerned to maximise votes, and bureaucrats their budgets, while the professionals have been less concerned with the welfare of their clients than with their own income, status, and working conditions.

Another argument against the welfare state has been that it has corrupted those it was intended to help. Recipients of benefits have become shirkers, who jump queues for houses by having children they can ill afford to look after. Welfare today, therefore, is said to be creating inequality and poverty rather than eradicating such evils. Robert Skidelsky has argued that the welfare state 'produces social pathologies summed up in the notion of "the underclass" ', while Frank Field believes that it is having 'a monstrous effect on human motivation and honesty'. Finally, others believe that it is an incubus on a strong economy, keeping growth down, making companies uncompetitive, and reducing our ability to compete in the global market.

What then is the true picture? While the Institute for Economic Affairs (IEA) and other right-wing think tanks paint a picture of gloom and doom, several leading experts insist that the crisis described by the revisionists is greatly exaggerated. For example, when the Joseph Rowntree Foundation funded an eight-year research project on the welfare state under the auspices of the prestigious Suntory-Toyota Centre for Economic and Related Disciplines (STICERD) at the LSE, the results were not very dramatic. It was clear that government social spending (including housing and education) had peaked around the mid-1970s and that the effects of demographic change or the growth in pension rights were less important than the recession caused by ERM membership in pushing up government deficits in the early 1990s. (Welfare spending, including housing and education, has remained more or less constant at around 25% or 26% of GDP since 1976.) Moreover it is still less than in most other EU countries, save Portugal. Hence it is not a growing burden on the economy in percentage terms of GDP, even if social security costs have risen. (These reflect the general level of unemployment and the stage of the economic cycle.)

Again, the STICERD research showed that the welfare state was not the engine of radical redistribution of income that it was often thought to be. In fact, two-thirds of welfare expenditure merely transfers income from one stage in an individual's lifetime to another. Only one-third involves transfers from one individual to another.

Nor is it true that the middle classes have deserted the welfare state. Private health care is limited in coverage and so growth has not been spectacular. Many private hospitals, for example, find it difficult to fill beds, whereas the NHS finds it difficult to find them. Again, fees for private schools are so high that only about 7% of children are educated there – the same proportion as for the last thirty years. And hard evidence for welfare cheating is still hard to come by. Moreover, it is surely obvious that the real reason for so many beggars on the streets and the increase in crime has been the massive unemployment and job insecurity of the last twenty years. Thatcherism certainly had its downside as well as its positive achievements.

The main debate over welfare costs and impending crises, however, has centred mainly on pension provision in the next century, since the growing numbers of elderly people in Western countries, all of which operate pay-as-you-go old age pension systems (i.e. the present generation of workers pays for present pensions), must represent an increasing burden on the shrinking working population. In June 1995 OECD highlighted this problem in a special report which pointed out that as a result of unfunded pension debt, America's government debt would rise from 38% of national income to 94% in 2030, Japan's from 13% to 289%, Germany's from 46% to 93% (with France and Italy on the same track). On the other hand, thanks to private pension provision here, a smaller baby boom in the 1940s, 1950s and 1960s, and Patrick Jenkin's decision to link pensions to price increases rather than wage increases, it predicted that Britain's debt ratio of 47% in 1995 would turn into a surplus of 9% by 2030.

This, by the way, is another argument against European Economic and Monetary Union. As Norris McWhirter pointed out in a letter to *The Times* on 31 July 1996, if European public debts were to be amalgamated as a result of monetary union, each new British child would be saddled not with £9,000 of unfunded pension debt – the situation in Britain today – but with

£39,000, a horrifying prospect, but one in line with OECD and IMF findings.

Le Grand is rather reassuring on the subject. He writes: '... for Britain at least, much of the increase (in OAPs) has already occurred. The numbers of elderly people will rise in the 20 years between 1991 and 2011 by less than half the increase that has already taken place since 1971.' The rise will be more dramatic after then but even by 2041, according to Le Grand, four-fifths of the population will still be under 65. The estimated age dependency ratio (the number aged over 65 for every 100 persons aged 15-64) shows no great change until 2020, remaining at around 25. By 2040 it will have increased to 33.1, but even then, according to Le Grand, it will be well below that faced by other advanced countries, including France (38.2), Japan (37.8) and pre-unification Germany (48.2). He concludes that the 'implications of an ageing population for future spending in the UK are not dramatic'. One estimate he quotes is that if spending on each elderly person were to remain the same as at present, welfare spending per head would increase in absolute terms by less than 17% by 2041 – a figure considerably less than the increase in average incomes over that period. John Hills of STICERD has written:

> We could, as a nation, decide to maintain or even improve welfare services in relation to particular needs, including maintaining the relative values of cash benefits and pay of welfare sector workers like doctors and teachers. To do this would mean that welfare spending would rise slowly as a percentage of national income, and with it the overall level of taxation. However, the rise implied would not take Britain's welfare spending above the average share of national income already spent in other industrialised countries.

The House of Commons select committee on health has also taken a less fevered view of developments, reporting on 7 August 1996 that 'The projections do not support claims that we face a "demographic time bomb" or at least one that is likely to explode over the next two to three decades.' It came down in favour of retaining present arrangements with regard to the elderly. Finally, Anatole Kaletsky, writing in *The Times* on 8 February 1996, pointed out equally logically:

> Any country can choose to spend whatever it wants on government programmes and still maintain both full employment and a balance in its trade with the rest of the world. The only proviso (admittedly a big one in Europe these days) is that the country must have an independent monetary policy and a floating exchange rate.

The arguments for continuing to provide for welfare as we do at present, therefore, are very strong. Moreover, there can be no doubt that this is what the public wants: paradoxically, as the economy becomes more flexible, they want it even more. Today, after all, less than 50% of the workforce, it is estimated, have permanent salaried jobs. The majority inhabit a flexible economy of part-time, temporary or contract jobs. The effects of this flexibility, of fewer people staying in full-time jobs for any length of time, as David Smith pointed out in the *Sunday Times* on 11 February 1996, are two-fold. First, employers can hire people well below a living wage and expect the state to top up their wages; secondly, very many people are not in a position to fund private pension schemes. Increasingly, they have to fall back on the state for help. Thus Kenneth Clarke could say in February 1996: 'people need to be reassured more than ever before, that, through thick and thin, their health will be looked after, their children educated and a safety net provided for their old age and periods of involuntary unemployment.'

The *Sunday Times* poll of 19 May 1996 on attitudes to the welfare state showed that 36% wanted higher benefits; 26% were satisfied with current levels; while only 18% favoured radical cuts in social spending. 68% were against the idea of replacing state-provided welfare with a private pension. Only 22% were in favour.

It is doubtful, however, whether we can afford to be as complacent over welfare as either public opinion or these estimates would suggest. For a start, they appear to overlook the fact that future generations will not tolerate old age pensions worth merely 7% of average wages. No one could live on such pensions. Already someone living solely on the old age pension is officially classed as living below the poverty line. The result is that many pensioners already have to have their pensions topped up through income support, housing benefit, and council tax benefit. However, if pensions fall by half, as they are now targeted to do – with the support of all the major parties – there will be riots in the streets during the next century. The social security budget will therefore have to go up and taxes with it, to levels which may not prove to be politically acceptable. The Institute for Fiscal Studies calculates, for example, that to provide a pension equivalent to one third of male earnings (about £120 a week) for all, even today, would cost an extra £17.6 billion to £22.9 billion a year or between 9p and 11.5p extra on the standard rate of income tax. To make up the gap twenty years from now would cost considerably more. Perhaps we should listen to commentators such as Bill Jamieson of the *Sunday Telegraph* when he writes (11 February 1996): 'We will rue the failure to defuse the pension time bomb.'

For those looking for a solution to the problem, one answer might be found in what is happening outside Europe and the USA, which has a much bigger pension time bomb than Britain. Singapore, for example, demands that all employees pay a large proportion of their income into a central provident fund, contributions which can later on be used for health care, retirement pensions, house purchases, school or college fees, or to tide them over periods of unemployment. Employees know at any given time how much they have saved and can decide how to spend their money.

The scheme undoubtedly encourages savings, not to mention personal choice and responsibility; it also avoids means-testing. But there are drawbacks. The difference between net and gross wages can reach 40%, and the government cannot resist plundering the fund for its own use and paying out only 2% interest (the fund is forced to invest in low-yield government bonds).

A much better system is the one adopted in Chile since 1981. This again links benefits to contributions, but is more flexible than the one in operation in Singapore, although it restricts itself to pensions. It came into being because the Chilean government realised that its own pay-as-you-go European/American-type pension system was facing bankruptcy, just as those of the advanced economies will be by 2030. The decision was taken to limit the maximum contribution to 10% of wages, although employees can contribute up to 20% tax free. The money is invested by private institutions and the returns are untaxed. By the time a worker reaches retirement age – 65 for men, 60 for women – a sizeable sum of capital has built up in his or her account. At retirement the employee transforms that lump sum into an annuity with an insurance company and can shop around different ones to find the plan best suited to his own needs. If he wants to retire early or have a bigger pension, he can contribute more than 10%. Individuals can retire when they want – 55, 65, or 85. Employees can always sit down at a computer terminal at their pension-fund company and work out their options. They discover how much they must contribute to retire at a certain age or with a certain pension and then inform their employers what percentage of their pay to deduct. If the employee's pension is not enough at the official retirement age, the government makes up the difference from general tax revenues.

The system is managed by competitive private companies called AFPs, each managing the equivalent of a mutual fund and investing in stocks, bonds and government debt. The AFP is separate from the mutual fund; thus, if an AFP goes bankrupt, the assets of the mutual fund – the employees' investments – are not touched. A regulatory board takes over their management and asks the employees to change to another AFP. Employees, by the way, can change from one AFP to another at any time. This makes them more competitive and encourages better returns, better service and lower commissions. Since the scheme started, no AFP has gone bankrupt. Employees have not lost a penny. The regulatory body helped by laying down strict rules for investment diversification, with limited proportions of funds being invested in any one kind of market and only then in companies with good credit ratings.

In order to get the scheme off to a good start, special transitional arrangements were made. Every employee was assured that the state would guarantee his pension; there was thus absolutely nothing to fear from the change. Secondly, employees who had already contributed to the old system were given the choice of remaining in it or changing to the new one. Those who moved over were given 'recognition bonds' which acknowledged their contributions to the old system and could be cashed in on retirement. New entrants to the employment market were made to participate in the new system since the old one faced bankruptcy. Hence the old system will die out when the last employee using it retires. Thereafter, the state of Chile will have no state pension system. The pensions of those still alive and who worked under the old system remain state-guaranteed. The transition costs amounted to about 3% of GNP and were financed by privatisations and borrowing.

After fifteen years, the system has provided spectacular results. Given that it pays compound interest, pensions are now 40-50% higher than those paid under the old system – in the case of disability and widows' pensions, also privatised, 70-100% higher. Employers have also benefited since they have been spared the old payroll tax on labour. Savings rates have risen from 15% to 26%. There is now an enormous pool of internal savings to finance investment strategies. Economic growth for the last ten years has averaged 7%, double the historic rate. This in turn has been the most powerful means of reducing poverty. 90% of workers are now enrolled in the new system, most by their own choice. There has also been cultural change. Workers see themselves as capitalists and are positively attached to their new freedom of determining their own futures. They feel they have a stake in their economy – real stakeholding by owning, as individuals, part of the nation's financial assets and are therefore much more attached to the free market, a free society and to democracy. One of the authors of the Chilean reforms, Dr Jose Pinera, has claimed it as a success 'beyond our wildest dreams', and perhaps unsurprisingly it has been copied by Argentina, Peru and Colombia. Given the pension time-bomb facing Britain, perhaps it should be copied here too.

The other area of concern in the field of welfare has been the National Health Service. Created in 1946 when Nye Bevan nationalised the hospitals, it was intended to provide health care free at the point of use and ensure that standards of health remained uniform throughout the whole country. Doctors resisted at first, but given assurances that they would have individual contracts and could practise privately if they so desired, not to mention the freedom allowed to the Royal Colleges to allow doctors and nurses to regulate their own professions, they soon participated happily. The scheme proved both an enormous success and economical to run. The latter feature depended largely on the relatively long hours and low wages of nurses and doctors (who were paid per patient rather than by visit or by consultation) and by small administrative costs. Soon the NHS became the sacred cow of the welfare state, and right up until the late 1980s no government dared to interfere with it. In 1987 health care in Britain took up only 6% of GNP compared with 11% in the USA and 9% in West Germany, France and the Netherlands and 7.7% in the western world as a whole. Yet in terms of life expectancy and infant mortality, the usual indices of international comparison, the NHS put Britain on a par with the Europe and the USA; in terms of insurance cover – unlike the USA – it covered every citizen in the country; while in terms of nursing it provided 85 nurses for every 100,000 citizens, compared with 50 in the USA, 45 in France, and 35 in West Germany. Moreover, British in-patients stayed in bed twice as long as their American counterparts. Part of the cost-effectiveness of the NHS was due to the fact that its doctors were paid only two-and-a-half times the average national wage compared with five times in the USA and over seven times in France. Yet contrary to popular belief, administrative costs were also very low. An OECD study found them to be about half those of other countries as a proportion of total health spending. Finally, research on health inequalities within thirty-two countries carried out by Professor Julian Le Grand and published by the LSE, found that 'England and Wales were among the countries with the *least* differences, with Scotland and Northern Ireland not far behind'.

The growth in numbers of the elderly, advances in medical technology, new illnesses and new treatments, however, all meant that governments came under unrelenting pressure to increase spending on the NHS. Despite record increases, Mrs Thatcher discovered that more was never enough and so in 1989 a White Paper entitled *Working for Patients* announced a series of 'reforms' to make the NHS more efficient. The main ones were the establishment of an 'internal market' in the NHS with purchasers (doctors, local authorities, etc.) being separated from providers (hospitals and other medical units); doctors being given the opportunity to run their own budgets as 'fundholders'; and hospitals being encouraged to do the same as 'NHS trusts'. The NHS, however, remained free at the point of use and continued to be financed through general taxation, although from April 1990 tax relief was available on private health insurance premiums to those over sixty. (The NHS had never been a monopoly; private health care had always been available in Britain after the war, although everyone still had to contribute to the upkeep of the NHS.)

These proposals were bitterly opposed by the British Medical Association and the Royal Colleges, who questioned how sick patients could be transferred around the country to cheaper hospital beds, foresaw the huge and expensive administrative upheavals that would inevitably be involved, and feared lest the ethic of service be replaced by the profit motive. There were also questions of a more general nature. John Hills of STICERD wrote:

First, the new 'internal markets' themselves use resources to establish and run, which may offset efficiency gains. Second, those who benefit from their access to a successful 'provider' may do so at the expense of others whose agent is less successful in the internal market place. Third, it is hard for central government to distribute resources without possibilities for 'cream-skimming' – providers making sure that their caseload is made up of those with lower costs than allowed for in the funding formula. Finally, who exercises the choices: is it really the users or someone acting on their behalf – do the reforms 'empower' users or the providers?

The jury, according to Le Grand, is still out. Yet newspapers are full of horror stories of 'community care' gone wrong, closed hospitals, closed wards, cancelled operations, lack of beds – especially intensive care beds – lack of nurses, burgeoning paperwork and an expanding army of highly paid administrators living in expensively refurbished offices carefully set apart from hospital corridors clogged full of patients lying on trolleys. According to the *Sunday Times* (17 December 1995) the number of acute care beds fell from 198,000 to 147,000 between 1983 and 1995. Only 2% of all hospital beds, it reported, catered for intensive care patients by the end of 1995. A survey by the British Paediatric Association found only 120 specialist intensive care beds for children across the whole country: in December 1995, 10-year-old David Geldard died after being shunted around three counties for 12 hours between four hospitals in a vain attempt to find him an intensive care bed. The *Daily Telegraph* on 26 June 1996 warned of 'doctor-free zones' in inner cities, as general practitioners fled from them. East London alone, it reported, had 140 vacancies; between 1990 and 1994 the overall number of GPs working full-time had fallen nationally by 700. Many were taking early retirement or turning to part-time work to avoid the stress. Young doctors saw no prospects as GPs either. Most medical men said they felt undervalued by the new trusts, whose presiding bureaucrats wanted quick, cheap results. The BMA helpline was receiving 80 calls a week from doctors who felt stressed and exhausted.

One could quote newspaper report after newspaper report to prove that the reforms have not worked, and the most weighty studies appear to confirm these. That of the Association of Community Health Councils, for example, claimed that after five years of the internal market most patients were still referred to their local hospital, so that the reforms had added £1.7 billion annually to administrative costs with no demonstrable improvements in patient care. These findings confirmed similar reports by the National Audit Office and the National Association of Health Authorities and Trusts. They also confirmed fears that a two-tier NHS was emerging, with patients of fundholding GPs getting much better treatment while health authority patients had to wait longer and got less attention. Generally, there were no improvements to patients' health. Dr Thomas Stuttaford, the medical correspondent of *The Times*, warned in an article commenting on the report that '(doctors') sense of service (was) being diluted by financial considerations' and concluded: 'Doctors have always shopped around, but for the best care and not the best bargain.'

On the other hand, the NHS is still the envy of finance ministers around the world, who have copied several aspects of its latest incarnation –

particularly budgetary control. None of them are very interested in the American model since that leaves 40% of the population uncovered and imposes huge costs on employers who pay much of the private insurance of the remaining 60%. There is also much inequality of provision, since large companies negotiate special deals. Finally, most US health insurance policies have important restrictions, often leaving families facing bankruptcy in certain contingencies or being forced to choose between education and health care for family members. The US system also encourages unnecessary medical testing, the unnecessary purchase of equipment, the duplication of administration, the narrow pooling of risk, and the inflation of salaries. Among health economists, there is still no doubt that the NHS is the best value for money internationally. However, the 1990 'reforms' will have to be carefully evaluated and perhaps reversed. The NHS will have to be provided with (probably) substantially increased resources that go to patients and not to bureaucrats, if Britain's citizens are to get the health care they deserve.

Other remedies for the welfare state have been devised recently. They range from 'legal welfare' – minimum wages and maximum hours of work – to 'partnership schemes', where the state matches contributions by individuals. None of these, however, seem very practical or revolutionary. The partnership schemes invented so far have rarely taken off. The only way forward that might solve the growing crisis of welfare costs is the privatisation of pensions.

Perhaps there is one other method, however – the integration of taxes and benefits. For example, the government pays £7 billion a year in child benefit. Yet until 1977 it paid no child benefit, giving parents tax allowances instead. Patricia Morgan has shown in a recent pamphlet (1996) from the Centre for Policy Studies, entitled *Are Families Affordable?*, that nearly all parents are worse off as a result and that average families have suffered big losses from Tory tax reforms. Yet, according to Anatole Kaletsky (*The Times*, 6 August 1996), the real point is that these benefits add £7 billion to public spending and thus to taxes, whereas the old system produced better results by *reducing* taxes. Surely, therefore, if it is possible to achieve better results by reducing taxes than by raising them, the correct course of action for the government should be to introduce a tax credit. (The tax cut would be smaller than the full £7 billion since not all parents who get benefits would be eligible for credits.) The same principle could apply to a whole range of benefits. According to Kaletsky, the main opponent of such change is the Treasury which demands that all taxes should be 'transparent' and 'neutral'. In short, lower taxes as a result of tax credits would disguise what the Treasury perversely considers to be the provision of state handouts – when in fact all that would really be involved would be allowing taxpayers to keep more of their own money. If this view were to be disregarded, however, taxes could be substantially reduced and benefits and taxes generally integrated.

In his article Kaletsky claimed: 'I could reduce the State's role to an Asian-style 30% of gross domestic product without hurting a single public service.' Why should this not be attempted? All the evidence from the Thatcher and Reagan years proves that tax cuts boost both income and revenue, as the Nobel prize-winning Harvard professor of economics, Martin Feldstein, demonstrated in a recent study in the *Journal of Political Economy*. In fact, with a combination of Chilean-style pension reform, tax credits leading to tax cuts and withdrawal from the European Union, Britain could easily rival any enterprise economy in the world and still provide better welfare for her citizens than any other country in the globe.

My own view is that in certain areas – particularly health and education – welfare services are absolutely essential if all citizens are to get an equal chance to develop to their full potential, a self-evident aim of national policy. However, in other areas – pensions and particular benefits – private provision or a mixture of state and private provision may be more efficient. After all, it is the aims of public policy which count, not the means of achieving them. These should be evaluated in terms of cost-effectiveness and efficiency of provision. Thus, given that insurance is cheaper when the maximum number of people pool the risks of ill health, the NHS remains the most efficient means available of providing health care, as comparative studies by health economists repeatedly demonstrate. On the other hand, the developing crisis in pension provision suggests that a predominantly private arrangement would be better placed to ensure pensions at a decent level for those about to retire.

The most radical critics of the welfare state have complained not merely about the costs and taxes involved, but about what they see as the pernicious role of the state. Their concern for suffering humanity is allied to the belief that citizens will always be better off if they take responsibility for their own affairs, whatever their economic circumstances, social disadvantages or physical disabilities. Such critics believe that welfare breeds dependency and that dependency breeds immorality and crime. Indeed, in an article in the *Sunday Times* of 12 January 1997, Charles Murray, the distinguished American sociologist, blamed 'the erosion of virtue' – or the rise in crime – in post-war Britain unambiguously on the welfare state. Yet before analysing crime in post-war Britain, it might be instructive to look at a related issue, namely the belief that the collapse in moral standards which 'welfarism' has supposedly encouraged has been aided by the 'moral revolution' of the 1960s and the creation of a 'permissive society'. This, together with welfare provision, has been held to have destroyed any concept of individual responsibility, replacing liberty with licence, family values with sexual promiscuity, and social solidarity with social indifference. Those who defend the welfare state and the social changes of the 1960s, on the other hand, wonder how those who would end social welfare can possibly talk of social solidarity and family values, when, as they believe, the very old, the very young and the socially vulnerable would be the obvious victims of what they depict as an illiberal, authoritarian, religiously fundamentalist, and socially reactionary nanny state. There can be no doubt, however, that the rise in crime and the expansion of the welfare state have led to a moral reaction in certain quarters against the so-called 'moral revolution' of the last quarter of a century.

Has Britain suffered a moral decline? Or is she experiencing a resurgence of narrow-mindedness and bigotry? These are interesting questions for the contemporary historian, but before we attempt to answer them we must define what morality is.

Fundamentally morality it is the code of conduct which regulates the behaviour of individuals towards one another. To some extent this is a matter of private practice, but public morals are enforced by law. This is especially true in matters of sexual conduct where, for example, the state imposes rules concerning the age of consent, contraception and homosexual behaviour. In matters closely related to sexual mores – abortion and divorce, for example – the state also intervenes. Yet there are many people who believe that the state intervenes either too much or too little, because there is a lack of consensus over the right of the state to interfere in what many regard as areas of strictly private choice. Ironically, it is often those who bitterly oppose state intervention on behalf of the poor who call most stridently not merely for tough state action on crime, but for state intervention to prevent individuals from exercising individual responsibility for their private lives. Many right-wing conservatives, for example, believe that while individuals should take responsibility for their economic fate, the state should strictly regulate their private lives, restricting what they see or read or who they should sleep or live with. Libertarians, on the other hand, believe that there should be neither a welfare state nor a nanny state and that individuals should take as much control of their personal destinies as possible.

The idea that Britain was on the brink of 'moral collapse' was most stridently put forward in the 1970s by Mrs Mary Whitehouse, the campaigner for television censorship (or against TV sex and violence, depending on one's point of view). She received vocal support from Lord Longford and Malcolm Muggeridge and later from powerful political figures like Norman Tebbit. The latter, as Tory Party Chairman used his Disraeli lecture of 13 November 1985 to denounce 'the valueless values of the Permissive Society', claiming that the 'trigger of today's outburst of crime and violence' lay in the 'era and attitudes of post-war funk which gave birth to the Permissive Society'. Thanks to 'permissives', he claimed, 'family life was derided as an outdated bourgeois concept. Criminals deserved as much sympathy as their victims …. Violence and soft pornography became accepted in the media. Thus was sown the wind; and we are now reaping the whirlwind.'

Yet Tory campaigns to claim 'family values' as their own would founder regularly during the next decade as Tory MPs – and even one Party Chairman – were exposed as having fathered illegitimate children, taken numerous mistresses, or conducted homosexual affairs. One was even found dead from self-asphyxiation, wearing ladies' underwear and with an orange stuffed in his mouth. At the start of 1997, having yet again proclaimed the Tories as the only party of 'family values', John Major was confronted by claims that a married Tory MP had had illegal sex with a gay teenage researcher. None the less, from the mid-1980s Mrs Thatcher and her party evidently believed that there was political mileage to be gained in pursuing this theme, however wide the gap between practice and pretension.

Needless to say, such attacks on permissiveness gave rise to counter-attacks. The columnist Julie Burchill, in an article in *New Society* on 13 June 1986, condemned all the fuss about family values and sex education: 'It is wicked of Mrs Thatcher,' she wrote, 'to put forward the family as the answer to a nation's prayer, considering that more than half of all violent assault, more than half of all child abuse, more than half of all murder takes place within the family.' Others simply wondered why Britain was being depicted as particularly permissive. In comparison with other countries, her so-called 'sexual revolution' seemed very restrained. London may have invented the mini-skirt, yet there were no live sex shows, gay bath houses, or singles bars as were found in Amsterdam, Copenhagen, San Francisco or New York. Probably as a direct result, the incidence of AIDS in Britain in the 1980s and 1990s was much lower than in America or in Continental Europe. The play *No Sex Please, We're British* was a not implausible box-office hit in London's West End, where it ran for years.

Sex, none the less, was at the very heart of Britain's debate about moral decline. As *Punch* once remarked, 'whenever sexual morality becomes the motif of public discussion, reason flies out of the window'. In the 1970s and 1980s the attack on permissiveness stemmed less from observation than from religious fears. Malcolm Muggeridge believed that 'the orgasm [had] replaced the Cross as the focus for longing.' Modern attitudes, he held, removed the need for God. By destroying any sense of guilt that attached to premarital, extramarital or 'perverse' sex, the need for redemption, and therefore the need for God had been removed. Sex, he believed, should be seen as a sacramental experience, with marriage consummating the physical and spiritual needs of men and women. Sex outside marriage was immoral, particularly homosexual sex. Indeed, Mrs Whitehouse was to bring an action for criminal blasphemy against *Gay News* over a poem suggesting a homosexual desire by the centurion at the foot of the cross for the crucified Christ.

The lack of support she received from the Church appalled Mrs Whitehouse, yet Christ himself never said anything about homosexuals and indeed had had very little to say about sex at all. His concern had been with life after death, demonic possession, faithfulness, honesty, love for neighbours and for enemies, forgiveness and the condemnation of hypo-crisy – themes with which the sexually obsessed anti-permissives never concerned themselves. Not that the official Church seemed particularly concerned with these values either. It was more concerned with demysti-fication. Indeed, the Bishop of Durham found surprising support when he suggested that the divinity of Christ, the virgin birth and the resurrection might all be theologically unsupportable. To many it seemed as if the Church wanted to take God out of religion and reduce Christianity to a spiritual version of social anthropology. In fact, the Church had accepted the contemporary change from ethics based on principles to those based on consequences (on which see more below). It may also have believed that support of Mrs Whitehouse and her like would have emptied its pews and cut off younger people from the Church. The anti-permissives believed precisely the opposite, that stricter moral attitudes (if only over sex) would restore Church membership. Yet after the 1960s, as we shall see, this was never very likely.

Had the permissive society in fact damaged the Church? Was there a need to return to 'Victorian values' as Mrs Thatcher believed? In the 1960s the proportion of the population who were communicants of churches was almost exactly the same as at the end of the eighteenth century, about 15%. True, more people had begun to attend church during the mid-Victo-rian era, but that had been largely due to a rise in the birth rate, the construction of more churches, and an influx of Irish and Scots into England. Most Englishmen never attended church except for weddings, funerals and baptisms; in fact, in 1851 only one in ten attended church regularly in the big cities. Charles Booth in his surveys of the working class in late Victorian England reported that 'the great masses of the people remain apart from all forms of religious communion'. He wrote: 'The very choirboys when their voices crack promptly claim the privileges of men and give up church going.' As a result missionaries were needed for 'darkest England' as well as 'darkest Africa'. The Lambeth Conference of 1897 simply declared that social and economic morality were subjects 'to which numberless Christians have as yet never thought of applying Christian principles'.

Indeed, the reaction against the Church had already set in before the end of Victoria's reign. Thus in 1886, 814 priests had been ordained in the Church of England, but only 569 in 1901. The decline was not, however, consistent. Between 1931 and 1941, for example, there was an increase of 29.8% in the number of priests ordained by the Catholic Church; between 1941 and 1951 an increase of 11%; and between 1961 and 1966 an increase of 6.8%. Only after 1966 was there an absolute decrease. The Anglican Church meanwhile saw a drop in annual ordinations between 1963 and 1973 from 632 to 373. In the 1960s, some 90% of the English population still claimed a religious affiliation: 60% Anglican; 12% Roman Catholic; 11% Free Church; 1% Jews; and 5% other faiths. Of those attending

Anglican services, 40% did not believe in life after death; 26% of doubters, agnostics and atheists prayed; although 20% of this group rejected Christ's divinity. By 1985, over 70% seldom or never read the Bible, no more than one person in seven attended church regularly; and no more than one in five was a convinced Christian. Yet three-quarters expressed a belief in God, 85% claimed membership of one of the main Christian denominations, while only 2% claimed to be convinced atheists. There was also widespread support for traditional morality as expressed in the Ten Commandments. The resulting rather confused picture was of a partially absorbed but declining Christianity.

If Victorian religious practice had fallen far short of acceptable standards, Victorian sexual practice had also left a lot to be desired. Rejection of premarital or extramarital sex had meant that young men had taken advantage of prostitutes (London had anything up to 100,000 during Victoria's reign) or exploited the family maid (infanticide was often the result). Even when sex was restricted to within marriage, it probably encouraged wife-beating, which constituted a major social problem, with 87,000 separation orders being issued between 1897 and 1906 on this ground alone. The lack of contraception meant yet another problem: the subjection of women. As one commentator has written: 'The prospect of a lifetime of childbearing and poverty lay ahead for most girls. At the turn of the century the life expectation of a woman of 20 was 46 years. Approximately one-third of this was likely to be given to the physiological and emotional demands of childbearing and maternal care of infants. Nor was the situation of upper-class women any different.' In 1857, for example, Lady Lyttleton was warned by her doctor that, having already borne 11 children, a twelfth pregnancy would mean her death. Yet she became pregnant and on being asked why she had neglected to inform her husband of the medical risk involved, she replied: 'my dear, we never speak of anything so nasty.' One suspects, therefore, that her experiences were less than 'sacramental'. It was their consequences that were to bring her closer to God.

In assessing the differences in moral values between the 1960s/1970s and the 1860s/1870s and whether a return to Victorian values might have been better than an accommodation with permissiveness, two points have to be borne in mind. First, the change in morals was of a particular kind; secondly, the so-called sexual revolution of the 1960s has been greatly exaggerated.

The basic legislation of the 1960s that gave rise to the 'permissive society' – the Obscene Publications Act of 1959, the Suicide Act of 1963, the Murder (Abolition of the Death Penalty) Act of 1965, the Abortion Act of 1967, the Sexual Offences Act of 1967, the Theatres Act of 1968 and the Divorce Act of 1969 – rested on the belief that morals should be based on the likely consequences rather than on the intrinsic righteousness of any act. This change of attitudes from moralism to 'causalism' was chronicled by Christie Davies in his book *Permissive Britain: Social Change in the Sixties and Seventies* (1975). In it he differentiated 'causalist' from utilitarian ethics, pointing out that the causalists seemed to have limited their consideration of consequences of any legislation in two ways: first, by considering only the short-term consequences of their decisions (assuming in practice that people's moral attitudes would not be affected by them); and secondly, by having regard to only negative utility and ignoring positive good or happiness. Hence, for example, with regard to the first limitation, divorce was made easier to obtain, without assuming that this would alter people's attitudes to marriage; or, with regard to the second limitation, the fact that many people claimed to achieve happiness from using cannabis did not prevent the ban on the use of this drug from being enforced.

Generally speaking, the aim of the legislation was to minimise the harm, suffering, conflict or distress caused by previous legislation: hence homosexuality was made legal, divorce made easier, capital punishment was abolished, and abortion made legally available. In all these cases what counted were the consequences. MPs did not suddenly approve of homosexuality; they merely no longer saw the point of persecuting a substantial minority of the population on account of different sexual preferences; likewise, in cases where marriages had already 'irretrievably' broken down, there seemed little point in refusing to allow divorce or in pinpointing a 'guilty party'. In the case of abortion reform, the arguments in a non-Catholic country, while partly centring on theological grounds, were actually won on points concerning back-street abortionists and medical and social consequences. Even the opponents of abortion used causalist arguments, insinuating for example that 'abortion on demand' would lead to euthanasia and mass extermination. The debate on the abolition of the death penalty followed similar lines. Points of principle were indeed discussed; yet, in the end, it was the belief that the death penalty was ineffective as a deterrent and that too many innocent people had been hanged already that clinched the argument for the abolitionists. Finally, with respect to censorship, the inability to get juries to convict and the tendency for the law to look ridiculous led to the relatively more liberal Obscene Publications Act of 1959 and the Theatres Act of 1968 which abolished the Lord Chamberlain's right to censor stage plays.

Had these reforms been based on moralist ethics, the results would have been much more radical. Yet there had been no attempt at all to exchange 'Christian' values for permissive ones. Indeed, it was very difficult to get this legislation through at all. The government saw these matters as largely irrelevant to its programme, despite Roy Jenkins's support, and all the reforms began life as private members' bills. In the words of one authority, 'they were the end results of a variety of different pressures: liberal reformism, pragmatic acceptance of the need for change, eccentric libertarianism, religious, especially Roman Catholic, counter-pressure and other sustained special interest agitation or opposition, channelled through Members of Parliament'. Each reform had to be argued on its own merits, each required mobilising a new parliamentary majority, and each had to avoid alienating moderate opinion.

The result was that the reforms achieved were limited ones. Homosexuals, for example, could only have sex if they were over the age of 21 and the act took place between consenting adults in private. Nor did the law change immediately when the age of majority was reduced to 18. Again, although abortion was allowed on social grounds in pregnancies up to 28 weeks, the Act fell far short of abortion on demand and the crucial issue was the medical opinion of the physician concerned. Later on the period allowed was reduced to 22 weeks, again on medical arguments.

Some topics proved too hot to handle altogether, such as sex and violence on television. The state of research in the 1970s suggested that pornography if anything reduced the number of sex crimes, whereas violence tended to increase violence in everyday life. Causalist legislators should therefore have encouraged the one, but censored the other. Yet, if anything, the opposite happened. This may have had to do with peculiarly British hang-ups about sex, but was probably the result of moral uncertainties and confusion. Secularisation, as we have seen, certainly cannot be blamed. Besides, the churches themselves began to offer a more permissive view of sex. In 1963 the report entitled *Towards a Quaker View of Sex* placed 'love' at the heart of morality rather than tradition, revelation or authority. According to the report, love, including homosexual love, could no longer 'be confined to a pattern', a viewpoint which all the other churches were eventually to accept.

If there was a shift to causalist ethics among legislators in the 1960s, to what extent did a 'sexual revolution' take place?

The twentieth century had seen several changes with regard to sexual attitudes and practices long before the 1960s: the growing influence of Freudian psycho-analysis which placed the sexual drive at the very centre of human development; the mores of the Bloomsbury Group, which were to a certain degree influential; the Kinsey reports of the 1940s which suggested that homosexual experience was far greater than hitherto suspected and which led to widespread discussion of sexual practices within the more tolerant atmosphere of general sexology; not to mention medical advances such as the sheath (used by the army during World War I) and the use of salvarsan (a compound of arsenic) after 1910 to reduce the incidence of syphilis. For the 1960s, however, the key medical developments were the use of antibiotics after 1945 for the cure of syphilis and gonorrhoea – venereal diseases could now be cured within weeks if not days – and the development of the oral contraceptive pill (freely available on the NHS by 1969), which meant that sex became increasingly risk-free. (Legalised abortion meant that yet another way of evading unwanted consequences became available.) These factors all meant that a 'sexual revolution' was possible. Yet others were necessary to bring one about.

One of these was the so-called 'youth revolution' of the 1960s which was composed of several elements: a 20% increase in the number of unmarried people between the ages of 15 and 24 (the post-war baby boom); a 50% increase in average real wages for adolescents since 1938; and a vast new market for 'youth products' such as record players, cosmetics and cheap exotic clothing. Many of these commodities were advertised with a more blatant emphasis on sex, since boys and girls were reaching sexual maturity about four to five years earlier than in the previous century largely as a result of rising living standards. The end of conscription at the start of the 1960s also brought changes: there was a reaction against military-style deference with uniforms becoming part of hippy gear and combat dress part of casual wear. The slogan of the time – in reaction to Vietnam – was, significantly, 'make love not war'.

In Britain, however, all this led more to a change in style and attitudes than in sexual practices. People tended to have sex earlier and girls had illegitimate babies at a slightly younger age, but this reflected physiological change rather than a a revolution in sexual mores. Similarly, although venereal disease rates rose by 34%, hospital admissions in general increased by 43%, demonstrating the availability of more facilities rather than a change in medical patterns. Michael Schofield in his book, *The Sexual Problems of Young People*, published in the mid-1960s, found a general conservatism: most boys still wanted to marry virgins; and the vast majority of Schofield's sample (boys and girls) were still virgins themselves. A *Sunday Times* survey of the late 1960s discovered that more than a quarter of men and nearly two-thirds of women interviewed had been virgins when they married. Research published in 1985 (M. Abrams, D. Gerard and N. Timms, *Values and Social Change in Britain*) demonstrated widespread support for traditional sexual values, with solid majorities among all classes and age-groups disapproving of under-age sex, pre-marital affairs, prostitution, homosexuality and abortion. And the latest weighty research on sexual attitudes in Britain and the USA published in 1994 (see Lawrence Stone's masterly review article, 'What, how often and with whom?' in the *London Review of Books*, 3 August 1995) demonstrates exactly the same. Although in both countries, there is a very wide range of sexual practices and values, a large majority of people – about 80% – think and behave in a very conservative, but mostly not intolerant way. Both societies are still strongly committed to the fading ideal of the heterosexual, monogamous union, whether marriage or steady cohabitation, but have ceased to be censorious about sex before marriage. There is no support for promiscuity or evidence that large numbers of people have multiple casual sexual partners.

The sexual revolution of the 1960s certainly changed attitudes and practices in some important ways – releasing speech, print and videotapes from almost all restrictions, leading to an explosion of soft porn and frank talk; making sexual cohabitation as a stage prior to, or as an alternative to marriage thoroughly acceptable; ending the nineteenth/early twentieth century panic over masturbation, which is no longer seen either as a shameful secret or a health hazard; and changing oral sex from a highly unusual practice to a perfectly normal and acceptable one, although the more educated people are, the more likely they are to enjoy it. (One conclusion of all research is that the higher the level of education, the more sexually adventurous and tolerant men and women are likely to be.)

However, in terms of morals the 1960s revolution had no visible effect on strong opposition to adultery, one-night stands and homosexual activity. (now reckoned to be restricted to only 3% of the population). Stone concludes, warily, as follows (he wisely wonders whether people tell the truth to interviewers when discussing their sexual histories):

> What we have ... is a picture of a sexual world still wedded to earlier values of fidelity and honesty. British and Americans agree that sex is not *the* key to a good relationship, but that monogamous relations lead to better and more frequent sex. They have also discovered that the sex drive does not altogether wither with age. The good news is that happiness with monogamous sex appears to be merely one aspect, although perhaps a very important one, of a state of happiness with life in general. Which is the cause and which is the result of this correlation, is, of course, not known. What is new is the rise not in promiscuity but in cohabitation before marriage, which among wives has risen from 6 to 65%. The number of those with only a single sex partner from the age of 18 has hardly altered over decades .... Judging by this evidence, family values are alive and well among the majority of citizens of Britain and America. Conservatives can be reassured.

Feminists and gays might well agree with this conclusion, given that women are still well under-represented in most professions and gays have been refused an equal age of consent. Yet conservatives will still worry over the fact that 32% of births in this country are illegitimate. This does not mean that these children are all brought up without fathers. According to the latest figures, as reported in the *Daily Telegraph* on 8 August 1996, eight out of ten white children will be brought up by married couples.

Marriage may have become less popular recently, but for most of this century this was not the case. The proportion of married women per 1,000 women has risen continuously during this century – from 340 in 1901, to 412 in 1931, to 487 in 1951, to 491 in 1979. In 1978 it was found that 95% of women and 91% of men were married by the age of forty. Even divorce did not put people off since by 1982 no less than 30% of all marriages were re-marriages, with roughly half of all divorced people remarrying, mostly within a year of of their divorce. In 1985 the Values Survey of Great Britain found that 84% disagreed with the statement that 'marriage is an outdated form of institution'. The Survey concluded:

It is not the fact of marriage that is being questioned, but rather the quality of married life .... Individuals do not divorce because marriage has become unimportant to them, but it has become so important to them that they have no tolerance for the less than completely successful marital arrangement... although increasing numbers of people are rejecting specific marriage partners, the institution of marriage is not threatened and this is underlined by the high rate of marriage following divorce.

If cohabitation is now becoming more the norm – although especially as a *pre-marital* situation – this may simply be a throwback to previous British practices. John Gillis, for example, in his book *For Better or Worse: British Marriages 1600 to the Present*, tells us that in the sixteenth and seventeenth centuries people cohabited before marriage forming 'little marriages' before the 'big' one (which might never take place). This practice was made illegal by the Hardwicke Act of 1753, leading to the high illegitimacy rates of early Victorian England. It was not until the early twentieth century that marriages became the norm for most people. Those who cohabit today may therefore be, in Gillis's words, 'honouring rather than defying society's standards and traditions'.

If British society had changed in some ways as a result of the 1960s revolution, it had also changed on account of coloured immigration. Yet once again, the fears of conservatives have hardly been borne out and the story has been more complex and reassuring than predicted by the pessimists of the 1960s and 1970s. In 1983, Bill Jones and Dennis Cavanagh, in their explanation of the social homogeneity of British political culture included in a Manchester University Press paperback guide for students they wrote entitled *British Politics Today*, wrote: 'Only 3% of the population are coloured, only 5% live in rural areas, two-thirds are members of the Church of England, and five-sixths live in England.' True, Philip Dodd in a confused Demos pamphlet of 1995, entitled *Battle over Britain*, could write: 'It may well be uncomfortable for the white English to have to consider themselves an ethnic group, but that's what they are.' Yet the British have coped with substantial immigration rather well without becoming just another ethnic group, although considerable problems remain both for them and for the immigrant populations.

Racism is certainly present in contemporary Britain, but not omni-present, and seems to be declining all the time. There are now black and Asian MPs, members of the House of Lords and local councillors. Black sportsmen and entertainers are popular heroes and heroines and the local Indian or Pakistani corner shop is a common feature of British life. Indeed, curry is now said to be the British national dish. At the 1992 general election the Conservatives issued a poster of a black man with the slogan: 'Labour see him as black. We see him as British', although the refusal of their Cheltenham constituency party to accept a black barrister as its candidate rather detracted from its potential impact.

Blacks have lived in Britain – albeit in small numbers – since Roman times and were the object of immigration control as early as the reign of Elizabeth I. The present black population, however, is largely the product of post-war immigration from the new Commonwealth – the West Indies, Bangladesh, India, Pakistan, Sri Lanka, parts of Africa, notably Kenya, Uganda and Nigeria, and parts of Asia, notably Malaysia, Singapore and Hong Kong. The peak period of immigration was the 1950s and 1960s. In 1951 only 0.2 million people in the UK were from the new Commonwealth. Twenty years later the figure had increased to 2.1 million. Today Britain's black population is over 3 million and, although often described as immigrant (it includes African and Caribbean blacks and Asians), half were in fact born here. By the year 2000, it is estimated, there will be nearly 3.5 million black Britons, making up nearly 6% of the population. (In 1995 in England – not the UK – there were 800,000 Indians, 500,000 black Caribbeans, 450,000 Pakistanis, 200,000 black Africans, 150,000 black others, 150,000 Bangladeshis, and 200,000 other Asians. There were also 550,000 from the Republic of Ireland and 450,000 born in the EU.)

Immigrants from the new Commonwealth came in the first place because they were needed. A Royal Commission in 1949 estimated that Britain would require 140,000 immigrants annually and the black British came to fill jobs in transport, the hospitals, textiles, clothing and foundries which fuelled the boom of the 1950s. Many had fought for Britain during World War II, spoke English and to a certain extent identified with 'the mother country'. Their own lack of employment prospects and growth of population were additional factors, as was the closure of the US labour market to British West Indians under the McCarren-Walter Act of 1952.

Yet this system seemed to suit everybody. Britain got cheap, hard-working labour for socially undesirable jobs; the newcomers got better jobs than they left behind and the prospect of saving to return home richer, later; the system also seemed self-adjusting – fewer vacancies would mean fewer immigrants. Yet more and more immigrants came after 1952 and few found that they could save enough to go home. By the late 1950s race riots had occurred in Notting Hill, although political pressure for immigration controls meant that more immigrants applied to enter Britain before they were excluded. From 20,000 in 1959 the figure rose to 58,000 in 1960 and 115,000 in 1961. The trouble was that one quarter of the world's population had the right to enter under the 1948 British Nationality Act. Hence immigration controls became unavoidable. The result was the 1962 Immigration Act which restricted entry to dependants of residents, students or those with an employment voucher (there were three types). The Act was temporary and required renewal. It was not overtly racist, although it did not apply to the 60-70,000 Irish citizens who entered Britain each year as immigrants. But as William Deedes, a government minister at the time, admitted in 1968: 'The Bill's real purpose was to restrict the influx of coloured immigrants. We were reluctant to say so openly.'

Labour opposed the Act, but once in power restricted immigration further. Two by-election defeats of Patrick Gordon-Walker, Labour's would-be Foreign Secretary, apparently on the racist issue, had made their impression. Labour renewed the 1962 Act and in a White Paper of 1965 promised to strengthen it. Labour did not want to seen to be 'soft' on race, although its own propaganda centred around 'taking race out of politics'. The result was the 1968 Commonwealth Immigrants Act, introduced in the wake of another right-wing campaign opposing the right of entry of Asians expelled from Kenya. This Act removed the right of entry from all British citizens who did not have a parent or grandparent born in Britain. Instead they could apply for special vouchers, 1,500 of which would be issued annually. Since immigrants from Canada, Australia, or New Zealand would, on the whole, have the patrial connection, while those of the new Commonwealth would not, the Act was clearly discriminatory on grounds of colour. It was passed against a background of speeches from Tory shadow cabinet member, Enoch Powell, warning against the destruction of British culture and sense of nationhood and hinting at future civil war. The Liberals still wanted unlimited immigration and seemed oblivious to racial tension in the country, but Powell had the support of the British working class. On 23 April 1968 the London dockers went on strike and marched to Westminster to support him. But Heath dismissed him from the shadow cabinet.

Labour's patrial distinction was reinforced by the Tories in 1971 in their own Immigration Act, designed to replace all previous legislation. The 'right of abode' was now given to all patrials or those resident in the UK for five years or more, and those born to or adopted by those born in the UK and spouses. All aliens and all non-patrial Commonwealth citizens needed permission and a work permit to enter Britain, although those already resident retained the right to bring in dependants. Citizens of the Irish Republic were not affected by the Act, which in fact increased those eligible for entry from the new Commonwealth. Moreover, whereas Labour had submitted to pressure to exclude Kenyan Asians, the Tories allowed those expelled from Uganda to enter in 1972. Once again in power in the late 1970s, Labour scarcely altered these provisions, although it ended virginity tests on women seeking entry.

Before winning the 1979 general election, Mrs Thatcher spoke in 1977 of 'holding out a clear prospect of an end to immigration' and in 1978 expressed the 'fear that [Britain] might be swamped' by immigration. Although primary immigration had slowed to a dribble, the British Nationality Act of 1981 established three categories of citizenship: British citizens (those with full rights of entry); British overseas citizens (new Commonwealth) and citizens of British dependent territories (Hong Kong, Bermuda). The latter two categories were to have restricted immigration and nationality rights.

Labour opposed this legislation, with Roy Hattersley claiming that its policies since 1962 had been mistaken. This view did not last. On the Tory right, the Monday Club proposed a plan for the repatriation of 100,000 black citizens annually.

Labour passed two Acts to defend coloured immigrants from discrimination. The Race Relations Act of 1965 established conciliation machinery to deal with discrimination which became unlawful on grounds of 'race, colour, ethnic or national origin' in places such as hotels, restaurants and public transport. The Act did not apply to housing or employment and its powers of enforcement were limited. Thus in 1968 a stronger Act was passed – this was the same year as Labour introduced tighter immigration controls – covering housing, employment, the provision of goods, facilities and services and the publication and display of advertisements. The Race Relations Board was given the duty to investigate complaints and the Act also established a Community Relations Commission to pursue community relations and oversee the work of local community relations councils. Yet there was little impact. The definition of discrimination was limited, enforcement procedures were still inadequate, and compensation small.

The Race Relations Act of 1976 extended the definition of discrimination to include 'indirect discrimination', and individuals were given the right to proceed to court without waiting for a decision of the Commission for Racial Equality. The latter body replaced the Race Relations Board and the Community Relations Committee and was given new powers, for example, of serving non-discrimination notices and enforcing them by injunctions. There was also a new clause on racial incitement. Various urban development programmes were instituted, under new legislation, to add to the scope of the campaign against racial discrimination, while schools and local councils were allocated extra funds to deal with special problems caused by immigration under separate legislation.

There is, scientifically speaking, only one race, the human race. Yet 'racial' tensions between the white majority and coloured immigrants and their descendants have been noticeable at different times and were bound to be. For a start, whatever governments thought the economic requirements of the country might be, and whatever was taught at school in the colonies, the ordinary people of Britain were neither in favour of, nor prepared for, mass third-world immigration in the 1960s – immigration which changed the nature of their cities (particularly the inner cities) – even if it brought them some unexpected advantages. The result was widespread discrimination against immigrants to begin with and a fairly weak response by governments to protect their rights. At times riots were the result – in Notting Hill in 1958, in Bristol in 1980, in most major cities in 1981, and in Handsworth and Broad Water Farm in 1985.

Yet the results could have been much worse. Instead, within a generation, partly as a result of immigration controls, partly as a result of government action, and partly simply as a result of different communities living together, being educated together and growing up together, 'racial' discrimination and tension in Britain gradually abated. Black faces were seen regularly on television screens among reporters and actors, entertainers and sportsmen; black lawyers, doctors and businessmen made up a growing middle class; successful black politicians belonged to the major parties; a black headed the largest trade union; and black students became part of the university population.

While it is true that blacks were also disproportionately unemployed and found in disproportionate numbers among the inmates of jails and mental institutions, research showed that whereas ethnic minorities in 1996 formed only 5.5% of the general population and only 5.2% of the economically active population, in 1995-6, 19% of the intake of the Bar Vocational Course were from ethnic minorities as were 18% of the 147,000 UK medical practitioners. Domestic ethnic students made up 21% of the total in medical schools – and all this occurred without any regulations requiring affirmative action or positive discrimination. It was a far from perfect record – especially when, according to official Home Office statistics released in October 1996, one white in 250 was subject to racial attacks in 1993, compared with one Afro-Caribbean in 25 and one Asian in 20. (The total number of racial attacks, recorded for the first time in the 1994 British Crime Survey to include racial attacks against whites, comprised 191,000 against whites, 31,000 against Afro-Caribbeans and 71,000 against Asians.) Yet it was a record of some consolation and hope.

Finally, one important indication of improving race relations – certainly as compared with France or Germany – was the total failure in British politics of explicitly racist political parties. The National Front (NF), for example, which was formed from a number of small racist sects in 1967, and which adopted a programme of opposition to the EEC, 'law and order' and, crucially, the compulsory repatriation of all black immigrants, got absolutely nowhere. In 1970 its ten candidates got 3.6% of the vote. After the decision by the Tories to admit the Ugandan Asians, it received 16% of the vote in the West Bromwich by-election. However, despite growing publicity, it received only 3% of the vote in the two general elections before splitting in 1976 and giving rise to the British National Party or BNP. After that it declined, moving away from parliamentary politics to street politics (often involving running battles with the Socialist Workers Party (SWP) or its front, the Anti-Nazi League) and in the general election of 1979 gained a mere 1.3% of the vote. In 1996 it changed its name to the National Democrats – although some branches objected to incorporating the word 'Democrats' – albeit to little effect. Compared with its French opposite number, led by Jean-Marie Le Pen, it proved a miserable failure. Its racism revolted the British people.

One reason why it got nowhere was the praiseworthy determination of the British political establishment to have nothing to do with such racism. Instead, the Conservative Party set up Anglo-Asian and Anglo-West Indian Conservative Societies, while the Labour Party offered a home to more politically radical members of the ethnic minorities, allowing them to contest safe seats. There was a battle for 'black sections' in the party in the 1980s, but, fortunately for the sake of good race relations, it was lost. The fact that the major parties chose to accommodate the ethnic minorities and received a positive response from them – although some blacks turned inwards to causes like Rastafarianism or Pan Africanism or simply preferred to take part in street riots when they occurred – bodes well for the future. The only way forward for British democracy was to incorporate the black British – most of whom by the 1990s had been born British – into the political system. Otherwise education was the best answer, although by the 1990s British education was in crisis.

British education in 1945 had generally been regarded as excellent. By 1997, on the other hand, few people had a good word to say for it and the Tory Secretary of State for Education, Gillian Shepherd, herself an ex-schoolteacher, was instituting all sorts of measures in a desperate attempt to achieve the basic standards in literacy and numeracy which her predecessors had allowed to slip over the previous decades. Newspapers published almost daily reports of grade inflation at O and A level, falling standards in schools, measured either by international comparisons or over time, or lack of discipline, literacy and numeracy among pupils, not to mention lack of resources and qualified teachers. Knowledge of English grammar seemed to have disappeared along with knowledge of British history and the ability to do mental arithmetic. The Tories themselves blamed comprehensive education, yet they themselves had not only expanded the number of comprehensive schools throughout the 1970s, but comprehensivised the universities in the 1990s, turning all sorts of polytechnics, colleges and institutes into universities simply to boost numbers. At the same time, funds for university education were drastically cut. The Tory strategy was simply to go for numbers – numbers of students, numbers of A levels and O levels achieved, numbers of A-grade passes awarded. They had no interest in standards and very little in education itself, which they did not regard as a vote-winner. It was a common political gibe that since the most important Tories sent their children to be educated at private (public) schools, they had no idea of what was going on inside state ones. This was very unfortunate, since, in some ways, attitudes in the state system had returned to those of the nineteenth century.

If by the late nineteenth century the middle classes had become aware that rising professional standards and modern universities required a higher standard of secondary schooling for their offspring, their main concern as far as the working classes were concerned was to ensure an elementary education that would teach them to know their place, acquire discipline, respect private property, and receive just sufficient instruction to enable them to carry out such limited tasks as were necessary in an expanding commercial economy. To some minds, the teaching profession by the late 1990s had even more limited ambitions – to teach the pupils to know their place and receive some basic instruction without worrying too much about instilling discipline or respect for private property.

A brief history of British education (in fact, English education – the Scottish system was always superior) since 1870 will be instructive. Before then, the provision of schools was left to the churches and private individuals. The Elementary Education Act of that year, however, empowered local authorities to fill the gap where voluntary schools did not exist. They were to do this by establishing school boards elected by ratepayers and entrusted to build and maintain schools with money from rates, school fees and government grants. In 1876 attendance was made compulsory for children living within two miles of any school. Elementary education was still thought to be sufficient and the responsibility of the boards ended when children reached the age of ten. Parents and independent schools looked after older children.

A major reorganisation came about with the 1902 Education Act which replaced 2,559 school boards with 330 local education authorities (LEAs) which were empowered to provide not merely elementary but also secondary education, something which expanded rapidly. Purpose-built secondary schools became known as 'high schools', while annexes to existing elementary ones were known as senior elementary schools. After the 1907 Education (Administrative Provision) Act a special place examination became known as the 'scholarship', then 'the eleven plus', and free places at grammar schools became general. In large towns, junior technical, junior commercial and junior art schools took pupils between the ages of thirteen and sixteen. The next major development was the 1918 Education Act (Fisher Act) which raised the school leaving age to fourteen. It was intended that children over fourteen should attend part-time 'day continuation schools' but this was not compulsory and did not happen much.

In 1926 the Haddow Report recommended that there should be a formal break in the education of children at eleven, with elementary education falling into primary and secondary stages. In 1938 the Spens Report considered the curriculum of grammar and technical high schools.

The Norwood Report, published in 1943, developed the idea that children fell into three types: those who loved learning for its own sake; those who loved applied science and applied art; and those who were more interested in concrete things than ideas. Logically, it recommended different types of schools for these three different types of pupils: secondary grammar schools, secondary technical schools, and secondary modern schools. Educationalists at this time were also impressed by recent developments in intelligence testing which reinforced these recommendations. The majority of LEAs followed Norwood thinking, but few technical schools were built and the outcome after 1944 was therefore a bipartite system of grammar and secondary moderns.

The 1944 Act (Butler Act) professed to introduce 'secondary education for all' by raising the school leaving age to fifteen (it was raised to sixteen in 1971), reducing the number of LEAs to 146, making religious education compulsory, and establishing the first Minister for Education. The British system became one of an eleven plus dividing pupils into a minority of 20% who went to grammar schools and a majority of 80% who went to secondary moderns.

Yet over the next quarter of a century doubts emerged as to the wisdom of this system: secondary modern schools lacked the prestige of grammar schools and were never seen as providing equal education; in any case there were never enough grammar school places for those who wanted them, leaving many parents and pupils dissatisfied; inevitably, an education system which failed 80% of its pupils was seen as undesirable; there was much geographical variation in any case allowing, for example, 40.3% of Merthyr's eleven-year-olds to go on to grammar school in 1962, but only 11.9% of Bootle's; the eleven plus depressed and emotionally unnerved generations of children and parents since so much depended on it; while even those working-class children who received grammar school places tended to do less well than their middle-class peers; finally, educationalists began to have serious doubts about the reliability of IQ tests, on which so much of the system seemed to rest. Until then intelligence, conceived as the ability to perform abstract thinking, was reckoned to be innate and probably inherited, an assumption, in the words of Lynton Robins, on whose work this survey is based, 'which had enormous social and political implications'.

If intelligence were inherited, then the existence of social classes was based on genetic factors and school results would simply reflect their social make-up. This factor lay behind the idea in the 1950s and 1960s that nothing very much could be done with the working classes or with secondary moderns.

Soon, however, these ideas were challenged. Sociologists insisted that environment, not genes, determined results – parental attitudes, the availability of space, privacy and books at home, and language development. These differences, they insisted, were the real ones determining IQ results – now seen as a measurement of social class rather than of intelligence. These insights were reinforced by other studies which showed that teachers were socially biased – perhaps unconsciously – against pupils who were scruffily dressed, assigning them to lower streams within schools than their abilities merited. In the end, therefore, these arguments, along with a call for a democratic educational system that placed all pupils in the same environment and allowed them to learn from one another, led to the comprehensive education system introduced from the late 1960s. Some radical educationalists, however, advocated the abolition of schools on the grounds that they merely taught pupils to conform, failed to teach basic skills, and employed 'qualified' teachers who could not teach instead of gifted teachers who were not qualified. Some advocated giving 'edu-credit cards' for pupils to pay for courses outside schools from whoever taught them to their personal satisfaction. Others preferred to work within the system using education vouchers to enhance parental choice.

Under the comprehensive system, however, – which in 1976 led Labour to abolish direct grant schools – new problems arose and in 1976 James Callaghan as prime minister opened a so-called 'great debate' on education. Standards were seen to be falling, and spending on education certainly stagnated after 1973, partly as a result of dramatically falling school enrolments as the baby boom died out.

The great debate centred around not so much on public versus private education – Labour never acquired the courage to abolish private schools – as around teaching methods, control of the curriculum, numbers of students staying on after sixteen, and teachers' pay. In retrospect, the key issue should have been teaching methods especially in primary schools, since 'progressive' methods there undermined much of the education system.

Once again, educational theory reflected social and political prejudice. Traditional teaching methods were held to be authoritarian and hierarchical with pupils largely playing a passive role, relying on the teacher as an expert. A 'closed classroom' was seen as an encouragement to conformity, whereas an 'open classroom' helped teachers to be friendlier, less authoritarian and able to participate with pupils in discovering knowledge by managing the learning process around them. This child-centred method of education was held to make pupils more self-confident and happy. The trouble was that it made them more self-centred, less disciplined, less literate and less numerate.

In the first place, it undermined the status and authority of the teacher, which in the past had derived from his or her being the person charged with transmitting a corpus of knowledge and values to a new generation. Child-centred learning substituted for this the importance of the child as learner discovering things for itself at its own pace, with the teacher reduced to the role of facilitator. Little wonder discipline collapsed since, as Gerald Roberts has written, teachers could not abdicate their authority one minute and then reassert it as glorified child-minders the next. Secondly, inordinate emphasis was placed on the child's creativity, usually at the expense of formal rules such as those required in learning grammar. The latter, for example, was seen as a curb on creativity. Yet all systems require rules. Thirdly, child-centred learning got the idea of the pupil's self-esteem quite wrong. It was reluctant to correct mistakes in case the child felt humiliated by being criticised in public while another child was praised for getting something right. Yet, to quote Roberts again, 'self-esteem in fact comes from being expected to get things right and actually getting them right. Not being expected to get them right actually lowers self esteem.' Another drawback was the refusal to use phonics as the best method to teach reading; instead, children were expected to absorb it by a process akin to osmosis called the 'real books' system. It failed miserably.

The refusal to allow boys to compete against one another for prizes was another failure (boys are not as dutiful as girls and need the spur of competition); so too, finally, was the reaction against whole class teaching in favour of group learning which both undermined the teacher's authority and was incompatible with streaming. These progressive methods had a lot to answer for.

Moreover, the effects carried over to secondary schools where teachers, trained in the same methods, did little to reverse these trends. Their task often enough became simply one of keeping undisciplined teenagers amused or occupied. It didn't matter if they learned very much, since if educational theory taught that schools were less important than social background in determining future prospects, working-class children could not be expected to learn much anyway. Standards under these conditions were bound to drop. Low standards encouraged poor discipline which lowered standards further which in turn reduced discipline. The end result was a vicious circle which had all sorts of social costs but apparently few political ones, since both major parties accepted the teaching methods involved.

When reform did come in the 1980s and 1990s, it was political. Less directed at teaching methods, it was more concerned to take the running of schools out of the hands of the local authorities and implement direct government control of education. Naturally, everything was dressed up to maintain the appearance of more individual choice – and some ministers may even have believed that that would be the end result – yet in the end the reality was one of more government control and falling standards.

The two main 'reforming' Acts were the Education Acts of 1988 and 1993. The first had 238 sections, the second 308. The first abolished the Inner London Education Authority, imposed a national curriculum on all pupils up to the age of 16 with regular testing at the ages of 7, 11, 14 and 16, and allowed schools to vote to withdraw from local authority control. Such schools would be known as 'grant maintained' and would be funded directly from Whitehall.

The national curriculum was designed around a set of core subjects – English, maths and science – surrounded by seven foundation subjects – technology, history, geography, music, art, physical education and a modern language. Religious education was thrown in as an afterthought. 'There was no gesture', in the words of Simon Jenkins, 'towards new subjects such as economics, accounting, design and graphics, catering, health and hygiene.' Ministers wanted pupils to learn what they themselves had learned at school. Programmes of study in each subject were to be published to demonstrate that the essentials were being covered. All were to be compulsory until 16 and examination results in them made public in the form of school league tables to encourage better future performance.

The national curriculum was to take up 90% of teachers' time. Their own views about teaching no longer mattered. Nor did the views of anyone else outside Whitehall, since once it became clear that the vast majority of schools would not opt out (only 1,000 out of 24,000 state schools in England and Wales had done so by 1995, half of them in only eight local education authority areas and most of them either small schools fearful of closure or former grammar schools eager to regain the ability to select), the government took further powers of control.

In 1992, sixth form and further education colleges were taken out of local authority control and placed under a Further Education Funding Council. Then a White Paper announced government plans to allow all schools to opt out of local authority control by 1996. The 1993 Act established a Funding Agency for Schools (FAS) with members appointed by the Secretary of State with unlimited powers over grant-maintained schools. It could sack or appoint governors, open or close schools, expand or contract them. It could also prevent local authorities from opening or expanding schools in competition with its own. The FAS was to be run by the Secretary of State as a kind of school planning body. It would assess schools on a cost-benefit analysis and ensure the provision of enough places in any given area. It could dictate the 'character' of a school and thus its selection system. In short, despite local competition between schools, central government could decide everything in the end. It was even laid down that in disputes between the FAS and the LEAs the Secretary of State would have the final word.

Given that most schools did not opt out of LEA control, however, the national system in practice fell back into a rather similar pattern to that established after 1944. There were private schools for the rich, a mixture of intermediate colleges and grammar schools (not to mention those other innovations, the city technical colleges, plus the assisted place schemes) for the middle classes, and the secondary modern (comprehensives) for the rest. The difference was that central government now closely controlled the middle tier.

One danger of this was the determination of the Department of Education and Science to establish a 'common funding formula' for pupils, i.e. a fixed sum to be spent on each pupil nationwide, in order to manufacture a standard budget for schools, which would then require either private funding or fees to exceed prescribed limits. This in fact would end any need for local management – so that schools, like police departments, local authorities or health authorities would merely work to spending formulae prescribed by central government. The end result was the education crisis of 1995 when the government allocated an extra 1% cash for school budgets but awarded schoolteachers a pay rise of 2.7%. Local authorities had to sack schoolteachers to balance their budgets. Logically, John Major began to talk more and more of restoring the old-fashioned grammar schools who could select children by charging their own fees.

In the end, the reforms were of the wrong kind. They merely established centralisation of curriculum and financial control. This meant that any government of the future with plans to indoctrinate children or to introduce new 'progressive' teaching methods could do so at a stroke, so great were the powers they would have over the day-to-day running of all schools. Only in 1996 did the government get round to looking at teaching methods and taking on the teacher training colleges and university education departments that had spread the ideology of child-centred learning in the first place. In the meantime, it had demoralised what spirit was left in the teaching profession by imposing huge administrative burdens, regular exams, league tables and ever-changing curriculums, for very little financial reward.

The universities suffered in exactly the same way. Once again, the emphasis was on centralisation, with the aim this time being to cut costs and increase numbers simultaneously – something that was only possible at the expense of academic standards. When the universities fought back, Oxford refusing Thatcher an honorary degree, for example, the campaign against them grew even more intense. It included the creation of the UFC (Universities Funding Council), the abolition of academic tenure, the reduction of university salaries, the introduction of research and teaching assessments, annual grants, and published league tables. Indeed, it was only with the greatest reluctance that the government accepted an amendment from Lord Jenkins to the 1988 Act agreeing that university contracts should 'ensure that academic staff have freedom within the law to question and test received wisdom and to put forward new ideas and controversial or unpopular opinions, without placing themselves in jeopardy of losing their jobs or privileges'.

The polytechnics were also taken out of local government control and placed under central direction. Yet they had one compensation. In the government's view universities should themselves have been polytechnics insofar as in its view their real tasks were commercial and vocational rather than academic. In the end therefore the two were merged under a Higher Education Funding Council (HEFC). Polytechnics became universities although in reality universities became polytechnics.

In 1989 a European report had rated British universities as the best in Europe on almost every score. But Thatcherism destroyed them. Between 1990 and 1995 expenditure per student fell by 25%; student numbers during the same period rose by the same amount. Academic salaries were kept down; quantity not quality of research became the criterion for obtaining funds; and the reputation of established universities was diluted by lumping them together with new ones, some of which taught subjects which were as far removed from the groves of academe as could possibly have been imagined and which accepted students without A levels or with grades as low as three Fs. So the age of university league tables arrived. People now demanded to know where a person had studied before accepting the quality of his or her degree as reliable. Indeed, foreign countries refused to fund students at any but the most established of the British universities.

*

A book such as this written twenty years ago would have been expected to analyse British politics and society from the point of view of social class. Today, this seems anachronistic. This is partly because after the fall of communism no one sees the class war as the instrument of political change; nor is anyone convinced that victory for the champions of the proletariat would bring more democracy or increased prosperity. Besides, the organised proletariat no longer exists, having been undermined by social and political change in the 1980s, not to mention massive unemployment. In Britain, in any case, its would-be champion, the New Labour Party, now has more middle-class members than the Tory Party and is committed to the same policies. The class war in politics is therefore over.

Did the British class system ever amount to very much? Britain always enjoyed great social mobility: Field Marshal Roberts, the head of the British army during World War I, rose through the ranks from the bottom; Benjamin Disraeli, although a baptised Anglican, was always regarded as a Jew, but one who in the nineteenth century at the height of British power could still become prime minister and a member of the House of Lords; Ramsay MacDonald, the illegitimate son of a fishwife, became prime minister in 1924. More recently, John Major rose from very humble origins to become premier in 1990; before him the prime minister was the daughter of a grocer. True, many of the cabinet colleagues of these people had been to public schools and Oxford or Cambridge, but what is wrong with graduates of the best universities gaining cabinet posts? Surely one would be more worried if a majority of cabinet members were graduates of the University of Bournemouth? The same might be said for top jobs in industry and elsewhere. Little more need be said. As one text book concluded in 1983: 'Britain, then, has a pattern of economic and social inequality which is characteristic of western industrialised countries. Private wealth is highly concentrated, particularly in the ownership of private-sector industry; income reflects the earner's role in the economy, and whilst in theory elite occupations are open to all, in practice they tend to go to those born higher up the social scale.'

The point to make is that there is as much – if not more – social mobility here than elsewhere in Europe; less income inequality than in America; and that class does not prevent anyone with talent from rising from the bottom of the social scale right to the top. Social classes are not biological attributes, passed on to offspring at birth; they are much more like hotels visited by different people at different times as they make their way through life. Different members of the same family will probably end up residing at different ones.

There is one class, however, that demands special attention, and that is the criminal class. Crime rates in Britain doubled in the 1980s and it is interesting to enquire why. Was it the lack of discipline in schools, the permissive society and the welfare state that between them created a lack of respect for authority? Did welfare breed contempt for the idea that wealth had to be earned, goods had to be bought and paid for? Did the breakdown of the traditional two-parent family mean a breakdown of parental discipline? Or did mass unemployment lead the poor and unemployed to break the law to acquire goods and wealth which would otherwise remain beyond their reach? Perhaps public policy was to blame. Perhaps the courts simply failed to lock sufficient people up. In any case, many people would say that one of the most important differences in Britain today compared to 1945 is the increase in crime.

8

Crime

Fear of crime is nothing new. In his influential book *Hooligan*, published in 1983, Professor Geoffrey Pearson offered a vivid history of 'respectable fears' throughout the ages. As Robert Reiner commented, 'He demonstrated how the post-middle-aged of every generation tend to look back nostalgically upon the days of their youth as a Golden Age of morality and tranquillity. In this rose-tinted grandadological perspective there is perpetual anxiety about the declining moral standards of the younger generation, with sharp condemnation of their incivilities and deviance.'

Often there have been outbreaks of what another criminologist, Professor Stan Cohen, has described as 'moral panic'. For example, Daniel Defoe, in a pamphlet addressed to the Lord Mayor of London in 1730, wrote: 'The Whole City, My Lord, is alarm'd and uneasy. Wickedness has got such a Head, and the Robbers and Insolence of the Night are such that the citizens are no longer secure within their own Walls or safe even in passing their Streets, but are robbed, insulted, and abused, even at their own Doors …. The citizens are oppressed by Rapin and Violence.' Little wonder Defoe found the idea of escaping to a desert island attractive! Later, another novelist and Chief Magistrate at Bow Street, Henry Fielding, described London as a 'vast wood or forest, in which a thief may harbour with as great security as wild beasts do in the deserts of Arabia or Africa'. Finally, another great literary figure, Horace Walpole, concluded in 1752 that 'one is forced to travel even at noon, as if one were going to battle.'

Fear of crime, therefore, has been with us for a long time and often tells us more about the state of mind of elderly citizens than anything else. Today it is very high indeed with well over 90% expressing a belief that crime has substantially increased, a percentage considerably higher even than those recorded in the 1980s. There is particular fear of burglaries, muggings and rapes. The question to be asked is: is such fear justified? How much crime is there today?

Unfortunately, according to Professor Robert Reiner, 'Overall there has been a huge increase in recorded crime since the mid-1950s, pretty well continuously, without any sustained periods of decline. In the last 40 years we have got used to thinking of crime, like the weather and pop music, as something that is always getting worse.' Yet this has not always been the case. In the second half of the nineteenth century, for example, levels of recorded crime began a long sustained decline until the eve of World War I. There was no clear upward direction in the statistics until the apparent inexorable rise which began around 1955.

Since then crime levels have risen, *but not at a constant rate*. Over the period as a whole, the rise appears staggering: from approximately 500,000 crimes recorded in 1950 to 5.7 million in 1993, i.e. from 1 crime per 100 population to almost 11 per 100. However, the rate of increase has been greater since the late 1970s than in the 20 years before that, although the earlier increase had already caused much alarm. During the 1980s the level of recorded crime doubled.

Under the Tories, predictably, the Home Office was only too eager to point out all the traditional pitfalls of relying on statistics for recorded crime. And criminologists are well aware of these. They certainly have to be careful, since according to the British Crime Surveys (BCS) conducted by the Home Office since the early 1980s there were over 15 million crimes committed against individuals and property in 1992, for example, compared to the mere 5.4 million recorded by the police. Such discrepancies, according to the Home Office, were to be explained by the fact that most crime is simply not reported at all and that while more crime is being reported one way or another, there is no evidence that the underlying rate of crime is increasing at all. Evidence for such an interpretation was drawn from the experience of the General Household Surveys (GHS) of the 1970s which demonstrated that most of the rise in recorded burglaries during the 1970s was indeed a recording phenomenon – due to the rise in the number of telephones and the policies of insurance companies, which insisted that burglaries now had to be reported to the police before compensation could be paid out.

For the 1980s, however, both the BCS figures and police figures for crimes of property doubled. As far as violent crime was concerned the police recorded that this too almost doubled, while the BCS increase, although substantial, was much smaller at 21%. In the area of violent crime, however, the BCS figures were less reliable: interviews took place at home and often therefore in the presence of the perpetrators of assaults. (Most violence against the person, child abuse, murder, etc., takes place within the family – a fact too often overlooked by those who make glib statements about 'family values'.) Improved treatment of rape and assault victims by the police also suggested that crimes which previously would never have been reported, began to be reported to the police during the 1980s. So the figures of reported crime were liable to various interpretations.

None the less, it is likely that violent crime increased very significantly indeed in the 1980s. Even if we are sceptical about the 100% increase in officially recorded violence, the BCS figures – which are likely to be a gross underestimate – show an increase of about a quarter in violent crime.

So there can be little doubt that the most serious and worrying types of crime are indeed increasing rapidly. There has been an almost continuous rise since the 1950s with especially rapid growth since the late 1970s and a spectacular increase in the 1990s. The public's increasing fear of crime has a substantial basis in the real risks of victimisation. (Reiner)

The chance of becoming a victim has always depended on where you live, how you live, who you are and who you know. There are dramatic differences between different parts of the country, with sharp contrasts between inner city and rural areas. Worst of all for property crime are gentrified middle-class areas in inner cities which combine the maximum of temptation with the maximum of opportunity.

With regard to violent crime, there are two common types: fights between young men and domestic assaults against women. Overall, the most frequent victim of violence has been the young man who goes out frequently and drinks heavily. Next most common has been the female victim of a man she is in a relationship with: 'Most victims of violence, especially if they are female, suffer at the hands of those they know, often their nearest and supposedly dearest' (Reiner).

Even today, relatively few crimes of violence are committed by strangers. Only 14% of female homicide victims (30% for males) are killed by strangers and only one third of recorded rapes are committed by strangers. Attacks by strangers, though, have become more frequent and now form the bedrock anxiety of public fears.

If we know who the victims are, it is more difficult, on the other hand, to determine who has victimised them. We know who goes to prison: essentially the young, male, poorly-educated and – disproportionately – black. Yet this does not tell us much about criminals in general.

Most crimes are never detected. Only 2% of crimes reported to the BCS by victims ever result in a conviction. Only a slightly higher proportion lead to any sort of identification of the offender. And we are leaving out of the picture the huge mass of white collar crime, hardly any of which comes to light at all. So we do not know very much about who criminals are apart from the tiny minority who are caught. How far their characters match those of all offenders, must remain a moot point. (Reiner)

Concerning the causes of crime there is much dispute. The Right blames everything on permissiveness and moral delinquency. The Left stresses social conditions. The Home Office stresses rising criminal opportunities. Fortunately, most of these causes can be integrated into a synthetic whole.

For a crime to be committed, four ingredients are necessary: motive, means, opportunity and lack of control. There must be a motivated offender with the means to commit the crime, the opportunity presented by a vulnerable victim and the offence must not be prevented by either external controls – police, security etc. – or by internalised controls, i.e.

conscience ('the inner policeman'). Rising crime rates since the mid-1950s must take at least three causal factors into account. The initial rise from the mid-1950s to the 1970s was probably the product of more criminal targets in an increasingly affluent society – more cars, radios, TVs, videos and other such stock-in-trade of thieves. Since the late 1950s, however, there has also been a change in cultural attitudes. Conservatives bemoan what they see as a Permissive Society subverting traditional family values and undermining social authority. Liberals and others welcome a freer society in which individuals can pursue a more varied life-style and escape the pressures of class-consciousness and social and religious conformism. However evaluated, the evidence is clear that since the 1960s social deference, conformism and unquestioning acceptance of the establishment has become passé. Once again, this factor may help explain the rise of recorded crime since the 1950s.

> However, the dramatic growth of crime in the 1980s ... is best explained by the socio-economic factors most often stressed by radical accounts. The crime explosion corresponds closely to the adoption of free market economic strategies ... These policies have increased poverty, inequality, and long-term unemployment especially among young people. (Reiner)

The American experience also bears this out. There criminals have always been anti-heroes of a kind and have often been glamorised as deviant examples of the American Dream. It is not surprising therefore that US values – particularly the stress on making money as the most important thing in life, not to mention the downplaying of social obligation during the Thatcher years ('There is no such thing as society') – should have brought American-style social problems (rising crime, race riots, etc.). After all, as the Americans have it, there is no such thing as a free lunch, and an economically generated underclass has formed which seems permanently cut off from legitimate opportunities. To quote Reiner once again:

> The rise in crime has social causes over which the police have little power. The initial crime take-off was probably due to the advent of mass consumerism, which created a bonanza of tempting and easy targets for quick and easy theft. It was fuelled further by a more liberal and less deferential culture, which simultaneously weakened inhibitions against offending and the authority of the police themselves.
> The other main ingredient has been the creation of an expanding underclass of young men, who have never been employed and are excluded from legitimate economic activities. It is this deadly combination of laissez-faire economics with laissez-faire morality which has generated massive increases in crime and disorder.

Many studies have now confirmed the link between Thatcherite economic policies and the growth in crime. Several of these were commissioned by the Home Office itself. Tory Home Secretaries are loath to admit this but the *Independent* reported (8 April 1994) that an internal Home Office document prepared as a 'draft speaking note' for a senior civil service seminar on law and order attended by Michael Howard explicitly recognised unemployment and relative deprivation as crucial explanations of rising crime.

Some of those who are unwilling to admit this make great play of lower crime rates in the 1930s. However, crime did rise during that decade. Besides, the social meaning of unemployment can vary considerably, and the criminogenic consequences will be very different if the unemployed are relatively insulated from contact with those in work and thus from experiencing a sense of relative deprivation, not to speak of opportunities for crime. The impact will be different according to the networks of communal or state support available to the unemployed. The length of unemployment – whether it is transitional or permanent – will also matter as will the age group affected. Middle-aged workers laid off after a lifetime's exposure to the discipline of work are far less likely to offend than young men who are at their peak age for crime.

In the 1930s just as many teenagers had criminal records as today, but family ties and the prospect of future work meant that they were reintegrated within society. Today – especially among young blacks who do not have the work experience or social deference of their elders who were prepared to take on very menial jobs as first-generation immigrants – teenage offenders often lack the family ties and work ethic that kept them from re-offending in the 1930s.

Another problem today which did not exist in the 1930s is drugs. These are reckoned to be at the heart of much of today's crime and in 1994 there were 72,000 arrests for possession of cannabis. Hundreds of millions of pounds are spent each year on enforcing the ban on drugs. Yet police and customs officials only manage to confiscate 10-20% of drugs imported into this country and the price of drugs remains fairly constant as market supplies remain stable. Curiously, cannabis – which accounts for 83% of all drug offences – is not associated with violence and there are no known deaths associated with it. Alcohol, on the other hand, is associated with 82% of public order offences and 43% of assaults. It is estimated to cause 25,000 deaths a year. Yet we are expanding pub opening hours. The probability is that it is the illegality of drugs rather than the drugs themselves which causes crime, something which the history of Prohibition in the United States would seem to bear out.

Leading policemen and security chiefs have spoken out for a debate in this country on drug laws. Labour, Liberal Democratic and Tory MPs have done the same. So too have newspapers of Left and Right. Yet generations which kill themselves with alcohol and tobacco react violently at the thought of legalising even soft drugs, with which they are unfamiliar but which are commonly smoked by their sons and daughters. The debate will not be postponed for ever, however, as police chiefs themselves see the fight against drugs as unwinnable and futile; even worse, it may actually increase criminal activity and divert hundreds of millions of pounds from more useful tasks of policing. Today the whole issue remains a taboo. On the other hand, an equally logical response – though no doubt an equally unenforceable one – would be to ban the sale of alcohol and tobacco. So what has been done?

Elected in 1979 on a law and order platform, the Tories initially made good on promises to increase police powers. In an era of public expenditure cuts, the police were protected. Yet, after record-breaking recorded crime increases, the Tories after 1989 cast around for a new approach. Throwing money at the problem had not worked.

The excuse was found that the police had not been 'businesslike' enough. In particular, it was hinted that if only the police would concentrate their efforts on catching criminals, crime could and would be conquered. Ministers accused the police of squandering the resources which had been lavished on them. As Kenneth Baker put it in his memoirs 'there was impatience that although we had spent more in real terms since 1979 there had been a substantial rise in crime. "Where is the value for money?" asked my colleagues.'

The answer to Baker's question came in a massive shake-up of police organisation and philosophy. The scale of this shake-up was concealed from most people since it was introduced piece-meal, without any statement of intent, without any Royal Commission, with little public debate and with little consultation with the police themselves. Yet the government developed a clear and coherent strategy to reconstruct the police.

This stategy was embodied in a string of official documents and reports that remade the criminal justice system without most people realising it: the White Paper on Police Reform and the Sheehy Report on police rewards and responsibilities, both of June 1993; the Police and Magistrates Courts Act and the Criminal Justice and Public Order Act of 1994; and the Home Office Report on the Police's Core and Ancillary Tasks of 1995. The only part of the process to involve outsiders was the Sheehy Report, led by Sir Patrick Sheehy, chairman of the multinational BAT corporation and thus known to the police as 'BATman'.

The rationale for change was set out in the 1993 White Paper: 'The main job of the police is to catch criminals', it declared, overturning the original purpose of the police force. (Sir Robert Peel in 1829 had instructed the new Metropolitan Police that 'the principal object to be obtained is the prevention of crime.') Yet the same paragraph of the White Paper stated that 'only 18% of the calls to the police are about crime and only about 40% of police officers' time is spent dealing directly with crime'. The government's aim was to make the police better criminal catchers by turning them into a tightly run, centralised police organisation, with value for money as its credo.

The post-Sheehy regime of pay and and conditions introduced the disciplines of the market place (short-term contracts, performance-related pay) in the belief that, as in hospitals or universities, these would ensure sharply motivated personnel. The revamped tripartite structure of police governance enshrined in the Police and Magistrates Court Act – locally elected members were no longer to dominate local police authorities – was intended to allow central government to set policing priorities. The police would be better able to concentrate on these, once relieved of the extraneous burdens and mundane tasks that interfered with catching criminals; that, at least, was the assumption of the Home Office working party on Core and Ancillary Tasks. Success or failure was to be monitored nationally by the Audit Commission, using league tables and ever more rigorous performance indicators, and locally by the retuned police authorities, legitimised by business experience rather than an electoral mandate.

So much for the government's grand design. Implementing it, however, did not prove easy. The opposition of the Police Federation forced the government to water down Sheehy's proposals; the opposition of several former Home Secretaries in the House of Lords forced a less centralised structure for setting national police priorities through the Police and Magistrates Courts Act; the Core and Ancillary Tasks working party failed to come up with an extensive list of powers of which the police could be deprived; while attracting busy local businessmen to serve on new police authorities proved difficult. Never the less, enough of the grand design remained to make the change of direction clear. 'Above all, central government had undiluted power to determine police budgets. It called the important tunes through its national policing plans, of which local authorities had to take account' (Reiner)

Government policy became a potent mix of centralisation (there were persistent rumours that it wanted to establish a sort of British FBI, no doubt as the British arm of Europol) combined with surreptitious privatisation. While the ethics of private enterprise were inculcated into the police force, it also faced competition from a burgeoning new private sector, the expansion of which was fuelled by holding back expenditure on public policing.

The police, equipped with task forces and special units, were increasingly asked to focus on clearing up crime using helicopters and fast cars. They were heavily equipped and distant from the public they served. The ordinary British bobby was reduced to a rump role: public order policing and the provision of a minimum core service. Those who were dissatisfied could join private security firms. However, it was not only private security companies which grew up in profusion; the government itself was reduced to organising the Neighbourhood Watch and advertising for special constables. People were encouraged more and more to provide their own policing as demand outstripped the government's willingness to pay for a proper police force. What was not inevitable, however, was the continued lack of democratic control over this process. Local government will have to have a greater say in all of this. So too will Parliament. As Reiner warned:

> Abandoning policing to the inequities of the private market threatens to push society into a new feudalism, as is already apparent in many North American cities. The well-heeled shelter in security bubbles shielded by space, architecture, technology, and private guards, while the underclass are consigned to the dreadful enclosures of the urban ghettos. The public police inherit the residual role of patrolling the frontiers between these. In this role they also act as sandwich boards for society's values of fragmentation and division.

So much for Tory policy towards the police. Tory policy with regard to criminals themselves went through two U-turns after they entered office in 1979. At first their policy was one of being tough on crime, spending more on the police, giving the police more powers, increasing the punitiveness of the penal system and making crime an explicitly partisan issue for the first time. Yet the evident failure of all this to check a more rapid increase in crime and disorder in the early 1980s led to a clear if unheralded U-turn. This culminated in the Criminal Justice Act of 1991, which ushered in means-related fines and stopped courts from taking into account more than two of an offender's previous convictions. With tight controls over the use of custody, fewer people were jailed. Tory Home Secretaries took the advice of Home Office researchers to adopt a more pragmatic approach. This combined an emphasis on crime prevention and a more community-based and problem-solving style of policing with a recognition that prison ('an expensive way of making bad people worse', in the famous words of the 1990 White Paper, *Crime, Justice and Protecting the Public*, which preceded the 1991 Act) was a last resort to house the most serious or dangerous offenders rather than a constructive response to crime.

Within six months of the 1991 Act, however, Tory policy underwent another U-turn in response to a moral panic over disorders in several inner city estates in the summers of 1991 and 1992 but particularly in the wake of the shocking murder of little James Bulger. The party's rhetoric now reverted to the period of 1979-81 and reached its climax in Michael Howard's dramatic 'Prison works' speech to the Tory Party conference of 1993. The 1993 Criminal Justice Act now allowed courts to take all previous convictions into account and policy shifted from reserving jail for the worst offenders – partly to avoid overcrowding – to a greater use of jail with heavier terms. The 1994 Criminal Justice and Public Order Act brought a host of tougher sentencing provisions for young offenders and tighter bail laws. Mr Major, therefore, in spite of heading a party which presided over the greatest crime wave in British history, planned to go to the country in 1997 as a law and order prime minister.

To ensure that people got the message, yet another White Paper was produced by Mr Howard in 1996 entitled *Protecting the Public: The Government's strategy on crime in England and Wales*. Its main provisions were incorporated in yet another Criminal Justice Act before the 1997 election. They included automatic life sentences for offenders convicted for a second time of attempted murder, threat or conspiracy to murder, manslaughter, wounding with intent to do grievous bodily harm, robbery involving the use of a firearm, rape, attempted rape and unlawful sexual intercourse with a girl under 13. The sentence was to be imposed even if the second offence was not the same as the first and any previous conviction for a relevant offence would count as a qualifying conviction, including crimes committed when under the age of 17 and before the new measure became law. However, a judge would be able to decide a lesser term if it was thought there were 'genuinely exceptional circumstances'. A judge would set the minimum term for 'deterrence and retribution' and when that was complete, the Parole Board, not a politician, would decide whether a person should be released. (This presumably followed from the recent decision of the European Court of Human Rights declaring the power of the Home Secretary to overrule the Parole Board to be illegal.)

Secondly, there were to be mandatory minimum sentences for drug dealers. Courts would have to impose a minimum seven-year sentence on an offender aged 18 years or over convicted for trafficking in a Class A substance who had two or more previous convictions for similar offences. Class A drugs included cocaine, heroin, and Ecstasy. The sentence would apply to offences of producing, supplying and possessing a Class A drug and importing or exporting. Any previous similar conviction would count as a qualifying offence, including those committed when under 17 and any committed before the proposals became law. But the minimum term was to be imposed only when the third conviction related to an offence committed after the White Paper proposals became law.

Thirdly, there would be mandatory minimum sentences for burglars. Courts would be required to impose a minimum sentence of three years on an offender aged over 18 convicted of domestic burglary who had two or more previous similar convictions. The mandatory sentence would apply to any previous convictions for similar offences committed after the measures became law. The three previous convictions had to relate to separate court appearances. (Presumably this was to allow police to continue to ask for other cases to be taken into account at each appearance so that they might inflate their clear-up rate.)

Fourthly, there was the abolition of automatic early release and parole. Offenders were to serve their full terms ordered by the court. For the first 12 months of a sentence or the whole of a year-long sentence, a prisoner would earn remission of six days a month. A prisoner sentenced to 12 months would earn maximum remission of about 2.5 months compared with the previous automatic release after six months. Over 12 months a prisoner would be able to earn three days a month by cooperation and a further three days a month for 'positive good behaviour'. The maximum earned early release would be 20% of a sentence. All offenders serving more than 12 months would remain under supervision after their release for a minimum of three months or 15% of the original prison sentence. The White Paper stated that the government did not expect an increase in the time offenders spent in jail. The Lord Chief Justice would be expected to issue a direction to judges urging them to take into account the abolition of parole and of automatic early release when handing down their sentences. (In other words the government was passing stricter laws and telling the judges to impose shorter sentences.)

Finally, as far as mentally disordered offenders were concerned, the courts would be allowed to pass a prison sentence and order immediate hospital admission. The government planned automatic life sentences for repeat serious offenders to be in force by October 1997 and the other proposals by October 1999.

These proposals were attacked by the judiciary not merely as interfering with their rights of sentencing but as counter-productive. The Lord Chief Justice, Lord Lane, described them as little more than a 'bonanza for prison architects' and warned that they could encourage rapists and others facing a mandatory life sentence to commit murder. There was little doubt that the majority of the legal profession had no faith in them and regarded them simply as playing to the gallery on the Home Secretary's part. Most people expected the crime rate to keep going up even if more people were sent to jail. (They also believed that the policy would be very expensive. California, which operates a similar one, now spends more on jails than on higher education.) A massive new investment in jails was expected in order to keep the extra 10,000 prisoners that the White Paper proposals would produce behind bars. Over 25 years the cost of extra prisons was estimated at £3 billion. Michael Howard did win Treasury support for a minimum of 12 new prisons, though he still needed to win Treasury cash for the implementation of the Learmont Report on prisons which called for the building of a 'supermax' prison to hold the country's 300 most dangerous criminals (estimated cost £120 million). It was understood that the White Paper's proposals were watered down before they were published on grounds of cost. Yet the 12 new jails were in addition to two new ones then being built and six new ones already planned. All the new jails were to be built under the Private Finance Initiative under which private sector companies would design, build, finance and manage the prisons. The taxpayer would then pay the private sector an annual fee for 25 years. In 1996 there were 135 jails in England and Wales holding 53,941 inmates compared with 43,036 when the Tories came to power. These proposals, as already stated, were expected to add at least another 10,000 inmates to the total. In 1996 it cost £23,000 a year to keep a prisoner compared with £12,900 a year to send a boy to Eton or £13,300 a year to send a boy to Winchester.

From 1993 the Home Office claimed that the new get-tough policy had cut crime rates by between 1 and 5%. Police officers, on the other hand, claimed that this was simply because the statistics were being 'massaged'. The *Sunday Telegraph* on 31 March 1996 ran the headline 'Crime figures a sham, say police'. According to a number of police officers quoted, all sorts of tricks were encouraged. The chairman of the Metropolitan Police Federation said: 'The crime figures are meaningless. Police everywhere know exactly what is going on.' According to one recently retired Scotland Yard officer, all crimes reported in any one block of flats were recorded as a single crime; pickpocketing was not recorded as a crime unless it was seen being done. Excess restrictions on car insurance meant that car thefts were now rarely reported, while it was 'common practice' for detectives to go to prisons and get false confessions from criminals. Crimes could be 'written off' under Home Office rules if detectives believed they knew who committed them but could not 'prove' it. Confessions made to police by prisoners were known as crimes cleared 'by secondary means'. These admissons were not placed on the prisoners' records. 'At least half' of these were reckoned by police to be false confessions. In February 1996, according to the *Sunday Telegraph*, two West Midlands detectives were suspended after allegations that they had 'solved' thousands of crimes by bribing prisoners to confess to them. It was difficult to believe that Mr Howard's policies were actually working any more than the get-tough policies of 1979-81 or the more lenient ones of the period in between.

Robert Reiner's view was as follows:

> Deterrence is known not to be a feasible option, except for gaining applause at Conservative Party Conferences. Research has demonstrated that even large increases in police numbers, resources, or powers will not make much difference to the probability of being caught, and, short of permanent and universal saturation, policing will not prevent offending. Target-hardening, crime prevention tactics will may work in a localised way, but this is a 'burgle-my-neighbour' approach rather than a crime policy for reducing rates overall. Ultimately the only solution that offers any substantial hope must address the social sources of crime.

Perhaps this is why so many people responded to Tony Blair's famous soundbite: 'tough on crime, tough on the causes of crime.' The problem is that both the consumer society and the permissive society (or the civilised society to give it its liberal name) are here to stay, while there is little evidence that free-market economics are about to go out of fashion. It may well be the case therefore that higher crime rates are here to stay.

On the other hand, the harder-line policies may work if persisted in. In a brilliant series of articles in the *Sunday Times* in January 1997, the Harvard sociologist Charles Murray pointed out that the reason why so many criminals were around in the 1980s was that four times fewer were sent to jail as in the 1950s. In fact, five times as many prisons would have to be built if the same proportion of criminals were to go to jail in the 1990s as did then. This was why in the 1950s crime rates were extremely low.

Michael Howard argued the same case, explaining that between 1954 and 1994 the clear-up rate for theft and burglary – which account for 72% of all crime – fell by half, while during the same period the odds on a prisoner being sent to prison fell by 80%. Thus it became much safer to commit crimes, and between 1954 and 1992 recorded crime in England and Wales rose by over 1000%. American policy became more liberal, with the same results. Then America changed track in the 1970s and crime fell during the 1980s by 10%. According to Howard, exactly the same thing had happened in Britain. As a result of his 'get tough' policies half a million fewer crimes were recorded in 1996 than in 1993 – the greatest drop since the nineteenth century. He also revealed that since two-thirds of crime was committed by a hard core of one-fifth of all criminals, Home Office research had indicated that between three and 13 offences could be prevented for every domestic burglar imprisoned for a year rather than given a community sentence.Yet before his 1997 Criminal Justice Act was passed, the average sentence for a third conviction was just 18.9 months, only half of which was actually served.

The question of how accurate his statistics were has already been raised. The financial cost of building such a huge number of prisons as Murray would like can also be imagined. Again, there is the problem of actually catching the criminals. Yet with many permanently behind bars, it should be easier to some degree to concentrate on catching the others. Finally, deterrence might start to become a factor in the equation. The new criminal justice system will certainly be scrutinised very carefully.

However, we should not despair over crime. Crime rates *can* go down as well as up. New tools such as DNA data bases, closed-circuit cameras in town centres and elsewhere can make a considerable difference. So too might lessons to schoolchildren instructing them on the difference between right and wrong and the need for civility, respect and tolerance in dealing with others. Reform of police complaints procedures and more democratic accountability by police forces might also restore some of the respect which the police have undoubtedly lost in recent years.

Some siren voices might speak out for the weapons of despair – guns for the police and identity cards for citizens, for example. Neither, however, would work. The first would merely encourage criminals to arm themselves as well. The second would infringe civil liberties, increase crime (forgery in particular), and undermine respect for the police. Wartime identity cards were abolished in 1951 for precisely that reason – law-abiding citizens became so fed up with being asked to produce them. They would become a form of passport and therefore an excuse for the EU to abolish border controls, making it still easier for drug dealers, terrorists and criminals to enter the country. Immigration and customs services would give way to Europol which would have a pan-European status as a sort of European FBI. Our own police may not be perfect, but they are less corrupt and better at solving crime than anything the European Union has to offer.

9

Defence

Historical background

Today's defence arrangements are a left-over from the period of the Cold War when, it should be recalled, the only threat to European peace came from the USSR and its allies in the Warsaw Pact. This threat was met by NATO, mainly by US, British and Canadian troops, since West Germany was not re-armed until 1955 and did not possess a functioning Bundeswehr until the 1960s.

The re-armament of West Germany came about against the wishes of the West German people and was only agreed to by France on certain strict conditions. These included the establishment of the British Army of the Rhine, BAOR (originally 77,000 men, reduced to 55,000 in the 1960s) with tactical air support; the banning of ABC weapons (atomic, biological and chemical) as far as Germany was concerned; and a ban on West German submarines, capital ships, rockets, etc. West German troops also had to come under the command of a French general on the Central front next to the East Germans, rather than the French.

In the meantime, France did not play a major role in European defence: from 1946-54 her army (paid largely by the Americans) was in Vietnam, while from 1958-62 it was fighting a dirty war in Algeria, which almost became a civil war. Then, in 1966, General de Gaulle withdrew French troops from NATO's military command (although France remained a NATO member) and kicked NATO out of its HQ at Fontainebleau to Brussels. One consequence of this was that there was no longer any direct route overland between Italy and Germany. Austria and Switzerland, like Ireland, Sweden, Finland, it should be recalled, all remained neutral during the Cold War. The point to note in all this is that when Europe was most in danger, she was saved by the Anglo-Saxons, not by the continental Europeans.

European integration and defence

The process of European integration was entirely irrelevant to the defence of Europe. When the whole issue of German re-armament arose in 1950, the French came up with the Pleven Plan (named after the French PM, but in fact concocted by Monnet). The aim of this was to 'rearm the Germans without rearming Germany', by integrating various national units within a European Defence Community (EDC). There was thus to be no German army, merely German units within a European one. Most Germans were against the scheme and a movement was started to resist it with the slogan *ohne mich*, i.e. 'without me', Yet the scheme was scuttled by the French themselves in 1954, for a number of reasons: Britain would not join it (Churchill thought it was mad, 'a sludgy amalgam', in his words); the French wanted to be on the same level as the British (so, if it was not good enough for us, it was not good enough for them); the resurgence of Gaullism after 1952 meant that French sovereignty had to be protected; in any case the French were occupied outside Europe, so that European defence would have to be left to the Americans and Germans; the French still did not trust the Germans. In the end, the British saved the day. By promising to establish BAOR permanently on German soil in peacetime and by agreeing with the Americans to limit German weapons, France allowed West Germany to enter NATO through a revived WEU.

From all of this, it should be clear that European integration contributed nothing to European defence. On the contrary, it held up the process. It should also be noted that Germany after 1945 was never a threat to European peace in any case. Most West Germans were opposed to their rearmament (an American Cold War demand encouraged by Adenauer to win an army which would be a symbol of renewed German sovereignty) while, even if they had had a machine gun and tank each, there were half-a-million NATO troops on their soil and another half-million Warsaw Pact troops in East Germany. Thus European integration did not serve to solve 'the German problem' either.

NATO

Immediately after World War II, the US intended to demobilise its army and get on with the usual business of running America. Roosevelt told Stalin at Yalta that his 'boys would be back home within two years'. The US army in Europe was run down from 3 million to 300,000 men by 1947, while the Soviet army was run down to 3 million. Among the first troops to go were the more important ones – the signals and intelligence corps. Churchill and de Gaulle were in despair – hence Churchill's 1944 carve-up of the Balkans with Stalin (the so-called Percentages Agreement which in fact saved Greece), and the Franco-Soviet Treaty of the same year. Yet nothing could be done to get the US to stay in Europe or to commit herself militarily to its defence.

Under these circumstances, the British and French concluded the 1947 Dunkirk Treaty (supposedly to defend each other against Germany – but it was of little account, since the French had no real army and what it had was already fighting in Vietnam), which in 1948 was joined by the Benelux countries under the Brussels Treaty Organisation, otherwise known as West European Union (WEU). WEU or BTO had the right to discuss economic and political matters in its ministerial council, but its main task was common defence against aggression, a task which it could hardly fulfil, since the French were fighting in South East Asia, the British were scattered around the world and the Benelux nations had no troops to speak of. In fact, the BTO plan, should the Soviets attack, was to withdraw to an 'arc of defence' running from London to Gibraltar to Trieste. In other words, continental Europe would be abandoned. If this was rather upsetting to the French, so too was the British refusal to cut them in on bilateral talks with the Americans on global issues. The Americans, for their part, were none too keen to defend Western Europe. Their plan in the case of a Soviet invasion was simply to fly their troops back home with the object of making any decision to intervene later. This contingency plan was known as Operation Half Moon. When the Berlin Crisis broke out in 1948, there was therefore practically nothing in place to resist a Soviet advance. The airlift was totally improvised and was not expected to work. The propaganda that atom bombs had been sent to Berlin was meant to boost Western morale; the Soviets knew from the shape of US planes that there were no US atom bombs in Berlin; while the Soviet spy, Donald Maclean, had (very usefully in retrospect) let Stalin know that Western policy was not aggressive towards the USSR.

None the less, the Berlin Crisis, the 1948 coup in Czechoslovakia and rumours of Soviet aggression being planned against Norway, meant that the US was persuaded in 1949 to sign the NATO Treaty. Yet, once again, this brought no automatic guarantee that America would safeguard Europe militarily. Three things have to be noted about the treaty. First, in the words of Acheson and Eisenhower, it was meant as 'a psychological boost' only, to stop the Europeans from flapping; secondly, it was strictly limited in territorial scope, with only North America, the North Atlantic, North West Europe and the Mediterranean countries being covered (French North Africa outside Algeria was excluded); finally, in case of an attack, all members were free to decide what to do collectively or individually in response. The US constitution gives Congress the final say in decisions on peace and war, so the Europeans could extract no automatic guarantee from the Americans.

Article 5 of NATO reads (and this should be memorised for debates against those federalist ignoramuses who maintain that our right to govern our own affairs was originally surrendered to NATO) that the contracting parties agreed that in future:

> an armed attack against one or more of them in Europe or North America shall be considered an attack against all of them and consequently agree that, if such an armed attack occurs, each of them, in excercise of his right of individual or collective self-defence … will assist the party or parties so

attacked, by taking forthwith, individually and in concert with other parties, such action as it deems necessary, including the use of armed force, to restore and maintain the security of the North Atlantic area.

US policy, therefore, was not predicated on the use of force in Europe. The Truman Doctrine merely provided for some funds and a military mission to go to Greece. The Marshall Plan – which was aimed partly to stop anyone getting the wrong idea about the Truman Doctrine – was designed to stabilise Western Europe economically (thus obviating the need for military intervention) and was linked to US plans to bring about a politically stable United States of Europe. (Hence CIA patronage of the European Movement which, to all intents and purposes, was a CIA front.)

American policy soon changed, however. The explosion of the Soviet atom bomb in 1949 (15 years earlier than predicted by the CIA) plus the fall of China led to a famous rethink, entitled NSC 68. America now prepared to double its defence budget and contain Communism around the globe. Then the outbreak of the Korean War in 1950 allowed NSC 68 to be put into operation. The USA now sought defence pacts and bases everywhere, while its attitude to Europe entirely changed. Eisenhower himself was sent over to NATO as Supreme Allied Commander (SACEUR) at the head of 300,000 troops; Franco was later rehabilitated as an ally; and West Germany was rearmed through WEU. America now protested that she would provide an automatic guarantee to Europe, but not everybody believed her. De Gaulle insisted on a separate French defence policy with an independent French *force de frappe*. Later on Helmut Schmidt insisted that US Cruise and Pershing missiles be brought to Europe under only US nuclear control, so that if these had to be fired the US would be automatically involved in nuclear war alongside her European allies. Yet during the Gulf War of 1991, it was the Germans who informed their NATO allies, the Turks, that should Turkey be attacked by Iraq, Germany would not offer her military support, quoting Article 5 of NATO. (The Germans also deliberately misinterpreted their constitution to avoid sending troops to the Gulf. They claimed quite wrongly, as their Supreme Court subsequently ruled, that they were forbidden to send troops out of the NATO area – a curious claim, given that they had no troops at all when their constitution had been written and had not even been members of NATO at the time.)

Clearly, therefore, under the NATO Treaty, Britain has the right to determine her own defence policy.

WEU

Today, this right is under threat due to the development of WEU. Under Article 4 of the treaty establishing WEU in 1948, all signatories were bound to aid any member attacked in Europe 'with all the military and other aid and assistance in their power'. However, the organization operated not on supranational principles, but through a consultative council, and in any case became more or less redundant when superseded by NATO in 1949. With the rearmament of West Germany in 1955, protocols were added to the 1948 treaty which made sure that WEU was not to overlap with NATO institutions and was to refer to NATO for all military information and advice. It came to describe itself therefore as 'the European pillar of NATO'.

In fact, WEU began to exist on paper only. Its social and economic committees were transferred to the Council of Europe in 1960, while during the 1960s it was the scene of constant quarrels between Britain and France. Its only real job was to oversee the relaxation of the limitations on German weapon production enshrined in the 1954-55 agreements. Between 1969 and 1984 it was boycotted by the French and sunk into complete diplomatic and military irrelevance. It was only resurrected by François Mitterrand for Euro-propaganda purposes in 1984 and although it has recently acquired new members (see below) it has never organised any military events and was completely sidelined during the Gulf War. Mrs Thatcher was only hazily aware of its existence although its HQ until recently was in London (I had to write a memo for her explaining what it was!), and it has less military experience that the average military band school. Yet this body is now expanding and being increasingly entrusted with European defence.

The Maastricht Treaty (Title 5, article J4) states:

> The (European) Union requests the West European Union (WEU), which is an integral part of the development of European Union, to elaborate and implement decisions and actions of the Union which have defence implications. The (European) Council shall, in agreement with the institutions of the WEU, adopt the necessary arrangements.

It should be recalled that the Maastricht Treaty also forbids member states to pursue foreign or defence policies which are counter to those of the Union. Moreover, in all areas of foreign and defence policies, the European Council can adopt a collective position. Thereafter, individual member states have to pursue this position and must represent it in all international bodies. (Denmark, for example, was prevented from putting forward tough demands regarding the transport of nuclear waste at the Rio Environmental Conference as a result of European decisions.) Finally, the Treaty hints that the common foreign and security policy might lead to a common defence. That is where WEU comes in. It is being transformed into a European Army. Thus all EU members have become either members of WEU or have observer status. Austria, Finland, Sweden and Greece joined in 1995, Spain and Portugal before that, while Denmark and Ireland have observer status. (Italy joined with Germany in 1955.)

Since Maastricht this process has continued. The Petersberg Declaration of 19 June 1992 pledged WEU states to strengthen the operative role of WEU. National units from the whole array of national forces are to be placed at the disposal of WEU. If multinational strikeforces are required these are also to be placed under WEU. Participation in such is for the time being still to depend on individual national governments. Yet the main demand of the Germans at the Maastricht Review Conference is that security and foreign policy decisions should be taken by majority vote. WEU also foresees itself as playing a role not only in defence but in peace-keeping, peace-making, rescue missions, humanitarian operations and international crisis management. Its Rome communiqué of 19 May 1993 demanded a rapid reaction force capable of moving on land, in the air or in the water. It already has several corps at its disposal, namely the Eurocorps (50,000 men strong – 18,000 German, 10,000 French, 5,000 Franco-German Brigade, 10,000 Belgian and 4,500 Spanish plus some Luxembourgeois); the Southern European forces of France, Spain and Portugal involved in EUROFOR (military, *c.* 10,000-15,000 men) and EUROMARFOR (naval, numbers unknown); and the British-Dutch Amphibian Force (between 5,000 and 10,000 men). On top of this there is the body described in the British 1991 defence White Paper as the Allied Command Europe Rapid Reaction Force, which is to be 60% British, include NATO and non-NATO troops, operate outside the NATO area, and be associated with WEU. It is described as a body 'which could serve as a bridge between the transatlantic security and defence structures of NATO and the developing common political and security policies of the Twelve ... but would be subordinate to neither'. On the other hand the White Paper condemns the idea of WEU as a separate body from NATO. The truth is, however, that all recent defence developments make sense only within the context of WEU replacing NATO as Europe's main defence structure, presumably after a US withdrawal. In short, they make no sense at all.

The defects of WEU policy

1. Recent developoments have been designed to turn the EU into a federal superpower with its own military arm including nuclear weapons. Karl Lammers, the Chairman of the CDU/CSU Bundestag Foreign Affairs and Defence Committee, has already called for an equal share for Germany in the control and targetting of British and French nuclear weapons. Horst Teltschik, Kohl's former chief foreign policy adviser, has called for Europe to be a superpower to keep the USA and Japan in check. As the German Green MP, Christian Sterzing, has noted: 'The integration of the military structures of the WEU in the EU would signify the militarisation of the hitherto civil structures of the EU. And militarisation of the EU would serve as a justification for the militarisation of German foreign

policy and give a new impetus to re-armament in the shape of a European army of intervention.'

2. This new army would probably mean the reintroduction of conscription in the United Kingdom, while majority voting or federal political structures would mean that British soldiers would have to die for causes perhaps not related to British interests. In short, it would drag us into foreign wars in Germany's or other countries' interests.

3. It would mean first the evacuation of US troops from Europe and then almost certainly friction with the US over foreign and defence policy. The first step would make European defence largely incredible; the second would make the world largely unstable. Britain would lose out in all sorts of ways.

4. Since both the Gulf War and the Bosnian Crisis have shown that EU countries have no common interests around which to frame common policies, there is no need to have them. They were shown to be hollow in the Gulf and counter-productive as far as peace-keeping in Bosnia has been concerned. (We first recognised the state of Bosnia-Herzegovina and then three times voted to partition it, despite our signature on the Helsinki Accords which outlaw the recognition of territorial gains made by the use of force.)

5. British policy therefore must be to work within the traditional structures of NATO as long as possible, to persuade the US to remain in Europe; to resist all moves at developing the WEU (in fact we should seek its abolition); and to quit NATO should WEU begin to take over from it. Its Article 4, its association with the Maastricht Treaty, and its likely transformation into a European Defence Community as a result of the Maastricht Review Conference, make it absolutely against our national interest to become further involved in it. Fortunately, once we quit the European Union, we shall quit WEU as well.

6. Britain must develop a defence policy whose first priority is the defence of the UK. We must also retain the ability to act abroad, but only to protect our own interests in cooperation with other powers who must never be in a position to override our own national interests.

7. The exact strength of the armed forces required to defend an independent UK is impossible to forecast. In fact, a defence review is urgently required even at present to match manpower with commitments. An independent UK would of course have to give priority to the navy and airforce, but a strong military would be required both for the defence of Ulster and to take part in operations abroad. Certainly, we would not need to station forces in Germany. We would, on the other hand, have to strengthen customs and immigration services as well as the coast guard and fisheries protection fleets.

8. An independent British government would retain command of an independent nuclear deterrent. There is controversy about the exact degree of independence the British Trident fleet actually has (quite apart

from top-secret agreements covering the conditions under which they might be used, the missiles are bought off-the-shelf from the USA and have to be returned there for repair and maintenance); however, in the modern world Britain should have the most up-to-date defence affordable and should be prepared to contribute to the costs of a defensive shield to be erected in space to protect the West from missile attacks from 'rogue' countries which may acquire nuclear weapons.

The extension of NATO to the Russian border

Russia is obviously still a problem militarily. She still has armed forces numbering over 3.5 million men. Some 14 million people are still employed in military-related activities – about one fifth of the labour force. About two to four times as many people as in the West will be employed in military activity until the year 2,000. Over and above this, Russian military doctrine holds that Russian interests include all the former territories and satellites of the former USSR. Imperial wars are being or have been waged in the 'near abroad', for example in Chechnia, Georgia and Tadzhikistan. Yeltsin's Kremlin is desperately trying to steal the patriotic card from the opposition and to impress middle Russia which has been humiliated by the collapse of the Soviet Union. Russia is also dumping raw materials, weapons, missiles and maybe even uranium on the world market in order to acquire the foreign currency it cannot hope to get from normal exports, given the crude nature of its consumer goods. Meanwhile, its economy is still extremely shaky. Its reintegration costs after the fall of the USSR have been enormous – possibly 20% of GDP. Its infrastructure is breaking down and Western demands for a rapid transition to capitalism may have outlawed queues, but have brought massive unemployment, insecurity and depression. Most Russians think the West is deliberately weakening its old enemy.

Meanwhile, the West believes that a changeround can occur partly because of recent developments in China. Yet China has operated within a stable political environment and has followed very different economic policies: agricultural reform, small-scale enterprise in the countryside, manufactured exports, high tariffs and little privatization. Russian policy has been almost the opposite. And so have been the results. China has witnessed 10% growth per year for fifteen years. Russia has seen a fall in production of 50% since January 1991. She now collects only 62% of her tax revenue and is financing her deficit by neglecting to pay state employees their wages. In July 1994, 3.4 trillion roubles had not been paid. Recently, Russia's miners went on strike to recover months of lost wages. So anything could happen in Russia.

How then should the West treat Russia? So far it has offered a 'strategic partnership', a strategic community ranging 'from Vancouver to Vladivostock', a 'partnership for peace'. The Russians have accepted, but warily. (They now have a general stationed permanently at NATO headquarters at Brussels.) They need Western technology, which they are beginning to acquire since the abolition of the Co-ordinating Committee for Multilateral Export Controls (the West's ban on the export of sensitive goods to the USSR), has been abolished) and they have been consulted, albeit intermittently, over Bosnia. The West, in turn, needs Russia's aid in the Middle East and perhaps against China.

My own view is that friendship with Russia is vital and that we must treat her both with respect – which she craves and which is her due – and with sympathy. She did have to suffer Lenin, Stalin and Hitler and deserves all the help she can get. (She also contributed most to the defeat of Nazism.) Hence we must treat Russia as an important, if different, part of our diverse European civilisation. Our policy should be one of restraining her military ambitions in the short term with US aid, but in the medium term of showing our good will by economic support and cooperation rather than prolonging military confrontation any longer than is necessary. We must ensure that we do everything possible to encourage democracy and stability in Russia, but at the same time – and this will require skill – ensure that we do not treat her as a permanent enemy. Russia, in short, should be treated as a future friend. Besides, we have a more immediate interest in all this. An atmosphere of military confrontation will only increase the pressure on all European countries to turn WEU into a supranational military alliance.

It is in this context then that we must now look at the question of incorporating the new states of Eastern Europe within NATO – a question which arose immediately after the collapse of the Warsaw Pact in March 1991. The first step was the creation of the North Atlantic Cooperation Council, a 38-member body made up of all members of NATO and the former Warsaw Pact. The problem was that, with the inclusion of Russia, this failed to address the differences in perceived defence requirements between the former superpower and its former satellites. Hence the Pentagon came up with the Partnership for Peace programme, under which the former Warsaw Pact countries would not be invited to join NATO, but to reach individual arrangements with it. 'Partners' could undertake joint training exercises with full members, have the right to be consulted by NATO, and be represented at NATO headquarters.

However, this scheme satisfied no one. Thus at a NATO summit at Brussels in June 1994, President Clinton, who had come under pressure from Americans of East European descent, announced that East European countries could join NATO. It was merely a question of 'when and how'. The then US ambassador to Germany, Richard Holbrooke, was brought back to Washington to work on the problem and in December 1994 a formal study on how membership was to come about was commissioned by NATO. This 'Study on Nato Enlargement' was published in September 1995, formally committing NATO to take on new members with all the rights and guarantees of current ones. The trouble with the plan was that it refused to say which new member states would be taken on or when. This has given rise to a huge debate between those who fear that new members must be taken on before Russia 'goes wrong' and those who want to proceed more slowly, while encouraging fears that some states will be left out altogether (Bulgaria, Romania, the Baltic states and the Ukraine). Russia, meanwhile, is furous at the prospect of NATO being extended right up to its border when the Cold War is supposed to be over.

The major arguments in favour of extension were: that it would help to promote stability in Central and Eastern Europe; that it would bring enthusiastic and highly Atlanticist states into an alliance needing rein-vigoration; that it would show Russian nationalists that the West is not afraid of threats; and that it would provide a military glacis should Russia become expansionist again. The main arguments against were that it could provoke the Russians into abandoning arms control agreements or signing an alliance with Communist China; that it could promote unrest in Eastern and Central Europe by taking in some states and not others; that it could dilute NATO's cohesion by allowing in new members with particular interests; that it would be very expensive to arm these new members with modern equipment and bring their military infrastructure (bases etc.) up to date; and that to do this in any case would saddle the new post-Cold War Europe with a very old-fashioned Cold War atmosphere based on the need for permanent military pacts.

Other questions are also pertinent. How close to the Russian border should Western troops be stationed? What happens in cases (already with us) when East European countries are once again ruled by Communist governments? Are these to be given access to NATO secrets?

The most serious problem is the reaction of Russia. President Yeltsin and his most senior military advisers have all made their displeasure known. Yeltsin has said that NATO enlargement will 'fan the flames of war'. Is it really in the West's interests to humiliate the new Russia, having won the Cold War? Do we want to push Russia into the arms of China, encourage her to sell nuclear materials to Iran and blackmail the Ukraine? After all, the West would have to take a strong stance if Russia reoccupied Eastern Europe, whether these states were NATO members or not. Making them full NATO members might deter Russia from doing so, but it might also encourage her to do so before they were fully incorporated into NATO and might land the Alliance with guarantees that were simply not credible. Would any US President risk nuclear war with Moscow over Vilnius, Kiev or Bucharest? Finally, how much of the pressure being exerted on the West is coming from vested interests – US immigrant groups and NATO bureaucrats afraid of a demilitarised Europe?

It seems to me that for the present, there is not sufficient reason to provoke the Russians. We should be far more prepared to risk friendship with the new Russia, since the future rewards are so much greater. Treating her as a permanent enemy could be a self-fulfilling policy. Besides, it makes no military sense to incorporate Communist-run states (Poland, Hungary, Romania) into NATO. If Russia should turn out to be dangerous it would make greater sense to issue guarantees to Eastern Europe later on. In the meantime, the West should be striving to relax tensions, accepting the end of the Cold War, and refusing to aid the military bureaucrats who want to use old fears to build up a new military power in Western Europe which would develop WEU into a European army. Britain's best policy does not demand that we have any illusions about the dangers still represented by Russia; rather that we should attempt to remove these by skilful, patient diplomacy, by retaining a NATO based on an American presence, and by avoiding any precipitate and unnecessary provocation of a Russia whose pride and insecurities we would do well to understand.

Our policy, in short, should be one of strength, watchfulness, patience, sympathy and intelligence; not one of pessimism and provocation. The last thing we need is a new Cold War. Nor do Eastern Europe and Russia.

Conclusions

This book has demonstrated, I hope, that Britain, on the brink of the twenty-first century, has put the relative decline from which she suffered during the period 1950-80 behind her. She no longer runs an empire, she no longer acts as a world policeman, the pound no longer serves as a world reserve currency, the effects of two world wars have been overcome, there is no longer any complacency that takes continued success for granted, and the endemically bad industrial relations which crippled her economy for decades have been relegated to the past. The only burden which now weighs her down is membership of the European Union, that bizarre set of undemocratic institutions which aspire to superstate status. Once liberated from these and trading freely with the world as a whole, she can look forward to a future of great prosperity.

Britain has no reason to fear independence, since she is once again an object of considerable respect internationally. She has the fifth largest economy in the world, £1.7 trillion invested around the globe (70% of it outside the EU), the most advanced nuclear weapons and the most professional armed forces in Europe. She has a stable political system and the English language. Behind her is perhaps the most successful history of any country in the world. She sits on the Security Council of the UN and is a member of G7 Group, the IMF, the World Bank and NATO.

Despite all this, there are British politicians who desire to change her institutions and international status out of all recognition. They would surrender her independence; destroy her constitutional unity; deprive her of Northern Ireland against the wishes of the majority of the population there; reduce her to provincial status in a foreign state; and give her foreign institutions. In short, they would deprive her of the prosperity and relative ascent that now await her out of defeatism and disloyalty. They must be resisted at all costs.

Other pessimists believe that domestic developments have so altered Britain internally that she will succumb to social fragmentation and unrest. Yet having reviewed the evidence, it would seem that the welfare state is still a manageable asset, that the permissive society has been limited in its effects, that racism is not an insuperable enemy and that crime might even come under control, although much will have to be done to restore the harm done to our education system by Tory governments.

The future will be best served, however, if it is made over to those who have not absorbed the defeatism of the major parties or the nationalists. It will be brightest under those who still believe in Britain.

Further Reading

The standard narrative account of post-war British history is Alan Sked and Chris Cook, *Post-War Britain: A Political History, 1945-1992*, Penguin, 1993. The most useful analysis of various aspects of the country since 1945 is in German, namely H. Kastendiek, K. Rohe and A. Volle (eds), *Landerbericht Grossbritannien: Geschichte, Politik, Wirtschaft, Gesellschaft*, Bundeszentrale für politische Bildung, vol. 327, Bonn, 1994. For Britain and the EU, the two best volumes are Christopher Booker and Richard North, *The Castle of Lies: Why Britain Must Get Out of Europe*, Duckworth, 1996, and B. Burkitt, M. Baimbridge and P. Whyman (eds) *There is an alternative: Britain and its relationship with the EU*, Campaign for an Independent Britain, 1996. On Scotland, see Patrick S. Hodge (ed.), *Scotland and the Union*, Hume Papers on Public Policy, vol. 2, no. 2, Summer 1994, Edinburgh University Press.

References

Abel-Smith, Brian, 1983: 'Assessing the balance sheet', in Glennester, H. (ed.) *The Future of the Welfare State*, London.

Abrams, M., Gerard, D. and Timms, N. (eds) 1985: *Values and Social Change in Britain*, Basingstoke.

Alford, B.W.E. 1981: 'New industries for old? British industry between the wars', in Floud, R. and McCloskey, D. (eds) *The Economic History of Britain since 1700*, vol. 2: *1860 to the 1970s*, Cambridge.

Alter, Peter 1978: 'Staat und Wissenschaft in Grossbritannien vor 1914', in Berding, H. et al. (eds) *Vom Staat des Ancien Regime zum Modernen Parteistaat*, Oldenburg.

Anderson, M.S. 1989: *The Ascendancy of Europe, 1815-1914*, London.

Bacon, R. and Eltis, W. 1976: *Britain's Economic Problem: Too Few Producers*, London.

Barnett, Correlli 1986: *Audit of War*, London.

Barnett, Correlli 1995: *The Lost Victory: British Dreams and Realities 1945-1950*, London.

Bean, C. and Crafts, N. 1996: 'British economic growth since 1945: relative economic decline ... and renaissance?' in Crafts, N. and Toniolo, G. (eds) *Economic Growth in Europe since 1945*, Cambridge.

Bell, Josephine 1962: *Crime in our Time*, London.

Brittan, S. 1975: 'The economic contradictions of democracy', *British Journal of Political Science*, vol. 5, no. 1.

Buxton, N.K. 1979: 'Introduction', in Buxton, N.K. and Aldcroft, D.H. (eds) *British Industry between the Wars: Instability and Industrial Development, 1919-1939*, London.

Cairncross, Alex 1981: 'The post-war years', in Floud, R. and McCloskey, D. (eds) *The Economic History of Britain since 1700*, vol. 2: *1860 to the 1970s*, Cambridge.

Cameron, D.R. 1985: 'Public expenditure and economic performance in international perspective', in Klein, R. and O'Higgins, M. (eds) *The Future of Welfare*, London.

Chalmers, Malcolm 1985: *Paying for Defence: Military Spending and British Decline*, London.

Coleman, D.C. 1969: *Courtaulds: an Economic and Social History, II: Rayon*, Oxford.

Crafts, N. 1996: 'Britain's productivity growth: comparative performance and future prospects', in Gillespie, P. (ed.) *Britain's European Question: The Issues for Ireland*, Institute for European Affairs, Dublin.

Dahrendorf, Ralph 1985: *Law and Order* (The Hamlyn Lectures for 1985), London.

Davies, Christie 1975: *Permissive Britain: Social Change in the Sixties and Seventies*, London.

Drummond, I. 1981: 'Britain and the world economy', in Floud, R. and McCloskey, D. (eds) *The Economic History of Britain since 1700*, vol. 2: *1860 to the 1970s*, Cambridge.

Edgerton, David 1996: *Myths of Decline*, Prospect, August/September, London.

Eltis, Walter 1996: *The Key to Higher Living Standards*, Centre for Policy Studies, London.

Fischer, Wolfram 1983: *Germany in the World Economy during the Nineteenth Century*, The Annual Lecture, The German Historical Institute, London.

Fraser, W. Hamish 1981: *The Coming of the Mass Market, 1850-1914*, London.

Gamble, Andrew 1981: *Britain in Decline*, London.

George, V. and Wilding, P. 1984: *The Impact of Social Policy*, London.

Gillis, John 1986: *For Better or Worse: British Marriages 1600 to the Present*, Oxford.

Glennester, Howard (ed.) 1983: *The Future of the Welfare State: Remaking Social Policy*, London.

Gomulka, Stanislaw 1978: 'Britain's slow industrial growth: increasing inefficiency versus low rate of technological change', in Beckerman, W. (ed.) *Slow Growth in Britain: Cause and Consequences*, Oxford.

Hannah, C. 1974: 'Managerial innovation and the rise of the large-scale company in inter-war Britain', *Economic History Review*, 2nd series, vol. 27.

Harris, Jose and Thane, Pat 1984: 'British and European bankers, 1880-1914', in Thane, P., Crossick, G. and Floud, R. (eds) *The Power of the Past (Essays for Eric Hobsbawm)*, Cambridge.

Hills, John 1994: *What Future for Welfare*, LSE Magazine, Spring, London.

Hinton, Thomas R. 1973 'German and English intellectuals: contrasts and comparisons' in Feuchtwanger, E.J. (ed.) *Upheaval and Continuity: A Century of German History*, London.

Hofstadter, Richard 1955: *The Age of Reform*, New York.

Hofstadter, Richard 1966: *Anti-intellectualism in American Life*, New York.

Jenkins, Simon, 1995: *Accountable to None: The Tory Nationalisation of Britain*, Harmondsworth.

Kinsey, A., Pomeroy, W. and Martin, C. 1948: *Sexual Behaviour in the Human Male*, Philadelphia.

Kinsey, A., Pomeroy, W. and Martin, C. 1953: *Sexual Behaviour in the Human Female*, Philadelphia.

Kirby, M.W. 1981: *The Decline of British Economic Power since 1870*, London.

Leach, Rodney (1996) *Monetary Union: A Perilous Gamble*, London.

Le Grand, Julian 1996: *The Thinkable*, Prospect, July, London.

Lipset, Seymour Martin (1996) *American Exceptionalism: A Double-Edged Sword*, New York.

Manser, W.A.P. 1971: *Britain in Balance: The Myth of Failure*, Harmondsworth.

McIlroy, John 1987: 'The politics of racism', in Jones, Bill (ed.) *Political Issues in Britain Today*, Manchester.

Minford, Patrick 1996: 'The conflict between British economic liberalism and continental statism' in Gillespie, Paul (ed.) *Britain's European Question: The Issues for Ireland*, Institute for European Affairs, Dublin.

Mount, F. 1982: *The Subversive Family, An Alternative History of Love and Marriage*, London.

Norman, E.R. 1976: *Church and Society in England 1790-1970: a Historical Study*, Oxford.

Pinera, Jose 1996: *Empowering Workers: The Privatisation of Social Security in Chile*, Adam Smith Institute, London.

Pollard, S. 1982: *The Wasting of the British Economy*, London.

Porter, Bernard 1975: *The Lion's Share: A Short History of British Imperialism 1850-1970*, London.

Read, D. 1979: *England 1868-1914*, London.

Reiner, Robert: regular column in *Policing Today*.

Richardson, H.W. 1962: 'The basis of economic recovery in the 1930s: a review and a new interpretation', *Economic History Review*, 2nd series, vol. 15.

Robins, Lynton 1987: 'Issues in education', in Jones, Bill (ed.) *Political Issues in Britain Today*, Manchester.

Rubenstein, W.D. 1974: 'British millionaires, 1809-1949', *Bulletin of the Institute of Historical Research*, vol. 48.

Rubenstein, W.D. 1981: 'New men of wealth and the purchase of land in nineteenth century Britain', *Past and Present*, vol. 92.

Sandberg, L.G. 1981: 'The entrepreneur and technological change', in Floud, R. and McCloskey, D. (eds) *The Economic History of Britain since 1700*, vol. 2: *1860 to the 1970s*, Cambridge.

Saul, S.B. 1979: *Industrialisation and De-industrialisation? The Interaction of the German and British Economies before the First World War*, The Annual Lecture, The German Historical Institute, London.

Smith, Keith 1984: *The British Economic Crisis*, London.

Stern, Fritz 1965: *The Politics of Cultural Despair, A Study in the Rise of the German Ideology*, New York.

Taylor-Gooby, P. 1985: 'The politics of welfare: public attitudes and behaviour', in Klein, R. and O'Higgins, M. (eds) *The Future of Welfare*, London.

Thomas, T. 1981: 'Aggregate demand in the United Kingdom, 1918-45', in Floud, R. and McCloskey, D. (eds) *The Economic History of Britain since 1700*, vol. 2: *1860 to the 1970s*, Cambridge.

Thompson, F.M.L. 1984: 'English landed society in the nineteenth century', in Thane, P., Crossick, G. and Floud, R (eds) *The Power of the Past (Essays for Eric Hobsbawm)*, Cambridge.

Tracey, M. and Morrison, D. 1979: *Whitehouse*, London.

Turner, H.A. 1969: *Is Britain Really Strike Prone?: a review of the incidence, character and costs of industrial conflict*, Cambridge.

Walker, Nigel 1965: *Crime and Punishment in Britain: an analysis of the penal system in theory, law and practice*, Edinburgh.

Warwick, Paul 1985: 'Did Britain change? An inquiry into the causes of national decline', *Journal of Contemporary History*, vol. 20, no. 1.

Weeks, Jeffrey 1981: *Sex, Politics and Society: the Regulation of Sexuality since 1800*, London.

Wiener, Martin J. 1981: *English Culture and the Decline of the Industrial Spirit, 1850-1980*, Cambridge.

Williams, E.N. 1972: *The Ancien Regime in Europe: Government and Society in the Major States, 1648-1789*, Harmondsworth.

Index

Index